FROM ARMY GREEN
TO CORPORATE GRAY

FROM ARMY GREEN TO CORPORATE GRAY

A Career Transition Guide for Army Personnel

Carl S. Savino, Major, USAR
Ronald L. Krannich, Ph.D.

IMPACT PUBLICATIONS
Manassas Park, VA

FROM ARMY GREEN TO CORPORATE GRAY
A Career Transition Guide for Army Personnel

Library of Congress Cataloging-in-Publication Data

Savino, Carl
    From army green to corporate gray : a career transition guide for army personnel / Carl Savino, Ronald L. Krannich
            p.   cm.
    Includes bibliographical references and index.
    ISBN 1-57023-006-4 : $15.95
    1. Career changes—United States. 2. Retired military personnel—Employment—United States. 3. Veterans—Employment—United States. 4. Job hunting—United States. I. Krannich, Ronald L., 1945—
II. Title.
HF5384.K693 1994
650.14—dc20   94—456
                                                                      CIP

For information on distribution or quantity discount rates, Tel. 703/361-7300, Fax 703/335-9486, or write to: Sales Department, Impact Publications, 9104-N Manassas Drive, Manassas Park, VA 22111-5211. Distributed to the trade by National Book Network, 4720 Boston Way, Suite A, Lanham, MD 20706, Tel. 301/459-8696 or 800/462-6420.

CONTENTS

iii

CHAPTER 4

Obtain Transition Assistance **71**

CHAPTER 5

Identify Your Skills & Abilities **84**

CHAPTER 6

Specify Your Interests & Values **95**

PREFACE

"**B**e all you can be" has special meaning for members of the Army. It says something simple yet important to potential recruits—an Army career is likely to bring out the very best in you; it will challenge you to be your very best self. It also says a great deal about career advancement within the Army—the Army provides you with unique opportunities to maximize your potential. You acquire new skills, take on new assignments, work in different positions, advance through the ranks, and relocate when required. The Army is a supportive family that understands and takes care of its own.

But what happens when you leave this family? Are you prepared to also "be all you can be" in the civilian world? While the Army is primarily concerned with recruiting, training, and maintaining a competent force to accomplish its missions, it also must deal with the critical issue of downsizing its forces in this new post-Cold War era. Each day thousands of enlisted personnel and officers face the reality of soon parting company with the Army. As their Army careers draws to a close, these soldiers must prepare for re-entry into the civilian world. They need sound advice so that this career transition will be a positive force in their lives.

Unlike previous downsizing periods in the Army's history, today's Army has a mandate as well as a budget to assist its members with the career transition process. As we outline in Chapter 4, it provides numerous in-house services to help Army personnel make a positive transition to the civilian world. Various Army, government, and association-sponsored programs provide job search workshops, one-on-one counseling, testing, and career resources for Army personnel. You will want to take advantage of these unique opportunities to prepare yourself for your career transition prior to leaving the Army.

So why write a book on this subject? We believe there is a need for a comprehensive self-directed career transition book that addresses the specific needs of transitioning Army personnel. We've written it with certain guiding principles in mind. The book must go beyond anecdotal job finding tales, include much more than the standard mechanics of writing resumes and interviewing for jobs, and speak to the unique situations facing Army personnel. It must speak truth about your future and assist you in finding your best fit in the civilian work world.

Indeed, such a book must first of all be based on the latest and most effective career development and job search methods used by leading professionals. Second, it must address the key problem facing most transitioning Army personnel—the need to conduct a thorough self-assessment that leads to setting clear-cut goals for orchestrating an effective job search campaign; this must be done *prior to* writing a resume or contacting potential employers. Third, it must deal effectively with the nuts-and-bolts of a job search—conducting research, writing resumes and cover letters, networking, interviewing, and negotiating salary. Fourth, it should incorporate special career and lifestyle concerns of interest to many transitioning Army personnel and their families—relocation and starting a business. Above all, such a book must dispel numerous myths that continue to misdirect transitioning Army personnel into unproductive job search channels.

We've attempted to do all of these things in the pages that follow. The book is both self-directed and comprehensive. While we recommend using career transition services at various phases of your job search, the book is designed so you can use it on your own in developing and implementing your own successful career transition plan. The book is also comprehensive without being overwhelming. Each chapter deals with a specific career transition issue which is closely related to issues in adjacent chapters. While ideally you should complete the chapters in sequence—especially Chapters 5 through 13—the book is designed to be used in a flexible manner. If, for example, you are interested in relocation, go directly to Chapter 14.

If you are interested in starting your own business, examine Chapter 15. If you have an interview scheduled for tomorrow, review the contents of Chapters 12 and 13. If you want a quick overview of the major issues addressed in this book, review the myths and realities in Chapter 2.

We wish you well as you make your transition from Army green to corporate gray. You will "be all you can be" in the civilian work world if you approach your career transition properly. If you put into practice the advice found in the following chapters, you will begin reshaping your career—and your life—in the direction of your major interests, skills, and goals. More importantly, you will be able to make critical job and career changes when necessary and at will—not just now but in the years ahead. Hopefully, this book will become a good friend with whom you can consult frequently. You will face your future with confidence and the knowledge that you have the power to shape your future.

ACKNOWLEDGEMENTS

Several people contributed to the success of this project. Colonel Charles B. Giasson, Carl's former boss, motivated him to undertake the project. Pat Day of the Fort Myer Job Assistance Center; Patricia Wells of the Fort Myer Job Employment Transition Services Office; Beth Forbes, formerly with The Retired Officers Association; and Deidre Watters and Phyllis Giasson provided valuable insights and editorial reviews for the initial draft of the book. Many members of the U.S. Army read the initial draft and encouraged Carl to proceed with the project.

The final version is based in part on Ron's *Careering and Re-Careering for the 1990s*, a book that has been widely used throughout the military for career transition purposes and a perennial nationwide bestseller. In collaboration with Carl, this book has been significantly adapted to respond to the unique career transition issues and situations facing Army members.

We especially wish to thank Robert G. Johnston, Deputy Director of Officer Placement Service, The Retired Officers Association, for his thoughtful and detailed comments on the final draft of this book.

Finally, we wish to recognize the assistance of our spouses—Susan (Carl) and Caryl (Ron)—for their continual support and constant encouragement. Caryl wrote most of the chapter on interview techniques and completed the final editing.

We are grateful for the opportunity to have worked with so many dedicated and supportive individuals. It is for them and all those Army soldiers who have served our country that we dedicate this book.

1

WELCOME TO THE REST OF YOUR LIFE

*L*et's talk truth about your future. Thus far you've had a successful career in the Army. But now you're making a career transition that has major life-changing implications for you and those around you. It's probably unlike any transition you have ever experienced before and unlike any you will ever experience again. We believe you could use some help in directing and managing this unique career transition.

That's what we're here for—provide you with the best assistance possible based upon our many combined years of Army, career transition, and job search experience. We want to make sure you do this right— clarify your goals, get you moving in the right direction, save you time and effort, minimize your costs, and connect you with an excellent first

1

post-Army job that leads to a rewarding new career. We've got lots of work to do in the hours, days, and weeks ahead. If you stay with us for the duration of this book, you should acquire several useful tips that will have a significant impact on you and your future worklife.

QUESTION YOUR FUTURE

All of life's transitions should begin with a series of basic soul-searching questions. For in posing the right questions you will begin developing appropriate responses to your career transition situation.

Let's begin questioning your future and your ability to shape it with these orienting questions:

- What do you want to do with the rest of your life?

- Are you leaving the Army for greener pastures elsewhere or are you uncertain about your future?

- Are you more concerned with finding a rewarding job or pursuing a satisfying lifestyle?

- What will you most likely do well and enjoy doing in the civilian world?

- How well prepared are you for finding jobs in the new job markets of today and tomorrow?

- Do you know how to write an excellent resume that translates your military experience into desirable civilian job qualifications?

- Do you know how to communicate your qualifications to employers in civilian work language?

- Are you prepared to research employers, write job-winning cover letters, network for job leads, conduct job interviews, and negotiate salary and benefits?

- Would you be better off starting your own business and writing your own paycheck or finding a job with an employer who regularly writes you a paycheck?

- Where do you plan to relocate and how much will it cost you?

- If you are married, how involved will your spouse be in your job search?

- Does your spouse share your transition concerns and new career goals?

- Can your spouse clearly articulate your greatest strengths, evaluate your job search progress, and generally support you at every stage in your job search?

We've got a big, challenging, and exciting task ahead of us. Together we will try to raise the right questions and guide you into answers appropriate to your situation. If you are like many others who have followed the advice of this book, you will discover your career transition work is both interesting and fun. It will make a difference in your life. It may change your life forever. You are likely to renew some old acquaintances and meet lots of new people who will probably make a significant difference in your life.

We're delighted to be two of the first new people you're meeting on this road to renewed career success. We're here to help—a good friend if you need one. So let's get started on what should be an exciting journey into a new world of rewarding work.

LIFE GOES ON AND ON AND ON

These and numerous other career transition questions and issues provide the central focus for this book. The reality of Army jobs and careers is that they eventually come to an end for everyone involved. And in today's rapidly downsizing and consolidating Army, jobs and careers are coming to an end faster than most people ever expected. Some day everyone in the Army must go through a career transition. Your time is now. So let's do something very positive about your situation by finding your first post-Army civilian job which will put you on the road to renewed career success.

Whether you are being pushed or pulled into the civilian job arena doesn't really make much difference. The fact is that you're making a career transition in which your past may provide little guidance on how to best chart your future. How you make that transition has important implications for both your personal and professional lives. Therefore, it's extremely important to focus on how you will manage this transition from military to civilian work worlds. It's the *transition process*—not different jobs or employers—that should be your central focus. You need a clear sense of where you have been, where you are at present, and where you want to go with the rest of your life. You do this by focusing on your career transition—past, present, and future.

All good things come to an end, and life does indeed go on. If you've really loved your jobs and career in the Army, chances are you will really love your next series of jobs and careers in the civilian world. But you'll have to work at finding your right "fit" in the civilian world. It won't happen overnight, and there are no magic pills to make what may be a difficult transition quickly go away. You'll need to do some serious thinking and planning, starting with setting goals, assessing your skills, and charting a course of action aimed at finding the right job for you. You may want to involve other people in this process. If you are happily married, make sure your spouse is involved early on in this process. If not, your career transition could become more difficult than it should.

CHANCES AND CHOICES

Chances are you are planning to do something rewarding in your next worklife. Some transitioning Army personnel retire completely; they have the means and motivation to enjoy a leisurely lifestyle. But most Army personnel go on to second, third, and fourth careers. Many become employees in large corporations, small businesses, and government. Others decide to start their own businesses immediately upon leaving the Army or after a few years of work experience in the civilian business world. For them, the most critical transition is made upon leaving the service for their first post-Army civilian job.

If done properly, this transition can lead to a most rewarding career. If done haphazardly, the transition may result in finding the wrong job, leaving after the first year, and wandering on to other inappropriate jobs. Some people become unhappy job-hoppers who communicate the wrong messages to potential employers. Unfortunately, they repeat this pattern of job disappointment and career failure for the rest of their worklife. This should not happen to you.

You have excellent skills and experience that are readily marketable in the civilian work world. But what you most need to know is how to best present and market your skills and experience in today's new job market. You do this by acquiring another set of skills you may or may not at present possess—job search skills. Do you know, for example, how to best write and market a job-winning resume? What is networking, and how do you use it in a job search? How will you locate the best employers for your experience and skills? What are the best ways to get job information, advice, and referrals? How can you negotiate a salary twenty percent higher than expected?

You have excellent skills and experience that are readily marketable in the civilian work world.

You can clearly answer these job search questions once you develop specific job search skills. The chapters that follow acquaint you with the most important job search skills for making that all-important first post-Army career transition.

WELCOME TO THE NEW JOB MARKET

Perhaps you've never really had to look for job. When was the last time you assessed your skills, formulated a job objective, conducted occupational research, wrote a resume and job search letters, responded to classified ads, networked for information, advice, and referrals, or negotiated a salary? These are things you must learn to do effectively if you are to make a satisfying career transition.

Chances are your job search skills are either nonexistent or very rusty. If you've been out of the civilian job market for five or more years, you'll quickly discover today's job market is very different from five or ten years ago. The jobs are different, employers are different, skill requirements are more demanding, and salaries and benefits are tougher than ever to negotiate. Good jobs—those that are secure, high paying, and enjoyable—are more difficult than ever to find. Once found, good jobs are more difficult than ever to keep. You may quickly discover the job you secure today may disappear within twelve to twenty-four months. Indeed, recent studies indicate that forty percent of the working population goes to bed each night worried about whether or not they will have a job tomorrow! This, too, should not happen to you.

One thing is very certain about today's job market—it is an uncertain

and insecure job market. It can be ruthless in its treatment of job seekers
and employees. Frequent layoffs, firings, and downsizings testify to its
insensitive and unforgiving nature. If not approached properly, the job
market may result in numerous bumps and bruises for you. You may
quickly discover your career success in the Army lacks a clear counter-
part in the civilian world.

GETTING STARTED RIGHT

Where do you start, and what should you do first? The process of making
a career transition or finding a job is not really difficult. Anyone can find
a job. But finding a good job is hard work which only a few people are
lucky enough to secure. Much of what is involved in finding a job is
commonsense and follows a rational decision-making model as outlined
in Chapter 3. As an Army member, you are used to setting goals,
developing plans, and focusing on accomplishing the mission. Therefore,
the job finding process should make good sense to you. You'll initially
recognize the process as nothing more than good planning and implementation meeting commonsense. You'll later discover the job search is much
more than this, too.

At the same time, you are dealing with a chaotic job market in which
information on job vacancies and employers is difficult to access, the
rules for finding jobs are inconsistent, and the screening process seems
unpredictable and unfair. Rational planning applied to a chaotic environment beyond your control can lead to numerous rejections, disappointments, and frustrations. As you attempt to accomplish a mission in such
an uncertain environment, you will discover the wonderful world of
serendipity—chance occurrences that may unexpectedly lead to the right
job for you. Always keep your mind and eyes open for serendipity. It's
what makes chaos tolerable, forgiving, and unexpectedly rewarding.

Our job finding process in Chapter 3 follows seven well-defined career
planning and job search steps involving investigation, written communication, and employer contact activities. Successful job seekers learn to plan
and implement each of these sequential steps. Each step involves
important planning, organization and communication skills. They require
constant practice through daily, routinized job search activities.

DON'T FORGET YOUR CONCERNED SPOUSE

Funny things happen on the way to a new job and career. Unemployed
people will tell you that looking for a job is no fun. It's difficult on both

the ego and the family. Rejections are terrible experiences, especially if you have been used to receiving respect based on your Army rank and position and if you have been feeling successful in what you do. Change your job and you'll quickly discover how different life can be. Rank and position not tied to demonstrated performance doesn't count for much in the civilian work world. You'll have to quickly sell yourself to strangers.

If you are married, don't forget your spouse on the way to finding a job. Time and again we've discovered many transitioning military personnel are very unrealistic about their career future. Believing in many myths, they have inflated expectations about their value to civilian employers. They expect unrealistic salaries. Used to being successful in the Army, they now expect the process of finding a job will be relatively easy—just develop a sound plan and implement it. But their spouses know better; they worry a lot about you and the family future. They may be more realistic about the future—that this transition will not come easy and the result could be less than satisfactory if not done properly. If extremely insecure and worried about the family finances, some spouses will pressure their spouse to quickly take any job. The results can be disastrous—a bad job fit, an unhappy work situation, frequent job-hopping, and increased family tensions. Nothing fits right!

Please believe us when we advise you to have someone beside you on this journey into a new world of work. This is not the time nor the place to play the Lone Ranger. On your own you may find you are unrealistic about your career future, and your spouse may put pressure on you that results in a bad career choice. If you involve your spouse early in the career transition process, you will probably find your spouse will be very helpful and supportive of your job search efforts.

If not approached properly, job finding can be an extremely ego deflating process. You will need supports along the way. As we will see in Chapter 4, the Army and other military organizations provide numerous supports to assist you with your career transition. These supports come in the form of job search assistance, from electronic resume databases to workshops and counseling. At the same time, you will discover the process of charting a new career is best done in close communication with your spouse. Use each other as a sounding board for exploring career alternatives, examining new ideas, assessing your progress, and keeping your job search both focused and realistic. Better still, you may want to conduct two job searches together.

Most important of all, set your career and lifestyle goals together. In so doing, you'll discover finding a job will go much easier. You will probably cut your job search time in half by involving your spouse in the career decision-making process—and you'll stay happily married!

PLANNING AND THE ART
OF SAILING INTO YOUR FUTURE

We wish you well as you embark on what should become an exciting yet challenging process of finding a job and career right for you. The chapters that follow are designed to guide you through the key steps in the career transition process. We include the latest job search strategies and techniques that work for thousands of job seekers each year. They will work for you if you organize yourself properly and take the time to put them into practice.

To be most successful, you will need to be purposeful, patient, persistent, enthusiastic, and a bit irrational in your approach to the transition process. We strongly recommend a positive attitude toward this process: approach your career transition as an exciting adventure that will result in a rewarding lifestyle for you and your family. While much of this process follows a rational planning model, much of it at times appears irrational and chaotic—just like the job market for which you are organizing your job search efforts.

The plan should not become the end—it should be a flexible means for achieving your stated job and career goals.

Please don't confuse job search planning with strategic military planning—a mistake often made by inexperienced job seekers. Such a planning analogy is inappropriate given the relatively unstructured nature of the civilian job market and the general lack of centralized decision-making points, coherent communication channels, and visible power centers. Planning and organization in a job search does not mean creating a detailed plan, blueprint, or road map for taking action. Implementation according to a detailed plan simply doesn't work when dealing with the civilian job market. If you strictly adhere to such a plan, you will most likely be disappointed with the outcomes and frustrated with the civilian work world.

The role of planning in your job search should approximate the art of sailing: you know where you want to go and the general direction for getting there. But the specific path, as well as the time for reaching your destination, will be determined by your environment, situation, and skills. Like the sailor dependent upon his or her sailing skills and environmental conditions, you tack back and forth, progressing within what is an acceptable time period for successful completion of the task.

While we recommend planning your job search, we hope you will avoid the excesses of too much planning. The plan should not become the *end*—it should be a flexible *means* for achieving your stated job and career goals. Planning makes sense, because it requires you to set goals and develop strategies for achieving the goals. However, too much planning can blind you to unexpected occurrences and opportunities, or that wonderful experience called *serendipity*.

After all, you are operating in a highly decentralized and fragmented job market where information is at best incomplete, where communication is at best difficult, and where planning is subject to numerous changes and unexpected occurrences. In the end, you'll discover sailing is really what your job search is all about.

If you stay with us long enough, you're going to learn to sail very well, perhaps beyond your wildest expectations. You'll learn a great deal about both yourself and others in the job market. Best of all, you're going to turn what may initially appear to be problem into one of the most exciting times of your life.

May you sail into your next job and career with the greatest of ease. As you change your job, you'll change your life in many ways. Trust us to be here to help you through your transition.

2

MYTHS, REALITIES, AND YOUR JOB SEARCH

*W*hat do you know about today's job market? What do you need to do to make it work for you? How can someone with military experience and skills best fit into this market? Do you speak the same language as civilian employers or do you need to translate your military experience into civilian language? Does this job market have many jobs for you? Do you have a one or two-page resume ready to give to new network contacts and potential employers? How will you approach this job market? What do you do when you get there? Whom do you talk to? What do you say? In other words, how competent are you to conduct an effective job search?

Let's talk truth about the job market and your potential to do well in making a career transition from army green to corporate gray. If you have been out of the civilian job market for several years, you probably have a lot to learn about jobs, career opportunities, and how to best communicate your qualifications to potential employers. For if you have a clear understanding of the structure and operation of the civilian job market, you will be well on your way to developing and implementing an effective job search. If you don't understand this job market, you are likely to founder in the process of making your career transition.

The job market is anything but organized, centralized, and coherent.

JOB MARKET MYTHS AND REALITIES

The abstract notion of "a job market" generates several images of structures, processes, decision points, and outcomes. In one sense it appears to be well structured for dispensing job information and assistance. After all, you will find various elements that supposedly make up the structure of the job market: classified ads listing job vacancies; personnel offices with vacancy announcements; employment agencies and electronic databases linking candidates to job openings; and a variety of helpers known as career counselors, employment specialists, and headhunters who make a living by serving as gatekeepers to the "job market." At the same time, we know various processes are key to making this job market function: self-assessment, research, applications, resume and letter writing, networking, interviewing, negotiating, and hiring. You need to become very familiar with each of these processes as well as relate each process into a coherent job search.

Understanding the job market is analogous to the blind person exploring an elephant: you may recognize a trunk, a leg, and a tail, but you're not sure what it is as a whole. As we will see shortly, the job market is anything but organized, centralized, and coherent. It is more an abstraction, or convenient short-hand way of talking about finding jobs, than a set of well-defined and related structures.

Most people have an image of how the job market works as well as how they should relate to it. This image is based upon a combination of facts, stereotypes, and myths learned from experience and from the advice of well-meaning individuals. It's an unfortunate image when it guides people into unproductive job search channels by advising them to spend most of their time responding to vacancy announcements and waiting to hear from employers. In so doing, it reconfirms the often-heard lament of the unsuccessful job searcher—"What more can I do—there are no jobs out there for me."

Let's examine 45 myths about jobs, careers, and the job search before you proceed to organize yourself for today's and tomorrow's employment realities. These myths illustrate important points for organizing and implementing your job search. The corresponding realities constitute a set of how-to principles for developing a successful post-Army job search.

MYTH 1:   **It's best to get out of the Army today before becoming a victim of further downsizing.**

REALITY: You and millions of others are facing several diffi-cult choices for restructuring your life in today's tough economy. If you really love your work, and future promotions appear within your reach, you should seriously consider staying in the Army. The grass may look greener on the other side, but it may not prove greener for you. You and your family need to seriously assess your future in the Army. While today's Army is drawing down, it also is becoming leaner and meaner for the decade ahead. Those who get promoted must be exceptionally skilled and dedicated. On the other hand, if you are being forced out, accept the fact that this phase of your worklife is over. It's time to focus attention on your future worklife. This will be an exciting and challenging adventure. Three years from now you will look back at today and say you made the right choices because you planned your career transition properly.

MYTH 2:   **The military doesn't pay well. I'll be able to make a lot more money in the corporate world.**

REALITY: To the surprise of many, starting corporate salaries for most departing military personnel (especially officers) are often less—at least in terms of take home pay—then their active duty pay. You've been doing much better than you think. If you don't believe us, let us know about your new civilian pay six months after you leave the Army.

MYTH 3:   **With my many years of military experience, I'll have no problem finding a well-paying civilian job. Within a year or two I'll probably double my income.**

REALITY: While your positive attitude is to be admired, you are probably overly optimistic and unrealistic about the transition process and your appeal to high-paying employers. You may be in for a real shock, especially when two years later you are only making ten percent more than in your last Army job. Many military personnel have unrealistic expectations about

While many civilian employers verbally may be "military-friendly," not many are waiting in line to give you a job nor pay you a high salary.

their marketability and their dollar worth in the civilian job market. Many don't understand civilian compensation—it's usually tied to productivity and profits rather than to age, experience, or rank. If you believe you should be worth $80,000, are you prepared to convince an employer that you will generate an additional $500,000 in income for the company to justify this salary figure? If you can't, then you shouldn't be talking about such a salary expectation. Many ex-military are surprised to learn they have not been as underpaid in the military as they thought, especially when they cash their first civilian paycheck and pay their new set of bills. Let's face it. While many civilian employers verbally may be "military-friendly," not many are waiting in line to give you a job nor pay you a high salary. You'll have to work at it, persuade employers of your value, experience the usual frustrations and rejections accompanying a job search, and then probably settle for less than what you expected. Your job search is likely to be a real sobering experience for both you and your family. And there's a high probability you will initially choose a job that is not right for you and thus you will need to repeat this job search process within a year or two. You may quickly discover that your military experience does not translate well into specific high-demand civilian jobs. Furthermore, you may not experience a significant increase in income even though your new salary may appear higher than your Army pay. If you've not been living totally on the local housing and consumer economy, you will find your new cost of living as a civilian may more than offset your higher income. You may even settle for a job that pays less than your previous Army job. Only a lucky few ever find this transition process quick and easy or results in a high-paying job. Consequently, it's best to start with a more realistic expectation and commitment about your transition—your job search creed:

> This process will probably require three to six months of hard work on my part. I should expect disappointments and rejections along the way, but I will not let these negative experiences deter me from achieving my central goal—finding a job I really do well and enjoy doing. I had better get myself organized by first answering the question "What do I really want to do the rest of my life?" After that I will do a complete self-assessment, conduct research, write a terrific

resume and job search letters, network, and interview for jobs. I'll do the very best I can to find a job that is right for me. While I have dreams and I am a can-do person, I will avoid engaging in wishful thinking that distracts me from my central goal.

> *You should be looking for a job that is right for you—one you do well and enjoy doing.*

MYTH 4: Nobody's hiring.

REALITY: Just as in the military, personnel turnover is a fact of life. Even during economic downturns, companies are always looking for quality people who can help their business grow. If you are a quality person who conducts a first-class job search, you should have little difficulty getting hired. But remember, you're not looking for just any job that happens to come your way. You want to make the best choices. You should be looking for a job that is right for you—one you do well and enjoy doing. The job should be consistent with the motivated skills and abilities you identify in Chapter 7.

MYTH 5: Finding a good job in the corporate world is very difficult.

REALITY: While it takes time to properly prepare for and conduct a successful job search, obtaining a job can be a relatively painless process if you organize yourself properly. It takes a disciplined, concerted effort focused on your job search objective(s).

MYTH 6:   **I'll look for a job abroad where the pay is much higher than in the States.**

REALITY: Numerous myths and misunderstandings surround international employment. The major myths are outlined in the Krannichs' *Complete Guide to International Jobs and Careers.* While you may have lived and worked abroad with the Army, living and working abroad on your own or with a private company is very different. It's real international living. You're no longer being sponsored by your government, especially if you must live off the local economy and reside with the locals. The financial rewards of international employment vary greatly. Some jobs—especially international consulting—can pay very well. Jobs with many nonprofit organizations pay poorly. For those living abroad, special financial benefits are often offset by additional expenses incurred in trying to maintain a certain lifestyle as well as lost opportunities for supplementing income, such as appreciation of property in the States or job opportunities for one's spouse. Make sure you check with your JAG office before seeking international employment. There are certain legal restrictions (see Chapter 4) on whom ex-military personnel can work for abroad.

MYTH 7:   **I need a college education to find a good job in the corporate world.**

REALITY: While a college education will normally give you a "leg up" on the competition, the lack of a degree does not close the door. Prospective employers are always looking for "hard chargers" who will work diligently and help their business prosper. Many employers seek former military personnel because of their reputation for hard work, few personal problems, and dedication to accomplishing the mission.

MYTH 8:   **Any company will want me because I went to ABC University, a prestigious and well known institution of higher learning.**

REALITY: While private companies respect a candidate's educational background and military experience, they are more interested in knowing what skills he or she has and how these skills can be applied to make their companies more profitable. Be sure to use your university and alumni connections for getting job information, advice, and referrals, but don't expect to get a job because of your university background. You still have to sell yourself based upon your past performance and predictability about your future productivity.

MYTH 9: **All I need to get a good job is a list of employers hiring in my field of expertise; I'll contact them and land a job quickly.**

REALITY: You probably need a lot more than just a list of names, addresses, and telephone numbers. Most job seekers first need a clear understanding of their interests, skills, and abilities *before* contacting potential employers. You gain this understanding by conducting a self-assessment involving a series of tests and self-directed exercises for identifying your motivated pattern of interests, skills, and abilities. Once you have a clear picture of who you are and what you really want to do, you will be prepared to communicate your qualifications to employers.

MYTH 10: **The corporate world works 9 to 5. Therefore, my work hours will be far fewer than in the military.**

REALITY: Yes, the standard corporate hours are normally in this vicinity. However, in order to excel and move up the corporate ladder, be prepared to put in far more than such minimum hours.

MYTH 11: **Because I was a mid-level manager in the military, I should be hired as a mid-level manager in the corporate world.**

REALITY: Maybe yes, maybe no, but don't be surprised if you end up in some other type of position. While private companies take into consideration past military experience, most will want you to prove yourself before placing you in a leadership position. Indeed, mid-level management positions usually go to those who have experience within the organization; few are direct-hire positions. Furthermore, competition for mid-level management positions continues to be very keen given the downsizing that is taking place in corporate America today and which has significantly shrunk mid-level management ranks during the past five years. Corporations have eliminated mid-level management positions faster than most other positions. If you did well in the military, there's no reason not to believe you won't quickly re-establish yourself as a leader in the corporate world. But don't expect to quickly become a mid-level manager in organizations that are continuing to downsize their management ranks. If, on the other hand, you did not reach your full potential while in the military, the slate is wiped clean and you have a new opportunity to excel in the corporate world.

MYTH 12: **I'm lost and afraid of what to do next. I could use some help, but no one is available to assist me with my transition.**

REALITY: You'll be pleasantly surprised how much excellent professional assistance is available to help with your job search. In Chapter 4, for example, we identify numerous transition services available just for Army personnel. Be sure to take advantage of these free services. In Chapter 18 we identify numerous books available on a variety of job search subjects to assist you with a self-directed job search. You'll also discover numerous government and private job search services, from electronic databases and workshops to career counselors and executive search firms. Unfortunately, you may also encounter many unscrupulous firms that want up-front fees to find you a job. Many of these firms advertise overseas jobs, prey on military personnel, and disproportionately operate from Florida and Canada. Most charge from $150 to $2,000 in exchange for broken promises; none have jobs for sale. Remember, any firm that wants up-front fees for the promise of giving you a job is probably engaged in fraud. You should never pay such a firm for the promise of a job. The best job search services are free. The best kept secret is that the best place to find the best free job search services are at community colleges. Also, if you are looking for jobs in the $15,000 to $35,000 range, don't forget to visit your local state employment office. They have numerous free job services available for you, including job listings for veterans. Many are linked to America's Job Bank which is a nationwide computerized job listing service.

Any firm that wants up-front fees for the promise of giving you a job is probably engaged in fraud.

MYTH 13: **Medical and dental benefits are better in the private sector.**

REALITY: The extent of medical and dental benefits offered will vary depending on the company. Most medium to large size companies offer a range of employee plans that cover the individual and their families. However, these plans often require a monthly employee contribution. Smaller companies often do not have the resources to be as generous as their larger counterparts and may offer only limited coverage.

MYTH 14: **Anyone can find a job; all you need to know is how to find a job.**

REALITY: This classic "form versus substance" myth is often
associated with career counselors who were raised on
popular career planning exhortations of the 1970s
and 1980s that stressed the importance of having
positive attitudes and self-esteem, setting goals,
dressing for success, and using interpersonal strategies for finding jobs. While such approaches may
work well in an industrial society with low unemployment, they constitute myths in a post-industrial,
high-tech society which requires employees to demonstrate both *intelligence and concrete work skills*
as well as a *willingness to relocate* to new communities offering greater job opportunities. For example,
many of today's unemployed are highly skilled in the
old technology of the industrial society, but they live
and own homes in economically depressed communities. These people lack the necessary *skills and
mobility* required for getting jobs in high-tech,
growth communities. Knowing job search skills alone
will not help these people. Indeed, such advice and
knowledge will most likely frustrate such highly
motivated and immobile individuals who possess
skills of the old technology.

MYTH 15: **The best way to find a job is to respond to classified ads, use employment agencies, and submit
applications to personnel offices.**

REALITY: Except for certain types of organizations, such as
government, these formal application procedures are
not the most effective ways of finding jobs. Such approaches assume the presence of an organized,
coherent, and centralized job market—but no such
thing exists. The job market is highly decentralized,
fragmented, and chaotic. Classified ads, employment
agencies, and personnel offices tend to list low
paying yet highly competitive jobs or high paying
highly skilled positions that are hard to fill. Most of
the best jobs—high level, excellent pay, least competitive—are neither listed nor advertised; they are
most likely found through word-of-mouth. Your most

fruitful strategy will be to conduct research and informational interviews on what career counselors call the "hidden job market."

The job market is highly decentralized, fragmented, and chaotic.

MYTH 16: A civilian Federal job will be a good second career for me.

REALITY: It may be for some transitioning Army personnel, but it is not a good alternative for others. If you are an officer, you are better off looking for a job in the private sector. The Dual Compensation Act of 1964 reduces the retirement pay of commissioned officers who elect to work for the Federal government; this legislation does not affect reserve officers and enlisted personnel. If you are an officer and you become a Federal employee, you will receive one-half of your annual retirement pay in excess of $9,310.17. Consequently, commissioned officers are financially penalized for "double dipping" as Federal employees. If you are a commissioned officer, be sure to do your math on *total compensation* before seeking a Federal job. You may discover you are working for much less than you anticipated. On the other hand, it may be easier for you to land a Federal job than other non-military applicants, because by law you are eligible for a special veterans preference which gives you extra points in the selection process.

MYTH 17: Few jobs are available for me in today's competitive job market.

REALITY: This may be true if you lack marketable skills and insist on applying for jobs listed in newspapers, employment agencies, or personnel offices. Competition in the advertised job market usually is high, especially for jobs requiring few skills. Numerous jobs with little competition are available in the hidden job market. Jobs requiring advanced technical skills often go begging. Little competition may occur during periods of high unemployment, because many people quit job hunting after a few disappointing weeks of concentrating job search efforts on working the advertised job market.

MYTH 18: **Army personnel have advantages in the job market because of their unique work attitudes, discipline, and work.**

REALITY: Maybe at McDonald's, UPS, or other organizations run along military lines. You may quickly discover you are not as unique as you think. Indeed, the "we/they" and NIH syndrome—Not Invented Here— are frequent orientations held by individuals who have little experience outside their own organizations or work cultures. It's best to expect an even playing field in the civilian job market. There are just as many non-military people competing in today's job market who have similar work attitudes, discipline, and behaviors as those held by Army members. In the eyes of many employers, you may have certain advantages because of your Army background, but talk is cheap. Indeed, your military experience is a double-edge sword. Some employers may flatter you and then attempt to exploit you by paying you less that what you are worth because they believe you will come cheaper given your history of military pay. Remember, you're competing in a tough job market with people who have specific skills and work experience; they know their way around civilian organizations. Your military experience may also create certain liabilities in the eyes of employers— stereotypes which become *objections to hiring you.* Indeed, employers are naturally suspicious about anyone they hire. Given their past experiences with employees who have quit or were fired, they think about the possible negative consequences of making another hiring decision. Employers know your military experience potentially has both positive and negative consequences for them. Keep in mind that many transitioning military people leave their first post-military job within the first twelve months—a negative "military" experience for some employers. Many also have difficulty adjusting to corporate work cultures. You should be prepared to overcome these stereotypes and objections. Whether these objections are applicable to you or not, nonetheless, some employers believe them and act accordingly:

- You worked in a military *bureaucracy* which is more noted for its consumption capabilities and perks than for achieving market results; you're not a profit-oriented person. Since our business is business, your business should be business. We're heavily into managing our bottomline—productivity, customer service, and accountability.

- You're not prepared for making a quick transition to today's fast-paced corporate cultures. We are in the midst of several revolutions—new and radical ways of organizing work, networked information technology, knowledge-based products, and globalization of the company and its products. We operate in a different world from where you come from as well as in which we operated only five years ago. You'll need direct corporate experience in these revolutions before you can move to the positions and salary you expect to receive.

- You may be able to respectfully receive and give orders as a military leader, but you're probably not creative nor do you take much initiative. You may not be familiar with our ways of organizing and coordinating work. Around here we want creative and innovative people who are willing to take risks that could result in losing their jobs.

- You may be obsessed with simplifying problems —you think in black and white terms and thus are ill-suited for dealing with chaos, uncertainty, numerous decision points, decentralized structures, or situations in which no one is in charge.

- You may be a take-charge "leadership" person, but you're probably insensitive to other professionals who are vital to our operation but who are not under your control. The concept and practice of leadership is very different in our organization; we don't have command and control structures.

- You are probably intolerant of civilian organizational politics or you don't play this type of politics well. You'll quickly become a casualty.

- You don't really know what you want to do—you just want to secure any job for now. Within three months you'll probably be unhappy here and then leave after the first year. We prefer avoiding this type of turnover.

Do you know what to say or do if an employer raises any of these objections to hiring you? Are you prepared for the corporate revolutions? What used to be seen as positive military work attitudes and behaviors may no longer be seen as suitable for many of today's rapidly changing corporations. Overall, you may have difficulty adapting your military attitudes and work behaviors to civilian organizational settings and cultures. Your most positive asset may be your willingness and ability to quickly learn and adapt to new situations.

MYTH 19: **I know how to find a job, but opportunities are not available for me.**

REALITY: Most people don't know the best way to find a job, or they lack marketable job skills. They continue to use ineffective job search methods, such as only responding to classified ads with resumes and cover letters. Opportunities are readily available for individuals who understand the structure and operation of the job market, have appropriate work-content skills, and use job search methods designed for the hidden job market. They must learn to develop an effective networking and informational interviewing campaign for uncovering promising job leads. And they must persist in prospecting for new job leads as well as learn to handle rejections.

MYTH 20: **I'm over-qualified in the eyes of many employers. They don't want to hire over-qualified individuals.**

REALITY: Yes, if you're seeking a $25,000 a year job but you have experience and qualifications for a $60,000 a year job! Why would you even want to consider such a job? Who wants to hire someone who is over-qualified and thus likely to leave for greener pastures once they get their wake-up call that they are under-employed and under-compensated? This is the classic self-fulfilling prophecy of many career changers and transitioning military personnel who don't know how to best communicate their qualifications to employers. You're never over-qualified if you seek jobs for your level of skills and experience. Employers who view you as over-qualified are the wrong employers to whom to apply. They do you a favor by not giving you a job. Thank them for being so discriminating. They serve as your wake-up call. You need to get a better sense of where you fit into the job market. Stop under-selling yourself and thus contributing to this over-qualification myth. You need some job market smarts before you approach any more employers.

MYTH 21: **Employers are in the driver's seat; they have the upper-hand with applicants.**

REALITY: Most often no one is in the driver's seat. Not knowing what they want, many employers make poor hiring decisions. They frequently let applicants define their hiring needs. If you can define employers' needs as your skills, you might end up in the driver's seat!

If you can define employers' needs as your skills, you might end up in the driver's seat!

MYTH 22:   **Employers hire the best qualified candidates. Without a great deal of experience and numerous qualifications, I don't have a chance.**

REALITY: Employers hire people for all kinds of reasons. Most rank experience and qualifications third or fourth in their pecking order of hiring criteria. Employers seldom hire the best qualified candidate, because "qualifications" are difficult to define and measure. Employers normally seek people with the following characteristics: competent, intelligent, honest, enthusiastic, and likable. "Likability" tends to be an overall concern of employers—will you "fit in" and get along well with your superiors, co-workers, and clients? Employers want *value* for their money. Therefore, you must communicate to employers that you are such a person. You must overcome employers' objections to any lack of experience or qualifications. But never volunteer your weaknesses. The best qualified person is the one who knows how to get the job—convinces employers that he or she is the *most* desirable for the job.

MYTH 23:   **My spouse will be just as supportive of my job search as she/he has been of my Army career.**

REALITY: Don't bet on it. Many spouses' justifiably feel insecure about such a career transition. After all, they know other spouses who have made career transition mistakes. This fear leads them to pressure their spouse to take the first job that comes along. If you don't manage this transition process properly, you may discover that your spouse is an obstacle to making a healthy career transition. Your spouse will be most supportive if directly involved at the early stages of your job search. Don't be the Lone Ranger and surprise your spouse by coming home and announcing a new worklife. This is not the time to go through mid-life crisis and create turmoil for those close to you. Spouses worry a great deal about the family future. Involve your spouse throughout your transition. Do the self-assessment and goal-setting exercises together, write your resume together, and conduct research and network together. You'll discover such involvement generates much needed support and assistance, minimizes pressures to make premature career decisions, and is healthy for a marriage. In so doing, your spouse may also launch a new career with you!

MYTH 24: **It is best to go into a growing field where jobs are plentiful.**

REALITY: Be careful in following the masses to the "in" fields. First, many so-called growth fields can quickly become no-growth fields, such as aerospace engineering, nuclear energy, and defense contracting. Second, by the time you acquire the necessary skills, you may experience the "disappearing job" phenomenon: too many people did the same thing you did and consequently glut the job market. Third, since many people leave no-growth fields, new opportunities may arise for you. Fourth, if you go after a growth field, you will try to fit into a job rather than find a job fit for you. If you know what you do well and enjoy doing (Chapters 5-7), and what additional training you may need, you should look for a job or career that is most conducive to your particular mix of skills, interests, and motivations. In the long-run you will be much happier and more productive finding a

job fit for you. If you find a job you really love, you
will be more compensated than if you only focused
on finding a job that pays a high salary.

If you go after a growth field, you will try to fit into a job rather than find a job fit for you.

MYTH 25: People over 40 have difficulty finding a good job;
employers prefer hiring younger and less expen-
sive workers.

REALITY: Yes, if they apply for youth jobs. Age should be an
insignificant barrier to employment if you conduct a
well organized job search and are prepared to handle
this potential negative with employers. Age should
be a positive and must be communicated as such.
After all, employers want experience, maturity, and
stability. People over 40 generally possess these
qualities. As the population ages and birth rates
decline, older individuals should have a much easier
time changing jobs and careers.

MYTH 26: It's best to use an employment firm to find a job.

REALITY: It depends on the firm and the nature of employment
you are seeking. Employment firms that specialize in
your skill area may be well worth contacting. For
example, many law firms use employment firms to
hire paralegals rather than directly recruit such personnel themselves. Many employers now use temporary employment firms to recruit both temporary and
full-time employees at several different levels, from
clerical to professional. Indeed, many temporary
employment firms have temp-to-perm programs that

link qualified candidates to employers who are looking for full-time employees. But make sure you are working with a legitimate employment firm. Legitimate firms get paid by employers or they collect placement fees from applicants only *after* the applicant has accepted a position. Beware of firms that want up-front fees for promised job placement assistance.

MYTH 27: **I must be aggressive in order to find a job.**

REALITY: Aggressive people tend to be offensive and obnoxious people. Try being purposeful, persistent, and pleasant in all job search activities. Such behavior is well received by potential employers!

MYTH 28: **There are no jobs available in California's recessionary economy.**

REALITY: While California's economy has been hard hit with the double-whammy of defense cutbacks and recessions in the Pacific Rim economies, California still has a large job market. California's current high unemployment rates will gradually recede during the next five years as the State's economy rebounds. Construction, attendant with the deadly January 1994 earthquake, may lead the way. However, don't expect California to return to the go-go employment years of the 60's, 70's, and 80's. It still has a tough job market. You'll simply have to spend more time looking for a job in California than in other states.

MYTH 29: **Given current and long-term cutbacks in military spending, I should avoid looking for employment with defense industries.**

REALITY: Like California, defense industries are experiencing their own recession. For some defense industries, the cutbacks will be deep and devastating. Some may go out of business altogether. Others will be bought out and consolidated with other more viable defense contractors. Expect to see even more layoffs among defense contractors during the next few years. Given the uncertainty surrounding the government's defense policy, the future of defense contractors appears uncertain. At the same time, this period of uncertainty is also one of great opportunities. Defense contractors are being forced by public policy and economic changes to undergo much needed restructuring. Like any business undergoing cutbacks, many defense contractors are cutting the fat, becoming more efficient, diversifying their businesses, and generally becoming more lean and mean. This process results in winners and losers. The defense contractors that are in real trouble are the ones that have more than 70 percent of their business tied to government contracts. Others, such as Booz, Allen & Hamilton Inc., Martin Marietta, SAIC, PRC, and General Electric learned long ago to diversify their businesses so that government contracts make up only part of their larger business base. Firms engaged in "defense conversion"—converting defense technologies to commercial use—can more easily absorb policy uncertainties; they are still hiring. Our advice: if your experience and skills appeal to defense contractors, focus your job search on those firms that have a diversified business base rather than on those that are totally dependent on defense contracts. You're less likely to experience downsizing in the highly diversified firms.

MYTH 30: **I should not change jobs and careers more than once or twice. Job-changers are discriminated against in hiring.**

REALITY: While this may have been generally true 30 years ago, it is no longer true today. America is a skills-based society: individuals market their skills to organizations in exchange for money and position. Furthermore, since most organizations are small businesses with limited advancement opportunities, careers quickly plateau for most people. For them, the only way up is to get out and into another organization. Therefore, the best way to advance careers in a society of small businesses is to change jobs frequently. Job-changing is okay as long as such changes demonstrate career advancement and one isn't changing jobs every few months. Most individuals entering the job market today will undergo several career and job changes regardless of their initial desire for a one-job, one-career life plan.

MYTH 31: **People get ahead by working hard and putting in long hours.**

REALITY: Success patterns differ. Many people who are honest, work hard, and put in long hours also get fired, have ulcers, and die young. Some people get ahead even though they are dishonest and lazy. Others simply have good luck or a helpful patron. Moderation in both work and play will probably get you just as far as the extremes. There are other ways, as outlined in the next chapter, to become successful in addition to hard work and long hours.

MYTH 32: **I should not try to use contacts or connections to get a job. I should apply through the front door like everyone else. If I'm the best qualified, I'll get the job.**

REALITY: While you may wish to stand in line for tickets, bank deposits, and loans—because you have no clout— standing in line for a job is dumb. Every employer has a front door as well as a back door. Try using the back door if you can. It works in many cases. Chapter 11 outlines in detail how you can develop your contacts, use connections, and enter *both* the front and back doors.

MYTH 33: **I need to get more education and training to qualify for today's jobs.**

REALITY: You may or may not need more education and training, depending on your present skill levels and the needs of employers. What many employers are looking for are individuals who are intelligent, communicate well, take initiative, and are trainable; they train their employees to respond to the needs of their organization. You first need to know what skills you already possess and if they appear appropriate for the types of jobs you are seeking.

MYTH 34: **Once I apply for a job, it's best to wait to hear from an employer.**

REALITY: Waiting is not a good job search strategy. If you want action on the part of the employer, you must first take action. The key to getting a job interview and offer is follow-up, follow-up, follow-up. You do this by making follow-up telephone calls as well as writing follow-up and thank you letters to employers.

MYTH 35: **I don't need a resume. I can get a job based solely on my network contacts.**

REALITY: While networking certainly is one of the most effective methods used to find civilian employment, it does not erase the need for a resume. The resume is your corporate calling card; it provides a prospective employer with a snapshot of your background and skills. Use it wisely to generate interest.

MYTH 36: **A good resume is the key to getting a job.**

REALITY: While resumes play an important role in the job search process, they are often overrated. The purpose of a resume is to communicate your qualifications to employers who, in turn, invite you to job interviews. The key to getting a job is the job interview. No job interview, no job offer.

MYTH 37: **I should include my salary expectations on my resume or in my cover letter.**

REALITY: You should never include your salary expectations on your resume or in a cover letter, unless specifically requested to do so. Salary should be the very last thing you discuss with a prospective employer. You do so only after you have had a chance to assess the worth of the position and communicate your value to the employer. This usually comes at the end of your final job interview, just before or after being offered the job. If you prematurely raise the salary issue, you may devalue your worth.

MYTH 38: **My resume should emphasize my work history.**

REALITY: Employers are interested in hiring your future rather than your past. Therefore, your resume should emphasize the skills and abilities you will bring to the job as well as your interests and goals. Let employers know what you are likely to do for them in the future. When you present your work history, do so in terms of your major skills and accomplishments.

Employers are interested in hiring your future rather than your past.

MYTH 39: **It's not necessary to write letters to employers—just send a resume or complete an application.**

REALITY: You should be prepared to write several types of job search letters—cover, approach, resume, thank you, follow-up, and acceptance. In addition to communicating your level of literacy, these job search letters enable you to express important values sought by employers—your tactfulness, thoughtfulness, likability, enthusiasm, and follow-up ability. Sending a resume without a cover letter devalues both your resume and your application.

MYTH 40: **I should have no problem writing a good resume. Given all my experience, it will probably run five to ten pages.**

REALITY: Employers are not interested in reading a lengthy military resume filled with unintelligible language, titles, and awards. Remember, you speak a special language that may be comprehensible within the service culture, but it may sound strange and unintelligible to the civilian world. That's your problem—not theirs. The first thing you need to do is get your language and thinking right—assume you're dealing with civilians who know nothing about your military background nor do they care much about your unique history of ranks and reassignments. They want to know what you can do for them tomorrow—your skills in exchange for position and money. And they want it all boiled down into a crisp, clearly-worded, and attractive-looking one to two-page resume—no more, please!

MYTH 41: **Networking doesn't work well for military personnel. I'm used to getting ahead based upon my performance rather than on my "pull".**

REALITY: Military personnel are some of the best networkers found in any organization. After all, the Army family takes care of one another. Given all the contacts they have developed from participating in training and professional groups to developing new relationships at different bases, they are especially good at long-distance networking. Many officers and NCOs understand the "ole boy" system and are familiar in using it to affect their training, promotions, and base assignments. One of the first things you will want to do in making your career transition is to identify your network of friends and colleagues you've developed over the years. Yes, it's time to call in your debts and take on new ones. Let people in your network know you are making a career transition. Ask them for their advice and assistance. You will be surprised what you will learn from this network.

These individuals may be your best sources for job leads. You may get a job through these contacts.

MYTH 42: **Salaries are pre-determined by employers.**

REALITY: Most salaries are negotiable within certain ranges and limits. Before you ever apply or interview for a position, you should know what the salary range is for the type of position you seek. When you finally discuss the salary question—preferably at the end of the final job interview—do so with this range in mind. Assuming you have adequately demonstrated your value to the employer, try to negotiate the highest possible salary within the range.

MYTH 43: **Bigger employers will provide better benefits than smaller employers.**

REALITY: It depends on the employer and situation. Overall, both large and small employers are cutting back on benefits, especially in the high costs areas of health care and pensions. You should expect to contribute a larger percentage of your compensation to employer-sponsored benefit packages. When negotiating salary, it's best to concentrate on the total annual salary figure.

MYTH 44: **It's best to relocate to an economically booming community.**

REALITY: Similar to the "disappearing job" phenomenon for college majors, today's economically booming communities may be tomorrow's busts. It's best to select a community that is conducive to your lifestyle preferences as well as has a sufficiently diversified economy to weather boom and bust economic cycles.

MYTH 45: **It's best to broadcast or "shotgun" my resume to as many employers as possible.**

REALITY: Broadcasting your resume to employers is a game of chance in which you usually waste your time and money. It's always best to target your resume on those employers who have vacancies or who might have openings in the near future. Your single best approach for uncovering job leads will be the process called networking.

ADDITIONAL REALITIES

You also should be aware of several other realities which will affect your job search or which you might find helpful in developing your plan of action for finding a job or changing a career:

- **You will find less competition for high-level jobs than for middle and low-level jobs.** If you aim high yet are realistic, you may be pleasantly surprised with the results.

- **Personnel offices seldom hire.** They primarily screen candidates for employers who are found in operating units of organizations. Knowing this, you should focus your job search efforts on those who do the actual hiring.

- **Politics are both ubiquitous and dangerous in many organizations.** If you think you are above politics, you may quickly become one of its victims. Unfortunately, you only learn about "local politics" *after* you accept a position and begin relating to the different players in the organization.

- **It is best to narrow or "rifle" your job search on particular organizations and individuals rather than broaden or "shotgun"** it to many alternatives. If you remain focused, you will be better able to accomplish your goals.

- **Employment firms and personnel agencies may not help you.** Most work for employers and themselves rather than for applicants. Few have your best interests at heart. Use them only after you have investigated their effectiveness. Avoid firms that require up-front money for a promise of performance.

- **Most people can make satisfying job and career changes.** They should minimize efforts in the advertised job market and concentrate instead on planning and implementing a well organized job search tailored to the realities of the hidden job market.

- **Jobs and careers tend to be fluid and changing.** Knowing this, you should concentrate on acquiring and marketing skills, talents, and abilities which can be transferred from one job to another.

- **Millions of job vacancies are available every day** because new jobs are created every day, and people resign, retire, get fired, or die.

- **Most people, regardless of their position or status, love to talk about their work and give advice** to both friends and strangers. You can learn the most about job opportunities and alternative careers by talking to such people.

As you conduct your job search, you will encounter many of these and other myths and realities about how you should relate to the job market. Several people will give you advice. While much of this advice will be useful, a great deal of it will be useless and misleading. You should be skeptical of well-meaning individuals who most likely will reiterate the same job and career myths. You should be particularly leery of those who try to *sell* you their advice.

Always remember you are entering a relatively disorganized and chaotic job market where you can find numerous job opportunities. Your task is to organize the chaos around your skills and interests. You must convince prospective employers that they will like you more than other "qualified" candidates.

3

GET
ORGANIZED
FOR NEW
SUCCESSES

*Y*ou are joining millions of other individuals who go through job and career transitions each year. Indeed, between 15 and 20 million people find themselves unemployed each year. Millions of others try to increase their satisfaction within the work place as well as advance their careers by looking for alternative jobs and careers.

If you are like most other Americans, you will make more than ten job changes and between three and five career changes during your lifetime. The fact that you have spent many years in the Army where you have already made several job changes probably means you will make at least two more career changes and six job changes during the rest of your worklife. You are now engaging in the first of what may become several job and career changes in your future.

PLANNING YOUR SUCCESSFUL TRANSITION

Most people make job or career transitions by accident. While luck does play a role in finding employment, we recommend that you *plan* for future job and career changes. As a member of the Army, you can begin planning your luck by using several free or low cost transition services designed for military personnel. We'll examine these in Chapter 4.

Finding a job or changing a career in a systematic and well-planned manner is hard yet rewarding work. The task should first be based upon a clear understanding of the key ingredients that define jobs and careers. Starting with this understanding, you should next convert key concepts into action steps for implementing your job search.

A career is a series of related jobs which have common skill, interest, and motivational bases. You may change jobs several times without changing careers. But once you change skills, interests, and motivations, you change careers.

It's not easy to find a job given the present structure of the job market. You will find the job market to be relatively disorganized, although it projects an outward appearance of coherence. If you seek comprehensive, accurate, and timely job information, the job market will frustrate you with its poor communication. While you will find many employment services ready to assist you, such services tend to be fragmented and their performance is often disappointing. Job search methods are controversial and many are ineffective.

Job finding skills are often more important to career success than job performance or work-content skills.

No system is organized to give people jobs. At best you will encounter a *decentralized and fragmented system* consisting of job listings in newspapers, trade journals, employment offices, or computerized job data banks—all designed to link potential candidates with available job openings. Many people will try to sell you job information as well as questionable job search services. While efforts are underway to create a nationwide computerized job bank which would list available job vacancies on a daily basis, don't expect such data to become available soon nor to be very useful. Many of the listed jobs may be nonexistent, or at a low skill and salary level, or represent only a few employers. In the end, most systems organized to help you find a job do not provide you with the information you need in order to land a job that is most related to your skills and interests.

UNDERSTAND THE CAREER DEVELOPMENT PROCESS

Finding a job is both an art and a science; it encompasses a variety of basic facts, principles, and skills which can be learned but which also must be adapted to individual situations. Thus, *learning how to find a job* can be as important to career success as *knowing how to perform a job*. Indeed, job finding skills are often more important to career success than job performance or work-content skills.

Our understanding of how to find jobs and change careers is illustrated on pages 41 and 42. As outlined on page 41, you should involve yourself in a four-step career development process as you prepare to move from one job to another.

CAREER DEVELOPMENT PROCESS

1. Conduct a self-assessment:

This first step involves assessing your skills, abilities, motivations, interests, values, temperaments, experience, and accomplishments—the major concern of this book. Your basic strategy is to develop a firm foundation of information on *yourself* before proceeding to other stages in the career development process. This self-assessment develops the necessary self-awareness upon which you can effectively communicate your qualifications to employers as well as focus and build your career.

2. Gather career and job information:

Closely related to the first step, this second step is an exploratory, research phase of your career development. Here you

THE CAREER DEVELOPMENT PROCESS

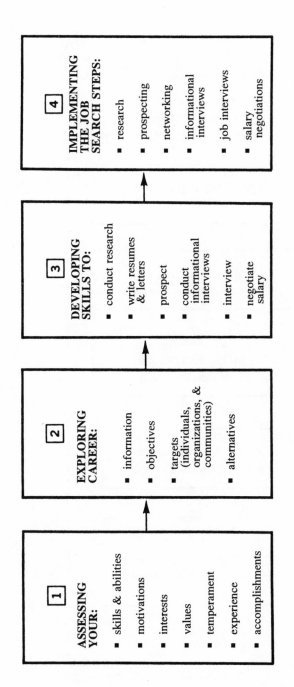

1

ASSESSING YOUR:

- skills & abilities
- motivations
- interests
- values
- temperament
- experience
- accomplishments

2

EXPLORING CAREER:

- information
- objectives
- targets (individuals, organizations, & communities)
- alternatives

3

DEVELOPING SKILLS TO:

- conduct research
- write resumes & letters
- prospect
- conduct informational interviews
- interview
- negotiate salary

4

IMPLEMENTING THE JOB SEARCH STEPS:

- research
- prospecting
- networking
- informational interviews
- job interviews
- salary negotiations

JOB SEARCH STEPS

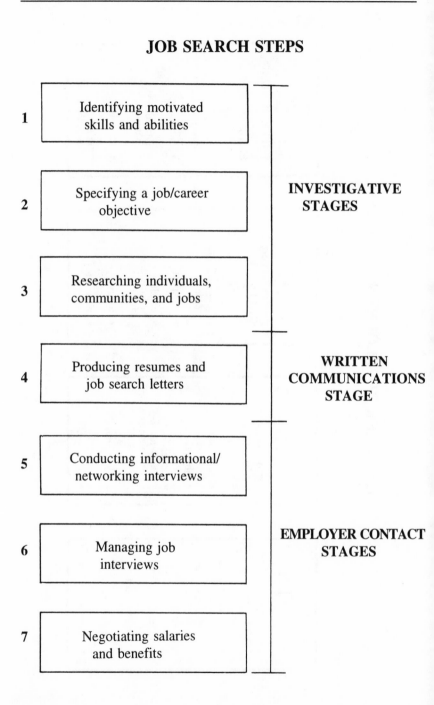

need to formulate goals, gather information about alternative jobs and careers through reading and talking to informed people, and then narrow your alternatives to specific jobs.

3. Develop job search skills:

The third step focuses your career around specific job search skills for landing the job you want. As further outlined on page 41, these job search skills are closely related to one another as a series of *job search steps*. They involve conducting research, writing resumes and letters, prospecting and networking, conducting informational interviews, interviewing for a job, and negotiating salary and terms of employment. Each of these job search skills involves well-defined strategies and tactics you must learn in order to be effective in the job market.

4. Implement each job search step:

The final career development step emphasizes the importance of transforming understanding into *action*. You do this by implementing each job search step which already incorporates the knowledge, skills, and abilities you acquired in Steps 1, 2, and 3.

ORGANIZE AND SEQUENCE YOUR JOB SEARCH

The figure on page 42 further expands our career development process by examining the key elements in a successful job search. It consists of a seven-step process which relates your past, present, and future. We will cover all of these steps in subsequent chapters which deal with skills assessment, research, resume writing, networking, interviewing, and salary negotiations.

Based on this concept, *your past* is well integrated into the process of finding a job or changing your career. Therefore, you should feel comfortable conducting your job search: it represents the best of what you are in terms of your past and present accomplishments as these relate to your present and future goals. If you base your job search on this process concept, you will communicate your *best self* to employers as well as focus on *your strengths* both during the job search and on the job.

Since the individual job search steps are interrelated, they should be followed in sequence. If you fail to properly complete the initial self-assessment steps, your job search may become haphazard, aimless, and costly. For example, you should never write a resume (Step 3) before first conducting an assessment of your skills (Step 1) and identifying your objective (Step 2). Relating Step 1 to Step 2 is especially critical to the successful implementation of all other job search steps. You *must* complete Steps 1 and 2 *before* continuing on to the other steps. Steps 3 to 6 may be conducted simultaneously because they complement and reinforce one another.

Try to sequence your job search as close to these steps as possible. The true value of this sequencing will become very apparent as you implement your plan.

The processes and steps identified on pages 41 and 42 represent key job and career changing processes used successfully with thousands of military and nonmilitary clients during the past 30 years. They should work for you as long as you recognize the importance of linking work-content skills with job search skills.

You must do much more than just know how to find a job. In the job markets of today and tomorrow, you need to constantly review your work-content skills to make sure they are appropriate for the changing job market. Assuming you have the necessary work-content skills for the civilian job market, you should be ready to target your skills on particular jobs and careers that you do well and enjoy doing. You will be able to avoid the trap of trying to fit into jobs that are not conducive to your particular mix of interests, abilities, skills, and motivations.

TEST YOUR JOB SEARCH COMPETENCIES

Knowing *where* the jobs are is important to your job search. But knowing *how to find a job* is even more important. Before you acquire names, addresses, and phone numbers of potential employers, you should possess the necessary job search knowledge and skills for gathering and using job information effectively.

Answers to many of your job related questions are found by examining your present level of job search knowledge and skills. Successful job seekers, for example, use a great deal of information as well as specific skills and strategies for getting the jobs they want.

Let's begin by testing for the level of job search information, skills, and strategies you currently possess as well as those you need to develop and improve. You can easily identify your level of job search competence by completing the following exercise:

YOUR JOB SEARCH COMPETENCE

INSTRUCTIONS: Respond to each statement by circling which number at the right best represents your situation.

SCALE: 1 = strongly agree   4 = disagree
2 = agree   5 = strongly disagree
3 = maybe, not certain

1. I know what motivates me to excel at work.   1 2 3 4 5

2. I can identify my strongest abilities and skills.   1 2 3 4 5

3. I have seven major achievements that clarify
    a pattern of interests and abilities that
    are relevant to my job and career.   1 2 3 4 5

4. I know what I both like and dislike in work.   1 2 3 4 5

5. I know what I want to do during the next
    10 years.   1 2 3 4 5

6. I have a well defined career objective that
    focuses my job search on particular
    organizations and employers.   1 2 3 4 5

7. I know what skills I can offer employers in
    different occupations.   1 2 3 4 5

8. I know what skills employers most seek in
    candidates.   1 2 3 4 5

9. I can clearly explain to employers what I do
    well and enjoy doing.   1 2 3 4 5

10. I can specify why employers should hire me.   1 2 3 4 5

11. I can gain support of family and friends
    for making a job or career change.   1 2 3 4 5

12. I can find 10 to 20 hours a week to
    conduct a part-time job search.   1 2 3 4 5

13. I have the financial ability to sustain a
    three- to six-month job search.   1 2 3 4 5

14. I can conduct library and interview research
    on different occupations, employers,
    organizations, and communities.   1 2 3 4 5

15. I can write different types of effective
    resumes and job search/thank you letters.   1 2 3 4 5

16. I can produce and distribute resumes and
    letters to the right people.   1 2 3 4 5

17. I can list my major accomplishments in
    action terms.   1 2 3 4 5

18. I can identify and target employers I
    want to interview.   1 2 3 4 5

19. I can develop a job referral network.   1 2 3 4 5

20. I can persuade others to join in forming
    a job search support group.   1 2 3 4 5

21. I can prospect for job leads.   1 2 3 4 5

22. I can use the telephone to develop prospects
    and get referrals and interviews.   1 2 3 4 5

23. I can plan and implement an effective
    direct-mail job search campaign.   1 2 3 4 5

24. I can generate one job interview for every
    10 job search contacts I make.   1 2 3 4 5

25. I can follow-up on job interviews.   1 2 3 4 5

26. I can negotiate a salary 10-20% above
    what an employer initially offers.   1 2 3 4 5

27. I can persuade an employer to renegotiate
    my salary after six months on the job.   1 2 3 4 5

28. I can create a position for myself
    in an organization.   1 2 3 4 5

                              TOTAL   _____

You can calculate your overall job search competencies by adding the numbers you circled for a composite score. If your total is more than 75 points, you need to work on developing your careering skills. How you scored each item will indicate to what degree you need to work on improving specific job search skills. If your score is under 50 points, you are well on your way toward job search success. In either case, this book should help you better focus your job search as well as identify job search skills you need to acquire or strengthen.

SEEK PROFESSIONAL
ASSISTANCE WHEN NECESSARY

While some people can successfully conduct a job search based on the advice of books such as this, many others also need the assistance of various professional groups that offer specific career planning and job search services. As we will see on pages 49-54 and in Chapter 4, these groups offer everything from testing and assessment services to offering employer contacts, including job vacancy information and temporary employment services. Some do one-on-one career counseling while others sponsor one to three-day workshops or six to twelve-week courses on the various steps in the career planning process. You should know something about these services before you invest your time and money beyond this and other career planning and job search books.

OPTIONS

You have two options in organizing your job search. First, you can follow the principles and advice outlined in this and many other self-directed books. Just read the chapters and then put them into practice by following the step-by-step instructions. Second, you may wish to seek professional help to either supplement or replace this book. Indeed, many people will read parts of this book—perhaps all of it—and do nothing. Unwilling to take initiative, lacking sufficient time or motivation, or failing to follow-through, many people will eventually seek professional help to organize and implement their job search. They will pay good money to get someone else to tell them to follow the advice found in this book. Some people need this type of expensive motivation and organization.

At the same time, we recognize the value of professional assistance. Especially with the critical assessment and objective setting steps (Chapters 5-8), some individuals may need more assistance than our advice and exercises provide. You may, for example, want to take a battery of tests to better understand your interests and values in relation to alternative jobs and careers. And still others, due to a combination of job loss, failed relationships, or depression, may need therapy best provided by a trained psychologist or psychiatrist rather than career testing and information services provided by career counselors. If any of these situations pertain to you, by all means seek professional help.

While many services are excellent, other services are useless.

You also should beware of pitfalls in seeking professional advice. While many services are excellent, other services are useless and some fraudulent. Remember, career planning and job assistance are big businesses involving millions of dollars each year. Many people enter these businesses without expertise. Professional certification in these areas is extremely weak to non-existent in some states. Indeed, many so-called "professionals" get into the business because they are unemployed. In other words, they major in their own problem! Others are frauds and hucksters who prey on vulnerable and naive people who feel they need a "specialist" or "expert" to get them a job. They will take your money in exchange for promises. You will find several services promising to assist you in finding all types of jobs. You should know something about these professional services before you venture beyond this book.

If you are interested in exploring the services of job specialists, begin by looking in the Yellow Pages of your telephone directory under these headings: Management Consultants, Employment, Resumes, Career Planning, and Social Services. Several career planning and employment services are available, ranging from highly generalized to very specific services. Most services claim they can help you. If you read this book, you will be in a better position to seek out specific services as well as ask the right questions for screening the services. You may even discover you know more about finding a job than many of the so-called professionals!

ALTERNATIVE SERVICES

At least twelve different career planning and employment services are available to assist you with your job search. Each has certain advantages and disadvantages. Use them, but also approach them with caution. Never sign a contract before you read the fine print, get a second opinion, and talk to former clients about the *results* they achieved through the service. With these words of caution in mind, let's take a look at the variety of services available.

1. **Customized Army transition services:**

   Several Army, Department of Defense, Department of Labor, and association-sponsored programs, such as the Army Career and Alumni Program (ACAP), Job Assistance Centers (JAC), Joint Employment Transition Services (JETS), Family Member Employment Assistance Program (FMEAP), Transition Assistance Program (TAP), Defense Outplacement Referral System (DORS), Association of the United States Army (AUSA), The Retired Officers Association (TROA), and the Non Commissioned Officers Association (NCOA), provide career transition services for service personnel. We provide information on these programs in Chapters 4 and 17.

2. **Public employment services:**

   Public employment services usually consist of a state agency which provides employment assistance as well as dispenses unemployment compensation benefits. Employment assistance largely consists of job listings and counseling services. However, counseling services often screen individuals for employers who list with the public employment agency. If you are looking for an entry-level job in the $15,000 to $35,000 range, contact this service. Most employers do not list with this service, especially for positions paying more than $35,000 a year. Although the main purpose of these offices is to dispense unemployment benefits, these offices also offer useful employment services, including self-assessment and job search workshops as well as job banks that match skills and experience with available job vacancies. Many of these offices are linked to America's Job Bank, an electronic database which includes job listings throughout the U.S. and abroad. Many jobs listed with state employment offices are for veterans. Go see for yourself if your state employment office offers useful services for you. Ask about job opportunities for veterans.

3. Private employment agencies:

Private employment agencies work for money, either from applicants or employers. Approximately 8,000 such agencies operate nationwide. Many are highly specialized in technical, scientific, and financial fields. The majority of these firms serve the interests of employers since employers—not applicants—represent repeat business. While employers normally pay the placement fee, many agencies charge applicants 10 to 15 percent of their first year salary. These firms have one major advantage: job leads which you may have difficulty uncovering elsewhere. Especially for highly specialized fields, a good firm can be extremely helpful. The major disadvantages are that they can be costly and the quality of the firms varies. Be careful in how you deal with them. Make sure you understand the fee structure and what they will do for you before you sign anything.

4. Temporary employment firms:

During the past decade temporary employment firms have come of age as more and more employers turn to them for recruitment assistance. They offer a variety of employment services to both employers and job seekers. Many of these firms recruit individuals for a wide range of positions and skill levels as well as full-time employment. If you are interested in "testing the job waters," you may want to contact these firms for information on their services. Employers—not job seekers—pay for these services.

5. College/university placement offices:

College and university placement offices provide in-house career planning services for graduating students. While some give assistance to alumni, don't expect too much help if you have already graduated. Many of these offices are understaffed or provide only rudimentary services, such as maintaining a career planning library, coordinating on-campus interviews for graduating seniors, and conducting workshops on how to write resumes and interview. Others provide a full range of well supported services including testing and one-on-one counseling. Indeed, many community colleges offer such services to members of the community on a walk-in basis. You can use their libraries and computerized career assessment programs, take personality and interest inventories, or attend special workshops or full-semester career planning courses which will take you through each step of the career planning and job search processes. You are well advised to enroll in such a course since it is likely to provide just enough structure and content to assess your motivated abilities and skills and to assist you in implementing a successful job search plan. Check with your local campus to see what services you might use.

6. Private career and job search firms:

Private career and job search firms help individuals acquire job search skills. They do not find a job for you. In other words, they teach you much—maybe more but possibly less—of what is outlined in this book. Expect to pay anywhere from $1,500 to $10,000 for this service. If you need a structured environment for conducting your job search, contract with one of these firms. One of the oldest and most popular firms is Haldane Associates. Many of their pioneering career planning and job search methods are incorporated in this book. You will find branches of this nationwide firm in many major cities.

7. Executive search firms and headhunters:

Executive search firms work for employers in finding employees to fill critical positions in the $60,000 plus salary range. They also are called "headhunters," "management consultants," and "executive recruiters." These firms play an important role in linking high level technical and managerial talent to organizations. Don't expect to contract for these services. Executive recruiters work for employers—not applicants. If a friend or relative is in this business or you have relevant skills of interest to these firms, let them know you are available— and ask for their advice. On the other hand, you may want to contact firms that specialize in recruiting individuals with your skill specialty. Several books identify how you can best approach "headhunters" on your own: *The Directory of Executive Recruiters* (Kennedy Publications); *How to Select and Use an Executive Search Firm* (A. R. Taylor); *How to Answer a Headhunter's Call* (Robert H. Perry); *The Headhunter Strategy* (Kenneth J. Cole); and *How to Get a Headhunter to Call* (Howard S. Freedman).

8. Marketing services:

Marketing services represent an interesting combination of job search and executive search activities. They can cost $2,500 or more, and they work with individuals anticipating a starting salary of at least $75,000 but preferably over $100,000. These firms try to minimize the time and risk of applying for jobs. A typical operation begins with a client paying a $150 fee for developing psychological, skills, and interests profiles. Next, a marketing plan is outlined and a contract signed for specific services. Using word processing equipment, the firm normally develops a slick "professional" resume and mails it along with a cover letter, to hundreds—maybe thousands—of firms. Clients are then briefed and sent to interview with interested employers. While you can save money and achieve the same results on your own, these firms do have one major advantage. They save you *time* by doing most of the work for you. Again, approach these services with caution and with the knowledge that you can probably do just as well—if not better—on your own by following the step-by-step advice of this book.

9. Women's Centers and special career services:

Women's Centers and special career services have been established to respond to the employment needs of special groups. Women's Centers are particularly active in sponsoring career planning workshops and job information networks. These centers tend to be geared toward elementary job search activities, because their clientele largely consists of homemakers who are entering or re-entering the work force with little knowledge of the job market. Special career services arise at times for different categories of employees. For example, unemployed aerospace engineers, teachers, veterans, air traffic controllers, and government employees have formed special groups for developing job search skills and sharing job leads.

10. Testing and assessment centers:

Testing and assessment centers provide assistance for identifying vocational skills, interests, and objectives. Usually staffed by trained professionals, these centers administer several types of tests and charge from $300 to $800 per person. You may wish to use some of these services if you feel our activities in Chapters 5-8 generate insufficient information on your skills and interests to formulate your job objective. If you use such services, make sure you are given one or both of the two most popular and reliable tests: *Myers-Briggs Type Indicator* and the *Strong-Campbell Interest Inventory.* You should find both tests helpful in better understanding your interests and decision-making styles. However, try our exercises before you hire a psychologist or visit a testing center. If you first complete these exercises, you will be in a better position to know exactly what you need from such centers. In many cases the career office at your local community college or women's center can administer these tests at minimum cost. You should also check with the various transition assistance programs outlined in Chapter 4; they can help you with these tests.

11. Job fairs or career conferences:

Job fairs or career conferences are organized by service associations (NCOA, AFCEA, AUSA—see Chapter 4) and employment agencies to link applicants to employers. Usually consisting of one to two-day meetings in a hotel or other conference facility, employers meet with applicants as a group and on a one-to-one basis. Employers give presentations on their companies, applicants circulate resumes, and employers interview candidates. Many such conferences are organized to attract hard-to-recruit groups, such as engineers, computer programmers, and clerical and service workers. While associations and private companies typically organize job fairs, the federal government increasingly uses job fairs for quickly recruiting many specialized personnel. These are excellent sources for job leads and information—if you qualify to participate in such meetings. We recommend that you contact

service associations for calendars of up-coming job fairs as
well as use the Transition Bulletin Board of DORS (see
Chapter 17) to get information on upcoming job fairs for
service personnel. The Non Commissioned Officers Association's (NCOA) job fair schedule for October 1993 through
June 1994, for example, includes eleven job fairs to be held in
Sacramento, San Diego, Ft. Walton Beach, San Antonio, N.
Charleston, Norfolk, Tucson, Colorado Springs, Jacksonville,
and San Antonio. To participate in an NCOA-sponsored job
fair, you must contact NCOA (Tel. 210/653-6161) and complete a mini resume using NCOA's computerized format. Employers usually pay for this service—not applicants.

12. Professional associations:

Professional associations often provide placement assistance.
Members of The Retired Officers Association (TROA) and the
Non Commissioned Officers Association (NCOA) can participate in excellent placement services designed specifically for
their members. If you are not a member, you are well-advised
to join the appropriate association as soon as possible—before
you leave the service. You should also check with other
professional associations. If, for example, you are a telecommunications, engineering, or computer specialist, you will find
several professional associations related to your professional
specialty. Some of these associations will have job search and
placement services available to their members. These services
usually consist of listing job vacancies and job information
exchanges at annual conferences. These meetings are good
sources for making job contacts in different geographic
locations within a particular professional field. But don't
expect too much. Talking to people (networking) at professional conferences may yield better results than reading job listings
and interviewing at conference placement centers.

CHOOSE THE BEST

Other types of career planning and employment services are growing and
specializing in particular occupational fields. You may wish to use these
services as a supplement to this book.

Whatever you do, proceed with caution, know exactly what you are getting into, and choose the best. Remember, there is no such thing as a free lunch, and you often get less than what you pay for. At the same time, the most expensive services are not necessarily the best. Indeed, the free and inexpensive career planning services offered by the Army, service associations, and many community colleges—use of libraries, computerized career assessment programs, testing, and workshops—are often superior to alternative services which can be expensive.

After reading this book, you should be able to make intelligent decisions about what, when, where, and with what results you can use professional assistance. Shop around, compare services and costs, ask questions, talk to former clients, and read the fine print with your lawyer before giving an employment expert a job using your hard earned money!

WHEN IN DOUBT, TAKE ACTION

The old adage "When in doubt, do something" is especially relevant when expanded to include a thoughtful plan of action related to the job search process: "When in doubt, engage in a concrete activity related to the sequence of job search steps." This might include conducting research on communities, companies, positions, and salaries; surveying job vacancy announcements; writing a resume and job search letters; or contacting three employers each day.

But developing a plan and taking action is much easier said than done. If conducted properly, a job search can become an extremely time consuming activity. It inevitably competes with other personal and professional priorities. That's why you need to make some initial decisions as to how and when you will conduct a job search. How much time, for example, are you willing to set aside each day or week to engage in each of the seven job search activities outlined at the beginning of this chapter? After you've spent numerous hours identifying your abilities and skills and formulating an objective, are you willing to commit yourself to 20 hours a week to network for information and advice? If you are unwilling to commit both your time and yourself to each activity within the process, you may remain stuck, and inevitably frustrated, at the initial stages of self-awareness and understanding. Success only comes to those who take action at other stages in the job search process.

USE TIME WISELY

If you decide to conduct your own job search with minimum assistance from professionals, your major cost will be your time. Therefore, you must find sufficient time to devote to your job search. Ask yourself this question:

> "How valuable is my time in relation to finding a job
> or changing my career?"

Assign a dollar value to your time. For example, is your time worth $3, $5, $10, $25, $50, or $100 an hour? Compare your figure with what you might pay a professional for doing much of the job search work for you. Normal professional fees range from $2,000 to $12,000.

The time you devote to your job search will depend on whether you want to work at it on a full-time or part-time basis. If you are unemployed, by all means make this a full-time endeavor—40 to 80 hours per week. If you are presently employed, we do not recommend quitting your job in order to look for employment. You will probably need the steady income and attendant health benefits during your transition period. Furthermore, it is easier to find new employment by appearing employed. Unemployed people project a negative image in the eyes of many employers—they appear to need a job. *Your goal is to find a job based on your strengths rather than your needs.*

However, if you go back to school for skills retraining, your present employment status may be less relevant to employers. Your major strength is the fact that you have acquired a skill the employer needs. If you quit your job and spend money retraining, you will communicate a certain degree of risk-taking, drive, responsibility, and dedication which employers readily seek, but seldom find, in candidates today.

Assuming you will be conducting a job search on a part-time basis—15 to 25 hours per week—you will need to find the necessary time for these job activities. Unfortunately, most people are busy, having programmed every hour to "important" personal and professional activities. Thus, conducting a job search for 15 or more hours a week means that some things will have to go or receive low priority in relation to your job search.

This is easier said than done. The job search often gets low priority. It competes with other important daily routines, such as attending meetings, taking children to games, going shopping, and watching favorite TV programs. Rather than fight with your routines—and create family disharmony and stress—make your job search part of your daily routines by improving your overall management of time.

Certain time management techniques will help give your job search high priority in your daily schedule. These practices may actually lower your present stress level and thus enhance your overall effectiveness.

Time management experts estimate that most people waste their time on unimportant matters. Lacking priorities, people spend 80 percent of their time on trivia and 20 percent of their time on the important matters which should get most of their attention. If you reverse this emphasis, you could have a great deal of excess time—and probably experience less stress attendant with the common practice of crisis managing the critical 20 percent.

Before reorganizing your time, you must know how you normally use your time. Complete the following inventory for a preliminary assessment of your time management behavior. While many of these statements are particularly relevant to individuals in managerial positions, respond to those statements that are most pertain to your employment situation.

YOUR TIME MANAGEMENT INVENTORY

Respond to each statement by circling "yes" or "no," depending on which response best represents your normal pattern of behavior.

1. I have a written set of long, intermediate,
   and short-range goals for myself (and family).   Yes   No

2. I have a clear idea of what I will do today
   at work and at home.   Yes   No

3. I have a clear idea of what I want to
   accomplish at work this week and month.   Yes   No

4. I set priorities and follow-through on the
   most important tasks first.   Yes   No

5. I judge my success by the results I produce
   in relation to my goals.   Yes   No

6. I use a daily, weekly, and monthly calendar
   for scheduling appointments and setting
   work targets.   Yes   No

7. I delegate as much work as possible.   Yes   No

8. I get my subordinates to organize their time
   in relation to mine.   Yes   No

9. I file only those things which are essential
   to my work. When in doubt, I throw it out.   Yes   No

10. I throw away junk mail.   Yes   No

11. My briefcase is uncluttered, including only
    essential materials; it serves as my office
    away from the office.   Yes   No

12. I minimize the number of meetings and con-
    centrate on making decisions rather than
    discussing aimlessly.   Yes   No

13. I make frequent use of the telephone and
    face-to-face encounters rather than written
    communications.   Yes   No

14. I make minor decisions quickly.   Yes   No

15. I concentrate on accomplishing one thing
    at a time.   Yes   No

16. I handle each piece of paper once and
    only once.   Yes   No

17. I answer most letters on the letter I receive
    with either a handwritten or typed message.   Yes   No

18. I set deadlines for myself and others and
    follow-through in meeting them.   Yes   No

19. I reserve time each week to plan.   Yes   No

20. My desk and work area are well organized
    and clear.   Yes   No

21. I know how to say "no" and do so.   Yes   No

22. I first skim books, articles, and other forms
    of written communication for ideas before
    reading further.   Yes   No

23. I monitor my time use during the day by
    asking myself "How can I best use my
    time at present?"   Yes   No

24. I deal with the present by getting things
    done that need to be done.   Yes   No

25.	I maintain a time log to monitor the best use of my time.	Yes	No
26.	I place a dollar value on my time and behave accordingly.	Yes	No
27.	I—not others—control my time.	Yes	No
28.	My briefcase includes items I can work on during spare time in waiting rooms, lines, and airports.	Yes	No
29.	I keep my door shut when I'm working.	Yes	No
30.	I regularly evaluate to what degree I am achieving my stated goals.	Yes	No

If you answered "no" to many of these statements, you should consider incorporating a few basic time management principles and practices into your daily schedule.

Don't go to extremes by drastically restructuring your life around the "religion" of time management. If you followed all the advice of time management experts, you would probably alienate your family, friends, and colleagues with your narrow efficiency mentality! A realistic approach is to start monitoring your time use and then gradually re-organize your time according to goals and priorities. This is all you need to do. Forget the elaborate flow charts that are the stuff of expensive time management workshops and consultants. Start by developing a time management log that helps you monitor your present use of time. Keep daily records of how you use your time over a two week period. Identify who controls your time and the results of your time utilization. Within two weeks, clear patterns will emerge. You may learn that you have an "open door" policy that enables others to control your time, leaving little time to do your own work. Based on this information, you may need to close your door and be more selective about access. You may find from your analysis that you use most time for activities that have few if any important outcomes. If this is the case, then you may need to set goals and prioritize daily activities.

A simple yet effective technique for improving your time management practices is to complete a "to do" list for each day. You can purchase tablets of these forms in many stationery and office supply stores, or you can develop your own "Things To Do Today" list. This list also should prioritize which activities are most important to accomplish each day.

Include at the top of your list a particular job search activity or several activities that should be completed on each day. If you follow this simple time management practice, you will find the necessary time to include your job search in your daily routines. You can give your job search top priority. Better still, you will accomplish more in less time, and with better results.

PLAN TO TAKE ACTION . . . AND GET LUCKY

While we recommend that you plan your job search, we also caution you to avoid the excesses of too much planning. Like time management, planning should not be all-consuming. Planning makes sense because it focuses attention and directs action toward specific goals and targets. It requires you to set goals and develop strategies for achieving the goals. However, too much planning can blind you to unexpected occurrences and opportunities—that wonderful experience called serendipity. Luck—being in the right place at the right time—plays an important role in the job search. However, we like to plan our luck. After all, luck is when preparation and opportunity meet.

> *Luck is when preparation*
> *and opportunity meet.*

Given the highly decentralized and chaotic nature of the job market, you want to do just enough planning so you will be in a position to take advantage of what will inevitably be unexpected occurrences and opportunities arising from your planned job search activities. Therefore, as you plan your job search, be sure you are flexible enough to take advantage of new opportunities and the luck that inevitably will come your way.

DEVELOP A TIMELINE

As with any military operation, it is important to establish a timeline and be disciplined in the execution of your planned activities. It is no less important when embarking on your employment campaign. Your mission is to obtain employment. Therefore, you need to consider doing the following:

1. Determine the number of weeks/months before you need to start the new job. It's not too early to start now!

2. Prioritize the employment search activities.

3. Determine which activities can be done concurrently and which activities must be done sequentially.

4. Place activities on a timeline.

5. Execute the plan.

6. Follow-up each job search activity with appropriate actions.

Developing a sound yet flexible search plan is critical to conducting a successful employment campaign. Regardless of how much time you have, the time spent planning and organizing your activities will result in a far more effective search.

A timeline is one useful technique you should include in your job search for planning each of your activities. Here's an example of the type of activities you may want to sequence on your timeline:

FIRST MONTH:

- Contact your organization's ethics attorney.

- Determine your employment desires (read job search books with major sections on self-assessment and goal setting).

- Contact ACAP, JAC, FMEAP—obtain schedule of transition classes.

- Enter in DORS (job data bank) through your ACAP office.

- Contact your college alumni services for assistance.

- Make a list of your friends and colleagues whom you believe would be willing to talk about the corporate world.

- Look at your wardrobe—think about what clothes you will need to buy. Begin watching the newspaper for sales.

SECOND MONTH:

- Attend transition classes offered by ACAP, JAC, FMEAP, and AFCEA. TROA conducts nearly 100 transition lectures a year.

- Prepare your resume.

    — Read books on our recommended reading list in Chapter 18.
    — Draft a resume for the positions you are seeking. (You will probably want to use a combination resume which highlights your functional skills and also tells the prospective employer the nature of your assignments.)

- Research employment fields.

    — Visit the library—learn about the different companies that exist in your fields of interest.
    — Follow our research advice in Chapter 9.

- Start informational interviews.

    — Contact your friends and associates on the list you made last month and make an appointment to meet with them.
    — Prepare for the interviews—think about questions you will ask; go to the library—read about their field/company.
    — At the interview—*listen*; ask intelligent questions; ask them if they will review your resume; thank them for their time.

- Prepare your wardrobe—the right suit for interviews.

THIRD MONTH:

- Contact an executive recruiter—establish a rapport; let him/her know about your background; ask for suggestions.

- Continue informational interviewing.

- Update your records—carefully track whom you've met, what transpired, future actions.

- Expand your wardrobe—purchase a second interview suit.

- Identify potential references—contact them; send copies of your resume.

- Write directly to those firms that are involved in the type of work in which you are interested.

- Respond to selected newspaper ads for employment (after researching firm at library).

- Attend local job fairs.

FOURTH AND SUBSEQUENT MONTHS:

- Follow-up on all employment leads.

- Stay in touch with your contacts, references, and executive recruiters.

Depending on your situation, you may want to develop a timeline which incorporates a different sequence of job search activities. However, your overall job search should follow the job search steps we previously discussed.

Your time line should incorporate the individual job search activities over a six month period. If you phase in the first five job search steps during the initial three to four weeks and continue the final four steps in subsequent weeks and months, you should begin receiving job offers within two to three months after initiating your job search. Interviews and job offers can come anytime—often unexpectedly—as you conduct your job search. An average time is three months, but it can occur within a week or take as long as five months. If you plan, prepare, and persist at the job search, the pay-off will be job interviews and offers.

While three to six months may seem a long time—especially if you are unemployed—you can shorten your job search time by increasing the frequency of your individual job search activities. If you are job hunting on a full-time basis, you may be able to cut your job search time in half. But don't expect to get a job that's right for you—within a week or two. Job hunting requires time and hard work—perhaps the hardest work you will ever do—but if done properly, it pays off with a job that is right for you.

STRATEGIES FOR SUCCESS

Success is determined by more than just a good plan or timeline getting
implemented. We know success is not determined primarily by intelligence, time management, or luck. Based upon experience, theory,
research, commonsense, and acceptance of some self-transformation principles, we believe you will achieve job search success by following many
of these 21 principles:

1. **You should work hard at finding a job:** Make this a daily
   endeavor and involve your family.

2. **You should not be discouraged with set-backs:** You are
   playing the odds, so expect disappointments and handle them
   in stride. You will get many "no's" before finding the one
   "yes" which is right for you.

3. **You should be patient and persevere:** Expect three to six
   months of hard work before you connect with the job that's
   right for you.

4. **You should be honest with yourself and others:** Honesty is
   always the best policy. But don't be naive and stupid by
   confessing your negatives and shortcomings to others.

5. **You should develop a positive attitude toward yourself:**
   Nobody wants to employ guilt-ridden people with inferiority
   complexes. Focus on your positive characteristics.

6. **You should associate with positive and successful people:**
   Finding a job largely depends on how well you relate to others.
   Avoid associating with negative and depressing people who
   complain and have a "you-can't-do-it" attitude. Run with
   winners who have a positive "can-do" outlook on life.

7. **You should set goals:** You should have a clear idea of what
   you want and where you are going. Without these, you will
   present a confusing and indecisive image to others. Clear goals
   help direct your job search into productive channels. Moreover,
   setting high goals will help make you work hard in getting
   what you want.

8. **You should plan:** Convert your goals into action steps that are organized as short, intermediate, and long-range plans.

9. **You should get organized:** Translate your plans into activities, targets, names, addresses, telephone numbers, and materials. Develop an efficient and effective filing system and use a large calendar to set time targets, record appointments, and compile useful information.

10. **You should be a good communicator:** Take stock of your oral, written, and nonverbal communication skills. How well do you communicate? Since most aspects of your job search involve communicating with others, and communication skills are one of the most sought-after skills, always present yourself well both verbally and nonverbally.

11. **You should be energetic and enthusiastic:** Employers are attracted to positive people. They don't like negative and depressing people who toil at their work. Generate enthusiasm both verbally and nonverbally. Check on your telephone voice— it may be more unenthusiastic than your voice in face-to-face situations.

12. **You should ask questions:** Your best information comes from asking questions. Learn to develop intelligent questions that are non-aggressive, polite, and interesting to others. But don't ask too many questions and thereby become a bore.

13. **You should be a good listener:** Being a good listener is often more important than being a good questioner or talker. Learn to improve your face-to-face listening behavior (nonverbal cues) as well as remember and use information gained from others. Make others feel they enjoyed talking with you, i.e., you are one of the few people who actually *listens* to what they say.

14. **You should be polite, courteous, and thoughtful:** Treat gatekeepers, especially receptionists and secretaries, like human beings. Avoid being aggressive or too assertive. Try to be polite, courteous, and gracious. Your social graces are being observed. Remember to send thank you letters—a very thoughtful thing to do in a job search. Even if rejected, thank employers for the "opportunity" given to you. After all, they may later have addi-

tional opportunities, and they will remember you. Thank you letters get remembered by employers.

15. **You should be tactful:** Watch what you say to others about other people and your background. Don't be a gossip, back-stabber, or confessor.

16. **You should maintain a professional stance:** Be neat in what you do and wear, and speak with the confidence, authority, and maturity of a professional.

17. **You should demonstrate your intelligence and competence:** Present yourself as someone who gets things done and achieves results—a *producer*. Employers generally seek people who are bright, hard working, responsible, communicate well, have positive personalities, maintain good interpersonal relations, are likable, observe dress and social codes, take initiative, are talented, possess expertise in particular areas, use good judgment, are cooperative, trustworthy, and loyal, generate confidence and credibility, and are conventional. In other words, they like people who score in the "excellent" to "outstanding" categories of the annual performance evaluation.

18. **You should maximize your contacts through networking:** Interpersonal networking still remains the key to getting the right job. It's not something you turn on and off when you need something from others—that's using others, not networking. You need to constantly renew old contacts, manage current contacts, and develop new contacts for maintaining and expanding your network of personal and professional contacts. These contacts will serve you well in your quests for finding a job, changing careers, or advancing on the job.

19. **You should not over-do your job search:** Don't engage in overkill and bore everyone with your "job search" stories. Achieve balance in everything you do. Occasionally take a few days off to do nothing related to your job search. Develop a system of incentives and rewards—such as two non-job search days a week, if you accomplish targets A, B, C, and D.

20. **You should be open-minded and keep an eye open for "luck":** Too much planning can blind you to unexpected and

fruitful opportunities. You should welcome serendipity. Learn to re-evaluate your goals and strategies. Seize new opportunities if they appear appropriate.

21. **You should evaluate your progress and adjust:** Take two hours once every two weeks and evaluate what you are doing and accomplishing. If necessary, tinker with your plans and reorganize your activities and priorities. Don't become too routinized and thereby kill creativity and innovation.

These principles should provide you with an initial orientation for starting your job search. As you become more experienced, you will develop your own set of operating principles that should work for you in particular employment situations.

TAKE RISKS AND HANDLE REJECTIONS

You can approach leaving the Army in various ways. Some actions have higher pay-offs than others. Many people waste time by doing nothing, reconstructing the past, worrying about the future, and thinking about what they should have done. This negative approach impedes rather than advances careers.

A second approach is to do what most people do when looking for a job. They examine classified ads, respond to vacancy announcements, and complete applications in personnel offices. While this approach is better than doing nothing, it is relatively inefficient as well as ineffective. You compete with many others who are using the same approach. Furthermore, the vacancy announcements do not represent the true number of job vacancies nor do they offer the best opportunities. As we will see in Chapter 9, you should use this approach to some degree, but it should not preoccupy your time. Responding to vacancy announcements is a game of chance, and the odds are usually against you. It makes you too dependent upon others to give you a job.

The third approach to making a job change requires *taking creative action* on your part. You must become a self-reliant risk-taker. You identify what it is you want to do, what you have acquired skills to do, and organize yourself accordingly by following the methods outlined in subsequent chapters. You don't need to spend much time with classified ads, employment agencies, and personnel offices. And you don't need to worry about your future. You take charge of your future by initiating a job search which pays off with job offers. Your major investment is *time*.

Your major risk is being turned down or rejected.

Job hunting is a highly ego-involved activity which will probably result in numerous rejections you may take personally. After all, you place your past, abilities, and self-image before strangers who don't know who you are or what you can do. Being rejected, or having someone say "no" to you, will probably be your greatest job hunting difficulty. We know most people can handle two or three "no's" before they get discouraged. If you approach your job search from a less ego-involved perspective, you can take "no's" in stride; they are a normal aspect of your job search experience. Be prepared to encounter 10, 20, or 50 "no's." Remember, the odds are in your favor. For every 20 "no's" you get, you also should uncover one or two "yeses." The more rejections you get, the more acceptances you also will get. Therefore, you must encounter rejection *before* you get acceptances.

This third approach is the approach of this book. Experience shows that the most successful job seekers are those who develop a high degree of self-reliance, maintain a positive self-image, and are willing to risk being rejected time after time without becoming discouraged. This approach will work for you if you follow our advice on how to become a self-reliant risk-taker in today's job market. Better yet, use the networking strategies outlined in Chapter 11 as well as more fully developed in the Krannichs' *Interview for Success* and *The New Network Your Way to Job and Career Success* books, and you can significantly decrease the number of "no's" you receive on your way to a job that's right for you.

JOIN OR FORM A SUPPORT GROUP

We believe most people can conduct a successful job search on their own by following the step-by-step procedures of this book. We know they work because these methods have been used by thousands of successful job hunters. But we also know it is difficult to become a risk-taker, especially in an area where few people have a base of experience and knowledge from which to begin. Therefore, we recommend sharing the risks with others.

Our self-directed methods work well when you join others in forming a job search group or club. The group provides a certain degree of security which is often necessary when launching a new and unknown adventure. In addition, the group can provide important information on job leads. Members will critique your approach and progress. They will provide you with psychological supports as you experience the frustration of rejections and the joys of success. You also will be helping others who will be helping you. Some career counselors estimate that membership in such groups can cut one's job search time by as much as 50 percent!

As a member of the Army, you are fortunate to be eligible for several career transition and job search services sponsored by the government and various service associations. Your participation in the ACAP program puts you in a support group where you can attend workshops, receive one-on-one counseling, and use electronic job banks. You also might check to see if the program on your base is organizing other types of support groups to assist participants in monitoring and following-up their job search progress. If not, you may want to organize your own informal support group consisting of four or five other Army members and their spouses who are going through the same transition process.

You can form your own group by working with your spouse or by finding friends who are interested in looking for a new job. Your friends may know other friends or colleagues who are interested in doing the same. Some of your friends may surprise you by indicating they would like to join your group out of curiosity. If you are over 40 years of age, check to see if there is a chapter of the 40-Plus Club in your community. This group is organized as a job search club.

Your group should meet regularly—once a week. At the meetings discuss your experiences, critique each other's approaches and progress, and share information on what you are learning or what you feel you need to know more about and do more effectively. Include your spouse as part of this group. We will return to this subject in Chapter 11 when we discuss how to develop your networks for uncovering job leads.

One other aspect of this self-directed book should be clarified. While we do not recommend that you immediately seek professional assistance, such as a career counselor, this assistance can be useful at certain stages and depending on individual circumstances. In fact, we outline in the next chapter several services available to assist transitioning Army personnel with their job search. You should immediately take advantage of these services since most are free and custom-designed to respond to your special needs. At the same time, this is a self-directed book that can be implemented with or without such assistance. For instance, in Chapter 5 we focus on skills identification. While we present the necessary information and exercises for you to identify your skills, some individuals may wish to enhance this step of the job search by seeking the assistance of a professional career counselor who may have more sophisticated testing instruments, such as the *Myers-Briggs Type Indicator* and the *Strong-Campbell Interest Inventory,* for meeting these needs.

On the other hand, if you bring to your job search certain health and psychological problems which affect your job performance, you should seek professional help rather than try to solve your problems with this book. This is especially true for those with alcohol or drug problems who really need some form of professional therapy before practicing this book. If you are in serious financial trouble or a separation or divorce is greatly troubling you, seek professional help. Only after you get yourself together physically and mentally will this book produce its intended results for you. Remember, no employer wants to hire alcohol, drug, financial, or marital problems. They want productive, job-centered individuals who are capable of handling their personal problems rather than bringing them to work.

You must be honest with yourself before you can be honest with others. The whole philosophy underlying this book is one of personal honesty and integrity in everything you do related to your job search.

4

OBTAIN
TRANSITION
ASSISTANCE

*Y*ou don't have to face your career transition alone. As noted in Chapter 3, you will find numerous organizations and individuals eager to assist you with career transition and job search services. Many of these services are free or require a nominal fee while others can be very expensive. The quality of these services varies widely, from outstanding to simply fraudulent. For the uninitiated, selecting the right services and choosing the best quality organizations and individuals to assist you can present truly bewildering choices. Let's try to sort through this maze.

You need to make the right choices for transition assistance. We recommend staying close to home by first looking to the government for such assistance. Indeed, the U.S. Army and the federal government sponsor a variety of high quality transition services you should use throughout your job search. We strongly recommend taking advantage of the courses, seminars, and testing services offered by these agencies.

We cannot over-emphasize the importance of taking advantage of these free or low-cost services early in the job transition process. The transition professionals staffing these services are highly skilled in their respective fields and will help steer you in the right direction. In this chapter we describe these transition services and reveal how to obtain additional information.

FORMS AND EMPLOYMENT RESTRICTIONS

One of the first actions you should take after making the separation/retirement decision is to visit the office of your post's Judge Advocate General (JAG). It's important to know the legal restrictions placed on Army members who separate or retire from active duty. This is especially true for retiring Regular Army officers and those officers who have served in the acquisition field. For example, if you are a retired regular officer, laws (37 U.S.S. 801[b] and 18 U.S.C. 281) prohibit you from collecting retirement pay while also engaging in selling, contracting, or negotiating with agencies of the uniformed services during the first two to three years of your retirement. These restrictions will initially eliminate you from certain jobs with government contractors. Therefore, you need to

1. **Know the rules:**

   - Pre-employment restrictions
   - Post-employment restrictions

2. **Report job contacts:**

   - Disqualification statements/refusals

3. **Acquire required forms prior to separation:**

   - **DD Form 1787:** retired regular officers file this report of Department of Defense and Defense Related Employment
   - **DD Form 1357:** Statement of Employment—Majors and above must file within 30 days after retirement if employed by prime defense contractors

You also need to understand foreign government employment prohibitions as well as the dual compensation formula affecting retired military personnel who choose to work for the federal government. You are prohibited from working for a foreign government unless given special congressional consent. If you are an officer and you choose to work for the federal government, you will receive your full federal salary but your Army retirement pay will be reduced according to the formula specified in the Dual Compensation Act. After you receive $9,310.17 in retirement pay, the remainder of your retirement pay will be reduced by 50 percent. Your JAG office can provide you with more detailed information on required forms and on employment prohibitions, and restrictions affecting your situation.

MILITARY TRANSITION SERVICES

Army Career and Alumni Program (ACAP)

The **Army Career and Alumni Program (ACAP)** is an excellent program that offers a wealth of free transition assistance services to all separating or retiring service members and their spouses. You should contact your local ACAP office early in the job search to more fully understand the range and depth of services offered, along with the schedule of classes. ACAP also has an 800 number: (800) 445-2049. Key services offered by ACAP's Transition Assistance Offices include:

- Transition counseling
- Career transition seminars
- Basic resume writing classes
- Career dressing classes
- Interviewing techniques
- Basic job hunting skills
- Job survival skills
- Job hunters support group
- National job database—**DORS** (Defense Outplacement Referral System)
- Electronic bulletin board—Transition Bulletin Board (TBB)

The following ACAP sites operate in the Continental United States (CONUS) and overseas:

CONUS ACAP Sites	Phone Number	Fax Number
Aberdeen Proving Grounds, MD	(410) 278-9669/9688	(410) 278-9685
Fort Belvoir, VA	(703) 806-5391	(703) 806-5431
Fort Ben Harrison, IN	(317) 542-4780/4779	(317) 542-4770
Fort Benning, GA	(706) 545-4902	(706) 545-7642
Fort Bliss, TX	(915) 568-4460/4461	(915) 568-5168
Fort Bragg, NC	(919) 396-2227/6826	(919) 396-1776

Fort Campbell, KY	(502) 798-5000	(502) 798-4232
Fort Carson, CO	(719) 526-5660/5661	(719) 526-1000
Fort Devens, MA	(508) 796-3423	(508) 796-3452
Fort Dix, NJ	(609) 562-3511	(609) 562-5255
Fort Drum, NY	(315) 772-3284/3286	(315) 772-5806
Fort Eustis, VA	(804) 878-2905	(804) 878-3063
Fort Gordon, GA	(706) 791-7356/8765	(706) 791-8767
Fort Hood, TX	(817) 288-6735/6736/6744	(817) 288-6745
Fort Huachuca, AZ	(602) 538-2214/2215	(602) 538-2224
Fort Irwin, CA	(619) 386-5645/5647/5648	(619) 386-5642
Fort Jackson, SC	(803) 751-6057/6062/6064	(803) 751-6126
Fort Knox, KY	(502) 624-2227	(502) 624-2687
Fort Leavenworth, KS	(913) 684-3072	(913) 684-3586
Fort Lee, VA	(804) 765-1438/1437	(804) 765-2293
Fort Leonard Wood, MO	(314) 596-0174	(314) 596-0177
Fort Lewis, WA	(206) 967-3250/3258	(206) 967-2072
Fort McClellan, AL	(205) 848-2227/6033	(205) 435-6032
Fort McPherson, GA	(404) 752-2129/2162/2172	(404) 752-2589
Fort Meade, MD	(301) 677-2227/5627	(301) 677-4447
Fort Monmouth, NJ	(908) 532-1906	(908) 532-1549
Fort Monroe, VA	(804) 727-4231	(804) 728-5051
Fort Myer, VA	(703) 696-2635	(703) 696-3352
Fort Ord, CA	(408) 242-5610	(408) 242-7539
Fort Polk, LA	(318) 531-1594/1595/1598	(318) 531-1588
Fort Richardson, AK	(907) 384-3500	(907) 384-3504
Fort Riley, KS	(913) 239-3946/3939/3844	(913) 239-6556
Fort Rucker, AL	(205) 255-2085/1068	(205) 255-6036
Fort Sam Houston, TX	(512) 221-2044/1402/2411	(512) 221-1671
Fort Sill, OK	(405) 442-6428	(405) 442-6423
Fort Stewart, GA	(912) 767-2611/5907	(912) 767-8681
Fort Wainwright, AK	(907) 353-2099	(907) 353-2114
Letterkenney Army Depot, PA	(717) 267-8887	(717) 267-9844
Picatinny Arsenal, NJ	(201) 724-2028	(201) 724-5605
Redstone Arsenal, AL	(205) 955-6490/6488/6487	(205) 955-6638
Rock Island Arsenal, IL	(309) 782-1227/1223	not available
Schoffield Barracks, HI	(808) 655-1942	(808) 655-1903
St. Louis, MO	(314) 263-3768	(314) 263-3327
Tooele Army Depot, UT	(801) 833-2639	(801) 833-3202

Overseas ACAP Sites	**Phone Number**	**Fax Number**
Baumholder, Germany	011-49-67836-6621/6360	011-49-67836-6301
Berlin, Germany	011-49-30819-7694/7696	011-49-30819-7695
Frankfurt, Germany	011-49-69151-7878/7540	011-49-6956-1987
Hanau, Germany	011-49-618188-8308/8257	011-49-618188-8304

Heidelberg, Germany	011-49-622157-8573	011-49-622139-0838
Kaiserslautern, Germany	011-49-631411-7401/7280	011-49-631411-6050
Korea (Camp Casey)	011-82-27913-3062	011-82-2796-4984
Nuernberg, Germany	011-49-911700-7221	011-49-91170-6619
Fort Clayton, Panama	011-507-787-5844	011-50-787-4350
Stuttgart, Germany	011-49-711729-2337	011-49-711729-2263
Vicenza, Italy	011-39-44451-7605	011-39-44451-7104
Vilseck, Germany	011-49-966283-2181	011-49-966283-2053
Wuerzberg, Germany	011-49-932170-2438	011-49-932170-2434

Job Assistance Center (JAC)

Like the Army Career and Alumni Program, the **Job Assistance Center (JAC)** has been established to assist military members and their spouses find employment—either in the private sector or the Government. Typical services provided by a JAC include the following:

- Individual counseling

- Job Assistance Center Workshops
  —Skill assessment
  —Job search strategies
  —Resume writing
  —Interview techniques

- Job database—Army Employer and Alumni Network
  —Database of firms seeking military personnel
  —Regional and national coverage

- Resume critique
  —Personal attention given to improving your resume

- Resume and cover letter preparation software

The following JAC sites are located in the Continental United States CONUS and overseas.

CONUS JAC Sites	Phone Number	Fax Number
Aberdeen Proving Grounds, MD	(410) 278-9674/9675	(410) 278-9685
Fort Ben Harrison, IN	(317) 543-6708	(317) 543-6713
Fort Benning, GA	(706) 545-2308	(706) 545-2307
Fort Bliss, TX	(915) 568-7168	(915) 568-3869

Fort Bragg, NC	(919) 396-7188/8169	(919) 396-9390
Fort Campbell, KY	(502) 798-4202	(502) 798-4232
Fort Carson, CO	(719) 526-1002	(719) 526-1000
Fort Devens, MA	(508) 796-2889	(508) 796-3566
Fort Dix, NJ	(609) 562-3465	(609) 562-5255
Fort Eustis, VA	(804) 878-4955/3027	(804) 878-4718
Fort Gordon, GA	(706) 791-8766/7356	(706) 791-8767
Fort Hood, TX	(817) 288-5627/6744	(817) 288-6745
Fort Huachuca, AZ	(602) 533-5764	(602) 538-2224
Fort Irwin, CA	(619) 386-5643	(619) 386-3906
Fort Jackson, SC	(803) 751-4109	(803) 751-4124
Fort Knox, KY	(502) 624-5222/4387/320	(502) 624-4812
Fort Leavenworth, KS	(913) 684-3463	(913) 684-3692
Fort Lee, VA	(804) 765-1435	(804) 765-2293
Fort Leonard Wood, MO	(314) 596-0175	(314) 596-0192
Fort Lewis, WA	(206) 967-3258	(206) 967-4416
Fort McClellan, AL	(205) 848-6036	(205) 848-6029
Fort McPherson, GA	(404) 752-2582/2577	(404) 752-2589
Fort Meade, MD	(301) 677-6802	(301) 677-5676
Fort Monmouth, NJ	(908) 532-6155/6156/6157	(908) 532-6124
Fort Myer, VA	(703) 696-0973	(703) 696-3352
Fort Ord, CA	(408) 242-7907/7908	(408) 242-6863
Fort Polk, LA	(318) 531-1591	(318) 531-4759
Fort Richardson, AK	(907) 384-3501/3502/3503	(907) 384-3504
Fort Riley, KS	(913) 239-2202/2278	(913) 239-2251
Fort Rucker, AL	(205) 255-2546/2558	(205) 255-9160
Fort Sam Houston, TX	(512) 221-1213/2422	(512) 221-1671
Fort Sill, OK	(405) 442-2713	(405) 442-5900
Fort Stewart, GA	(912) 767-8677	(912) 767-8689
Fort Wainwright, AK	(907) 353-2113	(907) 353-2114
Redstone Arsenal, AL	(205) 955-6486	(205) 955-6666
Rock Island Arsenal, IL	(309) 782-1301	(309) 782-0873
Schoffield Barracks, HI	(808) 655-1028/1853	(808) 655-1903
St. Louis, MO	(314) 263-3768	(314) 263-3327

Overseas JAC Sites	**Phone Number**	**Fax Number**
Baumholder, Germany	011-49-67836-6741	011-49-6783-5335
Berlin, Germany	011-49-30819-6451	011-49-30819-7874
Frankfurt, Germany	011-49-69151-7936	011-49-615169-7623
Hanau, Germany	011-49-618188-8298	011-49-618188-8304
Heidelberg, Germany	011-49-622157-7505	011-49-622157-7774
Kaiserslautern, Germany	011-49-631411-7089	011-49-631411-6050
Korea (Camp Casey)	011-82-351869-4033	011-82-351869-4037

Nuernberg, Germany	011-49-911700-6445	011-49-911700-6619
Panama	011-50-787-3147	011-50-787-5019
Schinnen, Netherlands	011-31-4328-4223	011-31-4328-4475
Stuttgart, Germany	011-49-711729-2255	011-49-711729-2254
Vicenza, Italy	011-39-44451-7188	011-39-44451-7104
Vilseck, Germany	011-49-966283-2055	011-49-966283-2057
Wuerzberg, Germany	011-49-932170-2462	011-49-932170-2434

Joint Employment Transition Services (JETS)

The Joint Employment Transition Services (JETS) office is a DOD-sponsored organization in the Washington DC area comprised of Family Member Employment and Transition Assistance specialists from all four branches of the uniform services. JETS offers monthly job fairs, workshops, and other employment assistance activities at no cost to separating or retiring military members and their spouses. JETS professionals are distributed throughout the greater Washington D.C. area and are located at the following military installations:

Virginia

- Fort Belvoir
- Fort Myer
- Henderson Hall Marine Base
- Dahlgren Naval Surface Warfare Center
- Quantico Marine Base
- Vint Hill Farms Station

Washington, DC

- Anacostia Naval Station
- Andrews AFB
- Bolling AFB
- Walter Reed Army Medical Center

Maryland

- Aberdeen Proving Ground
- Fort Meade
- U.S. Naval Academy
- Patuxent River Naval Station

For more information about JETS, contact the USO-Metro office at (703) 696-3279 or (703) 696-2552.

Family Member Employment Assistance Program

The Family Member Employment Assistance Program (FMEAP) is an integral part of the Army Community Service (ACS) organization and an important service provider to the Army Career and Alumni Program. FMEAP provides all active duty, retired, and transitioning military, federal civil employees, and family members with information on employment, educational, and volunteer opportunities.

The FMEAP offers the following transition services:

- Resume preparation
- Interviewing techniques
- Career counseling
- Job listings
- Job referrals

If you wish to use the FMEAP services, you should contact the FMEAP office nearest to you:

FMEAP Sites	Phone Number	AUTOVON Number
Aberdeen Proving Grounds, MD	(301) 278-4372	298-7474
Army Ammunition Plant, OK	(918) 421-3490	956-3490
Aviation Support Cmd, IL	(618) 452-4550	892-4260
Bayonne, NJ	(201) 823-6132	247-6132
Carlisle Barracks, PA	(717) 245-4357	242-4357
Dugway Proving Ground, UT	(801) 831-2387	789-2387
Fitzsimmons Army Med Ctr	(303) 361-3624	943-3624
Fort Belvoir, VA	(703) 664-6995	354-6995
Fort Ben Harrison, IN	(317) 542-4357	699-4357
Fort Benning, GA	(706) 545-7517/5516	545-7517/5516
Fort Bliss, TX	(915) 568-6332	978-6332
Fort Bragg, NC	(919) 396-8682	236-1534
Fort Campbell, KY	(502) 798-3032	635-3032
Fort Carson, CO	(719) 579-3862	691-3862
Fort Devens, MA	(508) 796-3379	256-2582
Fort Detrick, MD	(301) 663-2197	343-2197
Fort Drum, NY	(315) 772-5475	341-5475
Fort Eustis, VA	(804) 878-0912	927-3638
Fort Gordon, GA	(706) 791-4181	780-4181
Fort Greely, AK	(907) 873-3284	317-363-3284
Fort Hamilton, NY	(718) 630-4332	232-4332

Fort Hood, TX	(817) 288-2448	738-2448
Fort Huachuca, AZ	(602) 533-2993	821-5972
Fort Indiantown Gap	(717) 865-5444	277-2610
Fort Irwin, CA	(619) 386-3492	470-3492
Fort Jackson, SC	(803) 751-5708	734-5708
Fort Knox, KY	(502) 624-7561	464-7561
Fort Leavenworth, KS	(913) 684-5491	552-5491
Fort Lee, VA	(804) 734-3675	687-3675
Fort Leonard Wood, MO	(314) 596-4467	581-4467
Fort Lewis, WA	(206) 967-7408	357-7408
Fort McClellan, AL	(205) 848-4721	865-4721
Fort McCoy, WI	(608) 388-2412	280-3505
Fort McPherson, GA	(404) 752-2439	572-4070
Fort Meade, MD	(301) 677-6658	923-6658
Fort Monmouth, NJ	(201) 532-2076	992-2076
Fort Monroe, VA	(804) 727-3878	680-3878
Fort Myer, VA	(703) 696-3510	226-3047
Fort Ord, CA	(408) 899-4353	929-4353
Fort Polk, LA	(318) 531-1969	863-1969
Fort Richardson, AK	(907) 864-1129	317-864-1199
Fort Riley, KS	(913) 239-6029	856-6029
Fort Ritchie, MD	(301) 878-5194	277-5194
Fort Rucker, AL	(205) 255-5031	459-3309
Fort Sam Houston, TX	(512) 221-5705	471-2418
Fort Shafter	(808) 438-6826	438-6826
Fort Sheridan, IL	(312) 926-2272	459-3309
Fort Sill, OK	(405) 351-6801	639-6801
Fort Stewart, GA	not available	870-5058
Fort Story, VA	(804) 422-7311	438-7311
Fort Wainwright, AK	(907) 353-6918	317-353-6918
Hunter Army Airfield, GA	(719) 549-4432	749-4432
Letterkenny Army Depot, PA	(717) 267-9051	570-9051
Lexington Blue Grass, KY	not available	745-3235
MTMC, Bayonne, NJ	(201) 823-6132	247-6132
New Cumberland Depot, PA	(717) 770-6203	977-6203
Oakland Army Depot, CA	(415) 466-3459	859-3459
Picatinny Arsenal, NJ	(201) 724-2145	880-2145
Pine Bluff, AR	(501) 543-3317	839-2059
Pueblo Depot Activity, CO	(719) 549-4432	749-4432
Red River Army Depot	(214) 334-2806	829-2466
Redstone Arsenal, AL	(205) 876-0446	273-5903
Rock Island Arsenal	(309) 782-3828	793-3828
Sacramento Army Depot	(916) 388-2059	489-8388
Selfridge Air National Gd, MI	(313) 466-5903	273-5903
Seneca Army Depot, NY	(607) 869-0388	489-8388

Sierra Army Depot, CA	(916) 827-4425	974-5103
Tobyhanna Army Depot, PA	(717) 894-7509	795-7069
Tooele Army Depot, UT	(801) 833-2852	790-2852
Vint Hill Farm Station, VA	(703) 349-5914	229-5914
Walter Reed Med Ctr, D.C.	(202) 576-0620	291-3412
Watervliet Arsenal, NY	(518) 266-5103	974-5103
West Point, NY	(914) 938-4621	688-4621
White Sands, NM	(505) 678-6767	258-6767
Yuma Proving Ground, AZ	(602) 328-2513	899-2513

GOVERNMENT TRANSITION SERVICES

Transition Assistance Program (TAP)

The Department of Labor offers the **Transition Assistance Program (TAP)** to separating or retiring service members. The TAP operates at 168 sites in 44 states.

- Address: VETS
  Room S1313
  U.S. Department of Labor
  200 Constitution Avenue N.W.
  Washington, DC 20210

- Phone: (202) 523-5573

- TAP's three-day workshops include:

  —Information on conducting a successful job search
  —Information on career decision making
  —Realistic evaluations of employment options
  —Current occupational and labor market information
  —Information on veteran's benefits

NOT-FOR-PROFIT TRANSITION SERVICES

The Retired Officers Association (TROA)

The Retired Officers Association (TROA) provides an outstanding transition service called **TOPS** (TROA's Officer Placement Service). As discussed below, TOPS offers a wide range of transition services to former or retired officers (commissioned and warrant). To use the services of TOPS, you must be a member of TROA. For further information on membership and placement services, contact:

- Address: TROA/TOPS
  201 N. Washington Street
  Alexandria, VA 22314-2539

- Phone: (800) 245-8762 or (703) 838-8117 (0800-1600 Mon-Fri)

- Cost: $20 annually

TOPS offers the following transition services:

- Counseling
- Resume critique
- Transition lectures (U.S. and overseas)
- Employment reference library
  —Lists firms seeking candidates for specific positions
- Complimentary guide: *Marketing Yourself for a Second Career*
- Candidate database
  —To enter: submit resume (five originals) and a
    six-page registration form
  —Candidate/employer "matches" are mailed every Friday

Non Commissioned Officers Association (NCOA)

The **Non Commissioned Officers Association (NCOA)**, a federally chartered, non-profit fraternal association, provides its members with an impressive set of transition services. NCOA offers the *Veterans Employment Assistance (VEA) Program* to all active duty service members and their spouses, regardless of rank or whether they are members of NCOA. The program includes free Career Transition Seminars and Job Seekers Workshops, which are held throughout the world. For further information on NCOA and the VEA Program, contact:

- Address: Non Commissioned Officers Association
  10635 IH 35 North
  San Antonio, TX 78233

- Phone: (210) 753-6161

- Cost: $20 annually

Transition services offered through VEA:

- Job Fairs—conducted throughout U.S. and Europe
- Career Transition Seminars—held day before job fair
- NCOA mini resume—available at local NCOA service centers; provides access to all VEA services
- Mini Resume People Bank—online database that matches employers' needs with applicants' qualifications
- Job Seekers Workshops—conducted at military installations worldwide. Workshop focuses on all aspects of the job search, including goal setting, resume preparation, and salary negotiation.

Armed Forces Communications and Electronics Association (AFCEA)

The **Armed Forces Communications and Electronics Association** (**AFCEA**) has a **Career Planning Center** (**CPC**) which provides AFCEA members with a range of transition services, as discussed below. For information on AFCEA membership, contact:

- Address: AFCEA
  4400 Fair Lakes Court
  Fairfax, VA 22033-3899

- Phone: (800) 336-4583, ext. 6144 or (703) 631-6144

- Cost: $20 annually; open to all ranks

Transition services offered by the CPC:

- Career Transition Seminar ($25)
- Resume Preparation Guide ($5)
- Job Fairs
- AFCEA Career Planning Center—resume referral service and career transition assistance
- Topical Guide To AFCEA Member Companies and **Individual Company Listings**
- AFCEA Professional Development Center—courses in C^{4}I

Association of the United States Army (AUSA)

The **Association of the United States Army (AUSA)** offers its members a variety of transition services through the **AUSA Transition Assistance Program**. Provided below is the essential membership information on AUSA as well as a summary of the services provided by the **AUSA Transition Assistance Program**.

- Address: Association of the United States Army
  2425 Wilson Boulevard
  Arlington, VA 22201-3385

- Phone: (703) 841-4300

- Cost: $25 annually; open to all ranks

Transition services offered by the AUSA Transition Assistance Program:

- Address: AUSA Transition Assistance Program
  Suite 206
  3500 Virginia Beach Boulevard
  Virginia Beach, VA 23452

- Phone: (804) 486-2155

- Services:
  —Customer Assistance Service, (800) 233-1280
    Career Planning Kit
    Customized resume by *Nationwide Resumes of America:*
    • One proof copy for your review prior to typesetting
    • Five original resumes on high quality bond
    • Resume placed in Nationwide Employment Services for
      free employment referral to prospective employers

- Cost: $75

  —Discounted fee for enrolling in Job Bank, USA, one of the
    nation's premier employment database firms.

5

IDENTIFY YOUR SKILLS & ABILITIES

What skills to do you possess that are most relevant to today's job market? Are the skills you acquired in the Army attractive to many employers? What other skills do you possess which may or may not be relevant to your work in the Army? Do you need to acquire new skills? We live in a skills-based society where individuals market their skills to employers in exchange for money, position, and power. The ease by which individuals change jobs and careers is directly related to their ability to communicate their skills to employers and then transfer their skills to new work settings.

To best position yourself in the job markets of today and tomorrow, you should pay particular attention to refining your present skills as well as achieving new and more marketable skills. This may mean going back to school for a degree or certificate or taking advantage of employer-sponsored training programs.

IDENTIFY YOUR SKILLS

But before you can refine your skills or acquire additional skills, you need to know what skills you presently possess. What skills did you acquire in the U.S. Army that are directly transferable to the civilian work world? Unfortunately, few people can identify and talk about their skills even though they possess hundreds of skills which they use on a regular basis. This becomes a real problem when they must write a resume or go to a job interview. Since employers want to know about your specific abilities and skills, you must learn to both identify and communicate your skills to employers. You should be able to explain what it is you do well and give examples relevant to employers' needs.

What skills do you already have to offer employers? If you have just completed an educational program relevant to today's job market, the skills you have to offer are most likely related to the subject matter you studied. As you transition from the Army, the skills you wish to communicate to employers will be those things you already have demonstrated you can do in specific Army jobs.

The skills required for *finding a job* are no substitute for the skills necessary for *doing the job*. Learning new skills requires a major investment of time, money, and effort. Nonetheless, the long-term pay-off should more than justify the initial costs. Indeed, research continues to show that well selected education and training provide the best returns on individual and societal investment.

TYPES OF SKILLS

Most people possess two types of skills that define their accomplishments and strengths as well as enable them to enter and advance within the job market: work-content skills and functional skills. You need to acquaint yourself with these skills before communicating them to employers.

We assume you have already acquired certain *work-content skills* necessary to function effectively in today's job market. These "hard skills" are easy to recognize since they are often identified as "qualifications" for specific jobs; they are the subject of most educational and training programs. Work-content skills tend to be technical and job-specific in nature. Examples of such skills include proficiency in typing, programming computers, teaching history, or operating an X-ray machine. They may require formal training, are associated with specific trades or professions, and are used only in certain job and career settings. One uses a separate skills vocabulary, jargon, and subject matter for specifying technical qualifications of individuals entering and advancing in an occupation. While these skills do not transfer well from one occupation to another, they are critical for entering and advancing within certain occupations.

At the same time, you possess numerous *functional/transferable skills* employers readily seek along with your work-content skills. These "soft skills" are associated with numerous job settings, are mainly acquired through experience rather than formal training, and can be communicated through a general vocabulary. Functional/transferable skills are less easy to recognize since they tend to be linked to certain *personal characteristics* (energetic, intelligent, likable) and the ability to *deal with processes* (communicate, solve problems, motivate) rather than *do things* (program a computer, build a house, repair air-conditioners). While most people have only a few work-content skills, they may have numerous—as many as 300—functional/transferable skills. These skills enable job seekers to more easily change jobs. But you must first know your functional skills before you can relate them to the job market.

Most people view the world of work in traditional occupational job skill terms. This is a *structural view* of occupational realities. Occupational fields are seen as consisting of separate and distinct jobs which, in turn, require specific work-content skills. From this perspective, occupations and jobs are relatively self-contained entities. Social work, for example, is seen as being different from paralegal work; social workers, therefore, are not "qualified" to seek paralegal work.

Functional skills can be transferred from one job or career to another.

On the other hand, a *functional view* of occupations and jobs emphasizes the similarity of job characteristics as well as common linkages between different occupations. Although the structure of occupations and jobs may differ, they have similar functions. They involve working with people, data, processes, and objects. If you work with people, data, processes, and objects in one occupation, you can transfer that experience to other occupations which have similar functions. Once you understand how your skills relate to the functions as well as investigate the structure of different occupations, you should be prepared to make job changes from one occupational field to another. Whether you possess the necessary work-content skills to qualify for entry into the other occupational field is another question altogether.

The skills we identify and help you organize in this chapter are the functional skills career counselors normally emphasize when advising clients to assess their *strengths*. In contrast to work-content skills, functional skills can be transferred from one job or career to another. They enable individuals to make some job and career changes without acquiring additional education and training. They constitute an important bridge for moving from one occupation to another.

Before you decide if you need more education or training, you should first assess both your functional and work-content skills to see how they can be transferred to other jobs and occupations. Once you do this, you should be better prepared to communicate your qualifications to employers with a rich skills-based vocabulary.

Your goal should be to find a job that is fit for you rather than one you think you might be able to fit into.

YOUR STRENGTHS

Regardless of what combination of work-content and functional skills you possess, a job search must begin with identifying your strengths. Without knowing these, your job search will lack content and focus. After all, your goal should be to find a job that is fit for you rather than one you think you might be able to fit into. Of course, you also want to find a job for which there is a demand. This particular focus requires a well-defined approach to identifying and communicating your skills to others. You can best do this by asking the right questions about your strengths and then conducting a systematic self-assessment of what you do best.

ASK THE RIGHT QUESTIONS

Knowing the right questions to ask will save you time and steer you into productive job search channels from the very beginning. Asking the wrong questions can cripple your job search efforts and leave you frustrated. The questions must be understood from the perspectives of both employers and applicants.

Two of the most humbling questions you will encounter in your job search are "Why should I hire you?" and "What are your weaknesses?" While employers may not directly ask these questions, they are asking them nonetheless. If you can't answer these questions in a positive manner—directly, indirectly, verbally, or nonverbally—your job search will likely founder and you will join the ranks of the unsuccessful and disillusioned job searchers who feel something is wrong with them. Individuals who have lost their jobs are particularly vulnerable to these questions since many have lowered self-esteem and self-image as a result of the job loss. Many such people focus on what is wrong rather than what is right about themselves. Such thinking creates self-fulfilling prophecies and is self-destructive in the job market. By all means avoid such negative thinking.

Employers want to hire your value or strengths—not your weaknesses.

Employers want to hire your *value or strengths*—not your weaknesses. Since it is easier to identify and interpret weaknesses, employers look for indicators of your strengths by trying to identify your weaknesses. The more successful you are in communicating your strengths to employers, the better off you will be in relation to both employers and fellow applicants.

Unfortunately, many people work against their own best interests. Not knowing their strengths, they market their weaknesses by first identifying job vacancies and then trying to fit their "qualifications" into job descriptions. This approach often frustrates applicants; it presents a picture of a job market which is not interested in the applicant's strengths. This leads some people toward acquiring new skills which they hope will be marketable, even though they do not enjoy using them. Millions of individuals find themselves in such misplaced situations. Your task is to avoid joining the ranks of the misplaced and unhappy work force by first understanding your skills and then relating them to your interests and goals. In so doing, you will be in a better position to target your job search toward jobs that should become especially rewarding and fulfilling.

FUNCTIONAL/TRANSFERABLE SKILLS

We know most people stumble into jobs by accident. Some are at the right place at the right time to take advantage of a job or career opportunity. Others work hard at trying to fit into jobs listed in classified ads, employment agencies, and personnel offices; identified through friends and acquaintances; or found by knocking on doors. After 15 to 20 years in the work world, many people wish they had better planned their careers from the very start. All of a sudden they are unhappily locked into jobs because of retirement benefits and the family responsibilities of raising children and meeting monthly mortgage payments.

After 10 or 20 years of work experience, most people have a good idea of what they don't like to do. While their values are more set than when they first began working, many people are still unclear as to what they do well and how their skills fit into the job market. What other jobs, for example, might they be qualified to perform? If they have the opportunity to change jobs or careers—either voluntarily or forced through termination—and find the time to plan the change, they can move into jobs and careers which fit their skills.

The key to understanding your non-technical strengths is to identify your transferable or functional skills. Once you have done this, you will be better prepared to identify what it is you want to do. Moreover, your self-image and self-esteem will improve. Better still, you will be prepared to communicate your strengths to others through a rich skills-based vocabulary. These outcomes are critically important for writing your resume and letters as well as for conducting informational and job interviews.

Let's illustrate the concept of functional/transferable skills. Suppose that you are an Armor Non Commissioned Officer (NCO). Many NCOs view their skills in strict work-content terms—knowledge of an M1A1 main battle tank or experience in using and maintaining such a weapon system. When looking for jobs in the civilian world, these Armor NCOs know that they will find very few jobs that will allow them to build on this type of expertise. Instead, they must rely on the wealth of other skills they have acquired while in the Army to help them find suitable employment. Examples of these skills that are directly transferable to business and industry include:

- leadership
- discipline
- self-confidence
- teaching ability
- interpersonal skills
- writing

- perseverance
- general knowledge
- insight
- multicultural perspective
- critical thinking
- imagination

Most functional/transferable skills can be classified into two general skills and trait categories—organizational/interpersonal skills and personality/work-style traits:

TYPES OF TRANSFERABLE SKILLS

Organizational and Interpersonal Skills

___ communicating
___ problem solving
___ analyzing/assessing
___ planning
___ decision-making
___ innovating
___ thinking logically
___ evaluating
___ identifying problems
___ synthesizing
___ forecasting
___ tolerating ambiguity
___ motivating
___ leading
___ selling
___ performing
___ reviewing
___ attaining
___ team building
___ updating
___ coaching
___ supervising
___ estimating
___ negotiating
___ administering

___ trouble shooting
___ implementing
___ self-understanding
___ understanding
___ setting goals
___ conceptualizing
___ generalizing
___ managing time
___ creating
___ judging
___ controlling
___ organizing
___ persuading
___ encouraging
___ improving
___ designing
___ consulting
___ teaching
___ cultivating
___ advising
___ training
___ interpreting
___ achieving
___ reporting
___ managing

Personality and Work-Style Traits

___ diligent

___ patient

___ innovative

___ persistent

___ tactful

___ loyal

___ successful

___ versatile

___ enthusiastic

___ out-going

___ expressive

___ adaptable

___ democratic

___ resourceful

___ determining

___ creative

___ open

___ objective

___ warm

___ orderly

___ tolerant

___ frank

___ cooperative

___ dynamic

___ self-starter

___ precise

___ sophisticated

___ effective

___ honest

___ reliable

___ perceptive

___ assertive

___ sensitive

___ astute

___ risk taker

___ easy going

___ calm

___ flexible

___ competent

___ punctual

___ receptive

___ diplomatic

___ self-confident

___ tenacious

___ discrete

___ talented

___ empathic

___ tidy

___ candid

___ adventuresome

___ firm

___ sincere

___ initiator

___ competent

___ diplomatic

___ efficient

These are the types of skills you need to identify and then communicate to employers in your resume and letters as well as during interviews. This skills vocabulary helps you better translate your military work experience into civilian occupational language.

IDENTIFY YOUR SKILLS

If you were just graduating from high school or college and did not know what you wanted to do, we would recommend that you take a battery of vocational tests and psychological inventories to identify your interests and skills. Many of these tests are listed in Chapter 6. Since as a transitioning member of the Army you don't fall into these categories of job seekers, chances are you don't need complex testing. You have experience, you have well defined values, and you know what you don't like in a job. Nonetheless, check with the Job Assistance Center on your base as well as any other transition assistance program to see if they administer assessment tests. Such tests can provide you with a solid base of information on yourself for organizing and implementing an effective job search.

We outline several alternative paper-and-pencil skills identification exercises—from simple to complex—for assisting you at this stage. We recommend using the most complete activity—the Motivated Skills Exercise—to gain a thorough understanding of your strengths.

Use the following exercises to identify both your work-content and transferable skills. These self-assessment techniques stress your positives or strengths rather than identify your negatives or weaknesses. They should generate a rich vocabulary for communicating your "qualifications" to employers. Each exercise requires different investments of your time and effort as well as varying degrees of assistance from other people.

These exercises, however, should be used with caution. There is nothing magical nor particularly profound about them. Most are based upon a very simple and somewhat naive *deterministic theory of behavior* —understanding your past patterns of behavior are good predictors of your future behavior. Not a bad theory for most individuals, but it is rather simplistic and disheartening for individuals who wish to, and can, break out of past patterns as they embark on a new future. Furthermore, most exercises are *historical devices*. They provide you with a clear picture of your past, which may or may not be particularly useful for charting your future. Nonetheless, these exercises do help most individuals (1) organize data on themselves, (2) target their job search around clear objectives and skills, and (3) generate a rich vocabulary of skills and accomplishments for communicating strengths to potential employers.

If you feel these exercises are inadequate for your needs, by all means seek professional assistance from a testing or assessment center staffed by a licensed psychologist. These centers do in-depth testing which goes further than these self-directed skill exercises.

When using the following exercises, keep in mind that some individuals can and do change—often very dramatically—their behavior regardless of such deterministic and historical assessment devices. Most of the "motivation and success," "power of positive thinking," and "thinking big" literature, for example, challenges the validity of these standardized assessment tests that are used to predict or pattern future individual behavior. So be careful how you use such information for charting your career future. You *can* change your future. But at least get to know yourself before making the changes. Critiques of, as well as alternatives to, these exercises are outlined in the Krannichs' *Discover the Best Jobs for You!*

CHECKLIST METHOD

This is the simplest method for identifying your strengths. Review the different types of transferable skills outlined on pages 90-91. Place a "1" in front of the skills that *strongly* characterize you; assign a "2" to those that describe you to a *large extent*; put a "3" before those that describe you to *some extent*. After completing this exercise, review the lists and rank order the 10 characteristics that best describe you on each list.

SKILLS MAP

Richard N. Bolles has produced two well-known exercises for identifying transferable skills based upon John Holland's typology of work environments. Both are historical devices structured around a deterministic theory of behavior. In his book, *The Three Boxes of Life* (Ten Speed Press), he develops a checklist of 100 transferable skills. They are organized into 12 categories or types of skills: using hands, body, words, senses, numbers, intuition, analytical thinking, creativity, helpfulness, artistic abilities, leadership, and follow-through.

Bolles' second exercise, *"The Quick Job Hunting Map,"* expands upon this first one. The *"Map"* is a checklist of 222 skills. This exercise requires you to identify seven of your most satisfying accomplishments, achievements, jobs, or roles. After writing a page about each experience, you relate each to the checklist of 222 skills. The *"Map"* should give you a comprehensive picture of what skills you (1) use most frequently, and (2) enjoy using in satisfying and successful settings. While this exercise can take up to six hours to complete, it yields an enormous amount of useful data on past strengths. Furthermore, the *"Map"* generates a rich skills vocabulary for communicating your strengths to others. The *"Map"* is found in the appendix of Bolles' *What Color Is Your Parachute?* (Ten Speed Press), where it is placed within explicit deterministic and religious contexts, or it can be purchased separately in beginning, advanced, or new versions from Ten Speed Press. His books, as well as the latest version (1990) of his popular *New Quick Job Hunting Map*, can be ordered directly from Impact Publications by completing the order form at the end of this book.

AUTOBIOGRAPHY OF ACCOMPLISHMENTS

Write a lengthy essay about your life accomplishments. This could range from 20 to 100 pages. After completing the essay, go through it page by page to identify what you most enjoyed doing (working with different kinds of information, people, and things) and what skills you used most frequently as well as enjoyed using. Finally, identify those skills you wish to continue using. After analyzing and synthesizing this data, you should have a relatively clear picture of your strongest skills.

COMPUTERIZED ASSESSMENT SYSTEMS

While the previous self-directed exercises required you to either respond to checklists of skills or reconstruct and analyze your past job experiences, several computerized self-assessment programs are designed to help individuals identify their skills. Many of the programs are available in schools, colleges, and libraries. Some of the most popular and widely used programs include:

- *Career Information System (CIS)*
- *Career Navigator*
- *Choices*
- *Computerized Career Assessment and Planning Program*
- *Discover II*
- *Guidance Information System (GIS)*
- *SIGI-Plus (System of Interactive Guidance and Information)*

Most of these comprehensive career planning programs do much more than just assess skills. As we will see in Chapter 7, they also integrate other key components in the career planning process—interests, values, goals, related jobs, college majors, education and training programs, and job search plans. These programs are widely available in schools, colleges, and libraries across the country. You might check with the career or counseling center at your local community college to see what computerized career assessment systems are available for your use. They are relatively easy to use and they generate a great deal of useful career planning information. Many will print out a useful analysis of how your interests and skills are related to specific jobs and careers.

6

SPECIFY YOUR INTERESTS & VALUES

Knowing what you do well is essential for understanding your strengths and for linking your capabilities to specific jobs. However, just knowing your abilities and skills will not give your job search the direction it needs for finding the right job. You also need to know your work values and interests. These are the basic building blocks for setting goals and targeting your abilities toward certain jobs and careers.

Take, for example, the Army Personnel Specialist who types 120 words a minute. While this person possesses a highly marketable skill, if the person doesn't enjoy using this skill and is more interested in working outdoors, this will not become a *motivated skill*; the individual will most likely not pursue a typing job. Your interests and values will determine whether or not certain skills should play a central role in your job search.

VOCATIONAL INTERESTS

We all have interests. Most change over time. Many of your interests may center on your present job whereas others relate to activities that define your hobbies and leisure activities. A good place to start identifying your interests is by examining the information and exercises found in both *The Guide to Occupational Exploration* and *The Enhanced Guide to Occupational Exploration*. Widely used by students and others first entering the job market, it is also relevant to individuals who already have work experience. The guide classifies all jobs in the United States into 12 interest areas. Examine the following list of interest areas. In the first column check those work areas that appeal to you. In the second column rank order those areas you checked in the first column. Start with "1" to indicate the most interesting:

YOUR WORK INTERESTS

Yes/No (x)	Ranking (1-12)	Interest Area
____	____	**Artistic:** an interest in creative expression of feelings or ideas.
____	____	**Scientific:** an interest in discovering, collecting, and analyzing information about the natural world, and in applying scientific research findings to problems in medicine, the life sciences, and the nature sciences.
____	____	**Plants and animals:** an interest in working with plants and animals, usually outdoors.
____	____	**Protective:** an interest in using authority to protect people and property.
____	____	**Mechanical:** an interest in applying mechanical principles to practical situations by using machines or hand tools.

____   ____   **Industrial:** an interest in repetitive, concrete, organized activities done in a factory setting.

____   ____   **Business detail:** an interest in organized, clearly defined activities requiring accuracy and attention to details (office settings).

____   ____   **Selling:** an interest in bringing others to a particular point of view by personal persuasion, using sales and promotion techniques.

____   ____   **Accommodating:** an interest in catering to the wishes and needs of others, usually on a one-to-one basis.

____   ____   **Humanitarian:** an interest in helping others with their mental, spiritual, social, physical, or vocational needs.

____   ____   **Leading and influencing:** an interest in leading and influencing others by using high-level verbal or numerical abilities.

____   ____   **Physical performing:** an interest in physical activities performed before an audience.

The Guide for Occupational Exploration also includes other checklists relating to home-based and leisure activities that may or may not relate to your work interests. If you are unclear about your work interests, you might want to consult these other interest exercises. You may discover that some of your home-based and leisure activity interests should become your work interests. Examples of such interests include:

LEISURE AND HOME-BASED INTERESTS

____ Acting in a play or amateur variety show.

____ Advising family members on their personal problems.

____ Announcing or emceeing a program.

_____ Applying first aid in emergencies as a volunteer.

_____ Building model airplanes, automobiles, or boats.

_____ Building or repairing radio or television sets.

_____ Buying large quantities of food or other products for an organization.

_____ Campaigning for political candidates or issues.

_____ Canning and preserving food.

_____ Carving small wooden objects.

_____ Coaching children or youth in sports activities.

_____ Collecting experiments involving plants.

_____ Conducting house-to-house or telephone surveys for a PTA or other organization.

_____ Creating or styling hairdos for friends.

_____ Designing your own greeting cards and writing original verses.

_____ Developing film.

_____ Doing impersonations.

_____ Doing public speaking or debating.

_____ Entertaining at parties or other events.

_____ Helping conduct physical exercises for disabled people.

_____ Making ceramic objects.

_____ Modeling clothes for a fashion show.

_____ Mounting and framing pictures.

_____ Nursing sick pets.

_____ Painting the interior or exterior of a home.

_____ Playing a musical instrument.

_____ Refinishing or re-upholstering furniture.

_____ Repairing electrical household appliances.

_____ Repairing the family car.

_____ Repairing or assembling bicycles.

_____ Repairing plumbing in the house.

_____ Speaking on radio or television.

_____ Taking photographs.

_____ Teaching in Sunday School.

_____ Tutoring pupils in school subjects.

_____ Weaving rugs or making quilts.

_____ Writing articles, stories, or plays.

_____ Writing songs for club socials or amateur plays.

Indeed, many people turn hobbies or home activities into full-time jobs after deciding that such "work" is what they really enjoy doing.

Other popular exercises designed to identify your work interests include John Holland's *"The Self-Directed Search"* which is found in his book, *Making Vocational Choices: A Theory of Careers*. It is also published as a separate testing instrument, *The Self-Directed Search—A Guide to Educational and Vocational Planning*. Developed from Holland's Vocational Preference Inventory, this popular self-administered, self-scored, and self-interpreted inventory helps individuals quickly identify what type of work environment they are motivated to seek—realistic, investigative, artistic, social, enterprising, or conventional —and aligns these work environments with lists of common occupational titles. An easy exercise to use, it gives a quick overview of your orientation toward different types of work settings that interest you.

Holland's self-directed search is also the basic framework used in developing Bolles' *"The Quick Job Hunting Map"* as found in his *What Color Is Your Parachute?* and *The New Quick Job Hunting Map* books (see discussion on page 93).

For more sophisticated treatments of work interests, which are also validated through testing procedures, contact a career counselor, women's center, or testing and assessment center for information on these tests:

- Strong-Campbell Interest Inventory
- Myers-Briggs Type Indicator
- Career Occupational Preference System
- Kuder Occupational Interest Survey
- Edwards Personal Preference Schedule
- APTICOM
- Jackson Vocational Interest Survey
- Ramak Inventory
- Vocational Interest Inventory
- Career Assessment Inventory
- Temperament and Values Inventory

Numerous other job and career interest inventories are also available. For further information, contact a career counselor or consult Educational Testing Service which compiles such tests. *The ETS Test Collection Catalog* (New York: Oryx Press), which is available in many library reference sections, lists most of these tests. The *Mental Measurements Yearbook* (Lincoln, NE: University of Nebraska Press) also surveys many of the major testing and assessment instruments.

Keep in mind that not all testing and assessment instruments used by career counselors are equally valid for career planning purposes. While the Strong-Campbell Interest Inventory appears to be the most relevant for career decision-making, the Myers-Briggs Type Indicator has become extremely popular during the past five years. Based on Carl Gustav Jung's personality preference theory, the Myers-Briggs Type Indicator is used extensively by psychologists and career counselors for identifying personality types. However, it is more useful for measuring individual personality and decision-making styles than for predicting career choices. It is most widely used in pastoral counseling, student personnel, and business and religious organizations for measuring personality and decision-making styles. How these elements relate to career choices remains uncertain. For more information on this test, contact: Consulting Psychologists Press, Inc. at 3803 East Bayshore Road, Palo Alto, CA 94303, Tel. 800/624-1765. In the meantime, many career counselors find Holland's *The Self-Directed Search* an excellent self-directed alternative to such professionally administered and interpreted tests.

WORK VALUES

Work values are those things you like to do; they give you pleasure and enjoyment. Army personnel, for example, are noted for their loyalty, dedication, team playing, and willingness to work under pressure.

Most jobs involve a combination of likes and dislikes. By identifying what you both like and dislike about jobs, you should be able to better identify jobs that involve tasks that you will most enjoy.

Several exercises can help you identify your work values. First, identify what most satisfies you about work by completing this exercise:

MY WORK VALUES

I prefer employment which enables me to:

| _____ contribute to society | _____ be creative |
| _____ have contact with people | _____ supervise others |

____ work alone	____ work with details
____ work with a team	____ gain recognition
____ compete with others	____ acquire security
____ make decisions	____ make money
____ work under pressure	____ help others
____ use power and authority	____ solve problems
____ acquire new knowledge	____ take risks
____ be a recognized expert	____ work at own pace

Select four work values from the above list which are the most important to you and list them in the space below. List any other work values (desired satisfactions) which were not listed above but are nonetheless important to you:

1. _____

2. _____

3. _____

4. _____

Another approach to identifying work values is outlined in *The Guide to Occupational Exploration.* If you feel you need to go beyond the above exercises, try this one. In the first column check those values that are most important to you. In the second column rank order from 1 (highest) to 5 (lowest) the five most important values:

RANKING WORK VALUES

Yes/No (x)	Ranking (1-5)	Work Values
____	____	**Adventure:** Working in a job that requires taking risks.
____	____	**Authority:** Working in a job in which you use your position to control others.
____	____	**Competition:** Working in a job in which you compete with others.

____	____	**Creativity and self-expression:** Working in a job in which you use your imagination to find new ways to do or say something.
____	____	**Flexible work schedule:** Working in a job where you choose your work hours.
____	____	**Helping others:** Working in a job in which you provide direct services to persons with problems.
____	____	**High salary:** Working in a job where many workers earn lots of money.
____	____	**Independence:** Working in a job in which you decide for yourself what work to do and how to do it.
____	____	**Influencing others:** Working in a job in which you influence the opinions of others or decisions of others.
____	____	**Intellectual stimulation:** Working in a job which requires a great amount of thought and reasoning.
____	____	**Leadership:** Working in a job in which you direct, manage, or supervise the activities of others.
____	____	**Outside work:** Working out-of-doors.
____	____	**Persuading:** Working in a job in which you personally convince others to take certain actions.
____	____	**Physical work:** Working in a job which requires substantial physical activity.
____	____	**Prestige:** Working in a job which gives you status and respect in the community.

____ ____ **Public attention:** Working in a job in which you attract immediate notice because of appearance or activity.

____ ____ **Public contact:** Working in a job in which you daily deal with the public.

____ ____ **Recognition:** Working in a job in which you gain public notice.

____ ____ **Research work:** Working in a job in which you search for and discover new facts and develop ways to apply them.

____ ____ **Routine work:** Working in a job in which you follow established procedures requiring little change.

____ ____ **Seasonal work:** Working in a job in which you are employed only at certain times of the year.

____ ____ **Travel:** Working in a job in which you take frequent trips.

____ ____ **Variety:** Working in a job in which your duties change frequently.

____ ____ **Work with children:** Working in a job in which you teach or care for children.

____ ____ **Work with hands:** Working in a job in which you use your hands or hand tools.

____ ____ **Work with machines or equipment:** Working in a job in which you use machines or equipment.

____ ____ **Work with numbers:** Working in a job in which you use mathematics or statistics.

Second, develop a comprehensive list of your past and present *job frustrations and dissatisfactions.* This should help you identify negative factors you should avoid in future jobs.

MY JOB FRUSTRATIONS
AND DISSATISFACTIONS

List as well as rank order as many past and present things that frustrate or make you dissatisfied and unhappy in job situations:

Rank

1. _____ _____

2. _____ _____

3. _____ _____

4. _____ _____

5. _____ _____

6. _____ _____

7. _____ _____

8. _____ _____

9. _____ _____

10. _____ _____

Third, brainstorm "Ten or More Things I Love to Do". Identify which ones could be incorporated into what kinds of work environments:

TEN OR MORE THINGS I LOVE TO DO

Item   Related Work Environment

1. _____   _____

2. _____   _____

3. _____   _____

4. _____   _____

5. _____   _____

6. _____   _____

7. _____ _____
8. _____ _____
9. _____ _____
10. _____ _____

Fourth, list at least ten things you most enjoy about work and rank each item accordingly:

TEN THINGS I ENJOY THE MOST
ABOUT WORK

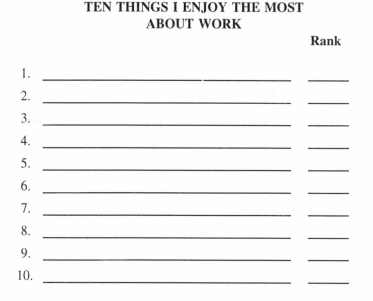

Rank

1. _____ _____
2. _____ _____
3. _____ _____
4. _____ _____
5. _____ _____
6. _____ _____
7. _____ _____
8. _____ _____
9. _____ _____
10. _____ _____

Fifth, you should also identify the types of interpersonal environments you prefer working in. Do this by specifying the types of people you like and dislike associating with:

INTERPERSONAL ENVIRONMENTS

Characteristics of people　　**Characteristics of people**
I like working with:　　　　　**I dislike working with:**

_____ _____

_____ _____

_____ _____

_____	_____
_____	_____
_____	_____
_____	_____
_____	_____
_____	_____
_____	_____
_____	_____

COMPUTERIZED SYSTEMS

Several computerized self-assessment programs largely focus on career interests and values. The two major systems outlined in Chapter 5 for identifying abilities and skills—*Discover II* and *SIGI Plus*—also include career interest segments. Other programs to consider including in your job search include

- *Career Interest Program*
- *Career Navigator*
- *Choices*
- *Computerized Career Assessment and Planning Program*
- *Computerized Career Information System*
- *Guidance Information System (CIS)*
- *Values Auction Deluxe*

You should be able to get access to some of these and other related computer programs through your local community college, career center, or library.

YOUR FUTURE AS OBJECTIVES

All of these exercises are designed to explore your past and present work-related values. At the same time, you need to project your values into the *future*. What, for example, do you want to do over the next 10 to 20 years? We'll return to this type of value question when we address in Chapter 8 the critical objective setting stage of the job search process.

7

KNOW YOUR MOTIVATED ABILITIES & SKILLS (MAS)

*O*nce you know what you do well and enjoy doing, you next need to analyze those interests, values, abilities, and skills that form a **recurring motivated pattern**. This "pattern" is the single most important piece of information you need to know about yourself in the whole self-assessment process. Knowing your skills and abilities alone without knowing how they relate to your interests and values will not give you the necessary direction for finding the job you want. You simply *must* know your pattern.

WHAT'S YOUR MAS?

The concept of motivated abilities and skills (MAS) enables us to relate your interests and values to your skills and abilities. But how do we identify your MAS beyond the questions and exercises outlined thus far?

107

Your pattern of motivated abilities and skills becomes evident once you analyze your *achievements or accomplishments.* For it is your achievements that tell us what you both did well and enjoyed doing. If we analyze and synthesize many of your achievements, we are likely to identify a *recurring pattern* that most likely goes back to your childhood and which will continue to characterize your achievements in the future.

An equally useful exercise would be to identify your weaknesses by analyzing your failures. These, too, would fall into recurring patterns. Understanding what your weaknesses are might help you avoid jobs and work situations that bring out the worst in you. Indeed, you may learn more about yourself by analyzing your failures than by focusing solely on your accomplishments.

For now, let's focus on your positives rather than identify your negatives. After you complete the strength exercises in this chapter, you may want to reverse the procedures to identify your weaknesses.

Numerous self-directed exercises can assist you in identifying your pattern of motivated abilities and skills. The basic requirements for making these exercises work for you are time and analytical ability. You must spend a great deal of time detailing your achievements by looking at your history of accomplishments. Once you complete the historical reconstruction task, you must comb through your "stories" to identify recurring themes and patterns. This requires a high level of analytical ability which you may or may not possess. If analysis and synthesis are not two of your strong skills, you may want to seek assistance from a friend or professional who is good at analyzing and synthesizing information presented in narrative form. Career counseling firms such as Haldane Associates (nationwide) and People Management, Inc. (Snohomish, WA) are known for their use of this type of motivated pattern approach; they should be able to assist you.

Several paper and pencil exercises help identify your pattern of motivated abilities and skills. We outline some of the most popular and thorough such exercises that have proved useful to thousands of people.

THE SKILLS MAP

Richard Bolles' *"Quick Job Hunting Map"* has become a standard self-assessment tool for thousands of job seekers and career changers who are willing to spend the time and effort necessary for discovering their pattern of motivated abilities and skills. Offering a checklist of over 200 skills organized around John Holland's concept of *"The Self-Directed Search"* for defining work environments (realistic, investigative, artistic, social, enterprising, and conventional), the *"Map"* requires you to identify seven of your most satisfying accomplishments, achievements, jobs, or roles. After detailing each achievement, you analyze the details of each in relation to the checklist of skills. Once you do this for all seven achievements, you should have a comprehensive picture of what skills you (1) use most frequently, and (2) enjoy using in satisfying and successful settings. This exercise not only yields an enormous amount of information on your interests, values, skills, and abilities, it also assists you in the process of analyzing the data. If done properly, the *"Map"* should also generate a rich "skills" vocabulary which you should use in your resumes and letters as well as in interviews.

The *"Map"* is available in different forms and for different levels of experience. The most popular versions are found in the Appendix of Bolles' *What Color Is Your Parachute?* and *The Three Boxes of Life* as well as in a separate publication entitled *The New Quick Job Hunting Map*. These three publications can be ordered directly from Impact Publications by completing the order information at the end of this book. The map is also available in three other versions: *The Beginning Quick Job-Hunting Map, How to Create a Picture of Your Ideal Job or Next Career*, and *The Classic Quick Job-Hunting Map*. These versions of the *"Map"* are most conveniently available directly from the publisher, Ten Speed Press (P.O. Box 7123, Berkeley, CA 94707).

We highly recommend using the Map because of the ease with which it can be used. If you will spend the six to 20 hours necessary to complete it properly, the *"Map"* will give you some important information about yourself. Unfortunately, many people become overwhelmed by the exercise and either decide not to complete it, or they try to save time by not doing it according to the directions. You simply must follow the directions and spend the time and effort necessary if you want to get the maximum benefit from this exercise.

Keep in mind that like most self-assessment devices, there is nothing magical about the *"Map"*. Its basic organizing principles are simple. Like other exercises designed to uncover your pattern of motivated abilities and skills, this one is based on a theory of historical determinism and probability. In other words, once you uncover your pattern, get prepared to acknowledge it and live with it in the future.

AUTOBIOGRAPHY OF ACCOMPLISHMENTS

Less structured than the *"Map"* device, this exercise requires you to write a lengthy essay about your life accomplishments. Your essay may run anywhere from 20 to 200 pages. After completing it, go through it page by page to identify what aspects of your Army experience you most enjoyed (working with different kinds of data, people, processes, and objects) and what skills you used most frequently as well as enjoyed using. Finally, identify those skills you wish to continue using. After analyzing and synthesizing this data, you should have a relatively clear picture of your strongest skills.

This exercise requires a great deal of self-discipline and analytic skill. To do it properly, you must write as much as possible, and in as much detail as possible, about your accomplishments. The richer the detail, the better will be your analysis.

MOTIVATED SKILLS EXERCISE

Our final exercise is one of the most complex and time consuming self-assessment exercises. However, it yields some of the best data on motivated abilities and skills, and it is especially useful for those who feel they need a more thorough analysis of their past achievements. This device is widely used by career counselors. Initially developed by Haldane Associates, this particular exercise is variously referred to as *"Success Factor Analysis," "System to Identify Motivated Skills,"* or *"Intensive Skills Identification."*

This technique helps you identify which skills you *enjoy* using. While you can use this technique on your own, it is best to work with someone else. Since you will need six to eight hours to properly complete this exercise, divide your time into two or three work sessions.

The exercise consists of six steps. The steps follow the basic pattern of generating raw data, identifying patterns, analyzing the data through reduction techniques, and synthesizing the patterns into a transferable skills vocabulary. You need strong analytical skills to complete this exercise on your own. The six steps include:

1. **Identify 15-20 achievements:** These consist of things you enjoyed doing, believe you did well, and felt a sense of satisfaction, pride, or accomplishment in doing. You can see yourself performing at your best and enjoying your experiences when you analyze your achievements. This information reveals your motivations since it deals entirely with your voluntary behavior. In addition, it identifies what is right with you by focusing on your positives and strengths. Identify achievements throughout your life, beginning with your childhood and

continuing through your present Army job. Your achievements should relate to specific experiences—not general ones—and may be drawn from work, leisure, education, or home life. Put each achievement at the top of a separate sheet of paper. For example, your achievements might appear as follows:

SAMPLE ACHIEVEMENT STATEMENTS

"When I was 10 years old, I started a small paper route and built it up to the largest in my district."

"I started playing chess in ninth grade and earned the right to play first board on my high school chess team in my junior year."

"Learned to play the piano and often played for church services while in high school."

"Designed and constructed a dress for a 4-H demonstration project."

"Although I was small compared to other guys, I made the first string on my high school football team."

"I graduated from high school with honors even though I was very active in school clubs and had to work part-time."

"I was the first in my family to go to college and one of the few from my high school. Worked part-time and summers. A real struggle, but I made it."

"I earned an Associate's Degree in Criminal Justice from Boston University while serving at Fort Hood, Texas. By taking evening courses over a two year period, I was able to satisfy all the degree requirements and also perform my military duties."

"Earned an 'A' grade on my senior psychology project from a real tough professor."

———————

"Designed plans for our house and had it constructed on budget."

———————

"Received the Soldier Medal for a heroic act during Operation Desert Shield."

———————

"When my Infantry unit entered Panama City during Operation Just Cause, I carried the company guidon for my commander."

———————

"The proudest day of my life occurred when I received the Army Ranger Tab. It was the most physically and mentally grueling training I've even been through."

———————

"Though I was the smallest soldier in my platoon, I won the intramural wrestling title for my weight group three straight years."

———————

"When I first joined the Army, I had never fired a weapon. After some good coaching from my NCOs, I scored expert the second time my unit went to the M-16 range."

———————

"As a participant in Operation Desert Storm, I will always remember the night our unit ambushed an Iraqi company and I captured five enemy soldiers singlehandedly."

———————

"Jumping from airplanes was an experience I'll never forget! As a member of the 82nd Airborne Division for over three years, I made 124 jumps and over 30 were done at night."

———————

"Being selected the honor graduate of my Officer Basic Course was a real honor."

2. Prioritize your seven most significant achievements.

YOUR MOST
SIGNIFICANT ACHIEVEMENTS

1. _____

2. _____

3. _____

4. _____

5. _____

6. _____

7. _____

3. Write a full page on each of your prioritized achievements.
You should describe:

- How you initially became involved.
- The details of *what you did* and *how you did it.*
- What was especially enjoyable or satisfying to you.

Use copies of the "Detailing Your Achievements" form on page 114 to outline your achievements.

DETAILING YOUR ACHIEVEMENTS

ACHIEVEMENT # __ : _____

_____

_____

A. How did I initially become involved? _____

_____

_____

_____

B. What did I do? _____

_____

_____

_____

C. How did I do it? _____

_____

_____

_____

D. What was especially enjoyable about doing it?

_____

_____

_____

4. **Elaborate on your achievements:** Have one or two other people interview you. For each achievement have them note on a separate sheet of paper any terms used to reveal your skills, abilities, and personal qualities. To elaborate details, the interviewer(s) may ask:

   - What was involved in the achievement?
   - What was your part?

- What did you actually do?
- How did you go about that?

Clarify any vague areas by providing an example or illustration of what you actually did. Probe with the following questions:

- Would you elaborate on one example of what you mean?
- Could you give me an illustration?
- What were you good at doing?

This interview should clarify the details of your activities by asking only "what" and "how" questions. It should take 45 to 90 minutes to complete. Reproduce the "Strength Identification Interview" form on page 116 to guide you through this interview.

5. **Identify patterns by examining the interviewer's notes:** Together identify the recurring skills, abilities, and personal qualities *demonstrated* in your achievements. Search for patterns. Your skills pattern should be clear at this point; you should feel comfortable with it. If you have questions, review the data. If you disagree with a conclusion, disregard it. The results must accurately and honestly reflect how you operate.

6. **Synthesize the information by clustering similar skills into categories:** For example, your skills might be grouped in the following manner:

SYNTHESIZED SKILL CLUSTERS

Investigate/Survey/Read Inquire/Probe/Question	Teach/Train/Drill Perform/Show/Demonstrate
Learn/Memorize/Practice Evaluate/Appraise/Assess Compare	Construct/Assemble/Put together
	Organize/Structure/Provide definition/Plan/Chart course Strategize/Coordinate
Influence/Involve/Get participation/Publicize Promote	Create/Design/Adapt/Modify

STRENGTH IDENTIFICATION
INTERVIEW

Interviewee _____   **Interviewer** _____

INSTRUCTIONS: For each achievement experience, identify the **skills** and abilities the achiever actually demonstrates. Obtain details of the experience by asking *what* was involved with the achievement and *how* the individual made the achievement happen. Avoid "why" questions which tend to mislead. Ask for examples or illustrations of what and how.

Achievement #1:

Achievement #2:

Achievement #3:

Recurring abilities and skills:

This exercise yields a relatively comprehensive inventory of your skills. The information will better enable you to use a *skills vocabulary* when identifying your objective, writing your resume and letters, and interviewing. Your self-confidence and self-esteem should increase accordingly.

OTHER ALTERNATIVES

Several other techniques also can help you identify your motivated abilities and skills:

1. List all of your hobbies and analyze what you do in each, which ones you like the most, what skills you use, and your accomplishments.

2. Conduct a job analysis by writing about your past jobs and identifying which skills you used in each job. Cluster the skills into related categories and prioritize them according to your preferences.

3. Purchase a copy of Arthur F. Miller and Ralph T. Mattson's *The Truth About You* and work through the exercises found in the Appendix. While its overt religious message, extreme deterministic approach, and laborious exercises may turn off some users, you may find this book useful nonetheless. This is an abbreviated version of the authors' SIMA (System for Identifying Motivated Abilities) technique used by their career counseling firm, People Management, Inc. (924 First Street, Suite A, Snohomish, WA 98290, Tel. 206/563-0105). If you need professional assistance, contact this firm directly. They can provide you with several alternative services consistent with the career planning philosophy and approach outlined in this chapter.

4. Complete John Holland's *"The Self-Directed Search."* You'll find it in his book, *Making Vocational Choices: A Theory of Careers* or in a separate publication entitled *The Self-Directed Search—A Guide to Educational and Vocational Planning.*

BENEFIT FROM REDUNDANCY

The self-directed MAS exercises generate similar information. They identify interests, values, abilities, and skills you already possess. While aptitude and achievement tests may yield similar information, the self-directed exercises have three major advantages over the standardized tests: less expensive, self-monitored and evaluated, and measure motivation *and* ability.

Completing each exercise demands a different investment of your time. Writing your life history and completing the Motivated Skills Exercise as well as Bolles' *"Map"* are the most time consuming. On the other hand, Holland's *"Self-Directed Search"* can be completed in a few minutes. But the more time you invest with each technique, the more useful information you will generate.

We recommend creating redundancy by using at least two or three different techniques. This will help reinforce and confirm the validity of your observations and interpretations. If you have a great deal of work experience, we recommend using the more thorough exercises. The more you put into these techniques and exercises, the greater the benefit to other stages of your job search. You will be well prepared to target your job search toward specific jobs that fit your MAS as well as communicate your qualifications loud and clear to employers. A carefully planned career or career change should not do less than this.

Past performance is the best predictor of future performance.

BRIDGING YOUR PAST AND FUTURE

Many people want to know about their future. If you expect the self-assessment techniques in Chapters 5, 6, and 7 to spell out your future, you will be disappointed. Fortune tellers, horoscopes, and various forms of mysticism may be what you need.

These are historical devices which integrate past achievements, abilities, and motivations into a coherent framework for projecting future performance. They clarify past strengths and recurring motivations for targeting future jobs. Abilities and motivations are the *qualifications* employers expect for particular jobs. Qualifications consist of your past experience *and* your motivated abilities and skills.

The assessment techniques provide a bridge between your past and future. They treat your future preferences and performance as functions of your past experiences and demonstrated abilities. This common sense notion is shared by employers: past performance is the best predictor of future performance.

Yet, employers hire a person's *future* rather than their past. And herein lies an important problem you can help employers overcome. Getting the job that is right for you entails communicating to prospective employers that you have the necessary qualifications. Indeed, employers will look for signs of your future productivity *for them*. You are an unknown and risky quantity. Therefore, you must communicate evidence of your past productivity. This evidence is revealed clearly in your past achievements as outlined in our assessment techniques.

The overall value of using these assessment techniques is that they should enhance your occupational mobility over the long-run. The major thrust of all these techniques is to identify abilities and skills which are *transferable* to different work environments. This is particularly important if you are making a career change. You must overcome employers' negative expectations and objections toward career changers by clearly communicating your transferable abilities and skills in the most positive terms possible. These assessment techniques are designed to do precisely that.

8

DEVELOP EMPLOYER- CENTERED OBJECTIVES

As a member of the Army, you are used to setting objectives. However, the objectives you set in the Army are normally closely associated with the Commander's mission. They're not really *your* objectives. Now it's time to formulate objectives based on *your* desires and goals. What do *you* want to do? This question will help guide your job search campaign.

Once you identify your interests, skills, and abilities, you should be well prepared to develop a clear and purposeful objective for targeting your job search toward specific organizations and employers. With a renewed sense of direction, and versed in an appropriate language, you should communicate to employers that you are a talented and purposeful individual who *achieves results.* Your objective must tell employers what you will *do for them* rather than what you want from them. It targets your accomplishments around employers' needs. In other words, your objective should be employer-centered rather than self-centered.

GOALS AND OBJECTIVES

Goals and objectives are statements of what you want to do in the future. When combined with an assessment of your interests, values, abilities and skills related to specific jobs, they give your job search needed direction and meaning for the purpose of targeting specific employers. Without them, your job search may founder as you present an image of uncertainty and confusion to potential employers.

---

*Your objective should be
employer-centered rather
than self-centered.*

When you identify your strengths, you also create the necessary data base and vocabulary for developing your job objective. Using this vocabulary, you should be able to communicate to employers that you are a talented and purposeful individual who achieves results.

If you fail to do the preliminary self-assessment work necessary for developing a clear objective, you will probably wander aimlessly in a highly decentralized, fragmented, and chaotic job market looking for interesting jobs you might fit into. Your goal, instead, should be to find a job or career that is compatible with your interests, motivations, skills, and talents as well as related to a vision of your future. In other words, try to find a job fit for you and your future rather than try to fit into a job that happens to be advertised and for which you think you can qualify.

EXAMINE YOUR PAST,
PRESENT, AND FUTURE

Depending on how you approach your job search, your goals can be largely a restatement of your past MAS patterns or a vision of your future. If you base your job search on an analysis of your motivated abilities and skills, you may prefer restating your past patterns as your present and future goals. On the other hand, you may want to establish a vision of your future and set goals that motivate you to achieve that vision through a process of self-transformation.

The type of goals you choose to establish will involve different processes. However, the strongest goals will be those that combine your motivated abilities and skills with a realistic vision of your future.

The strongest goals will be those that combine your motivated abilities and skills with a realistic vision of your future.

ORIENT YOURSELF
TO EMPLOYERS' NEEDS

Your objective should be a concise statement of what you want to do and what you have to offer to an employer. The position you seek is "what you want to do"; your qualifications are "what you have to offer." Your objective should state your strongest qualifications for meeting employer's needs. It should communicate what you have to offer an employer without emphasizing what you expect the employer to do for you. In other words, your objective should be *work-centered*, not self-centered; it should not contain trite terms which emphasize what you want, such as give me a(n) "opportunity for advancement," "position working with people," "progressive company," or "creative position." Such terms are viewed as "canned" job search language which say little of value about you. Above all, your objective should reflect your honesty and integrity; it should not be "hyped."

Identifying what it is you want to do can be one of the most difficult job search tasks. Indeed, most job hunters lack clear objectives. Many engage in a random, and somewhat mindless, search for jobs by identifying available job opportunities and then adjusting their skills and objectives to fit specific job openings. While you can get a job using this approach, you may be misplaced and unhappy with what you find. You will fit into a job rather than find a job that is fit for you.

Knowing what you want to do can have numerous benefits. First, you define the job market rather than let it define you. The inherent fragmentation and chaos of the job market should be advantageous for you, because it enables you to systematically organize job opportunities around your specific objectives and skills. Second, you will communicate professionalism to prospective employers. They will receive a precise indication of your interests, qualifications, and purposes, which places you ahead of most other applicants. Third, being purposeful means being able to communicate to employers what you want to do. Employers are not interested in hiring indecisive and confused individuals, especially transitioning military personnel who do not know what they want to do; such individuals may become unhappy employees who quit after only a few months on the job. Employers want to know what it is you can do for them. With a clear objective, based upon a thorough understanding of your motivated skills and interests, you can take control of the situation as you demonstrate your value to employers.

Finally, few employers really know what they want in a candidate. Like most job seekers, employers lack clear employment objectives and knowledge about how the job market operates. If you know what you want and can help the employer define his or her "needs" as your objective, you will have achieved a tremendously advantageous position in the job market.

BE PURPOSEFUL AND REALISTIC

Your objective should communicate that you are a *purposeful individual who achieves results.* It can be stated over different time periods as well as at various levels of abstraction and specificity. You can identify short, intermediate, and long-range objectives and very general to very specific objectives. Whatever the case, it is best to know your prospective audience before deciding on the type of objective. Your objective should reflect your career interests as well as employers' needs.

Objectives also should be *realistic.* You may want to become President of the United States or solve all the world's problems. However, these objectives are probably unrealistic. While they may represent your ideals and fantasies, you need to be more realistic in terms of what you can personally accomplish in the immediate future. What, for example, are you prepared to deliver to prospective employers over the next few months? While it is good to set challenging objectives, you can overdo it. Refine your objective by thinking about the next major step or two you would like to make in your career advancement.

PROJECT YOURSELF INTO THE FUTURE

Even after identifying your abilities and skills, specifying an objective can be the most difficult and tedious step in the job search process; it can stall the resume writing process indefinitely. This simple one-sentence, 25-word statement can take days or weeks to formulate and clearly define. Yet, it must be specified prior to writing the resume and engaging in other job search steps. An objective gives meaning and direction to all of your other job search activities.

Your objective should be viewed as a function of several influences. Since you want to build upon your strengths and you want to be realistic, your abilities and skills will play a central role in formulating your work objective. At the same time, you do not want your objective to become a function solely of your past accomplishments and skills. You may be very skilled in certain areas, but you may not want to use these skills in the future. As a result, your values and interests filter which skills you will or will not incorporate into your work objective.

Overcoming the problem of historical determinism—your future merely reflecting your past—requires incorporating additional components into defining your objective. One of the most important is your ideals, fantasies, or dreams. Everyone engages in these, and sometimes they come true. Your ideals, fantasies, or dreams may include making $1,000,000 by age 45; owning a Mercedes-Benz and a Porsche; taking trips to Rio, Hong Kong, and Rome; owning your own business; developing financial independence; writing a best-selling novel; solving major social problems; or winning the Nobel Peace Prize. If your fantasies require more money than you are now making, you will need to incorporate monetary considerations into your work objective. For example, if you have these fantasies, but your sense of realism tells you that your objective is to move from a $40,000 a year position to a $43,000 a year position you will be going nowhere, unless you can fast-track in your new position. Therefore, you will need to set a higher objective to satisfy your fantasies.

You can develop realistic objectives many different ways. We don't claim to have a new or magical formula, only one which has worked for many individuals. We assume you are capable of making intelligent career decisions if given sufficient data. Using redundancy once again, our approach is designed to provide you with sufficient corroborating data from several sources and perspectives so that you can make preliminary decisions. If you follow our steps in setting a realistic objective, you should be able to give your job search clear direction.

Four major steps are involved in developing a work objective. Each step can be implemented in a variety of ways:

STEP 1: Develop or obtain basic data on your functional/transferable skills, which we discussed in Chapter 7.

STEP 2: Acquire corroborating data about yourself from others, tests, and yourself. Several resources are available for this purpose:

A. From others: Ask three to five individuals whom you know well to evaluate you according to the questions in the "Strength Evaluation" form on page 126. Explain to these people that you believe their candid appraisal will help you gain a better understanding of your strengths and weaknesses from the perspectives of others. Make copies of this form and ask your evaluators to complete and return it to a designated third party who will share the information—but not the respondent's name—with you.

B. From vocational tests: Although we prefer self-generated data, vocationally-oriented tests can help clarify, confirm, and translate your understanding of yourself into occupational directions. If you decide to use vocational tests, contact a professional career counselor who can administer and interpret the tests. We suggest several of the following tests:

- Strong-Campbell Interest Inventory
- Myers-Briggs Type Indicator
- Career Occupational Preference System
- Edwards Personal Preference Schedule
- Kuder Occupational Interest Survey
- APTICOM
- Jackson Vocational Interest Survey
- Ramak Inventory
- Vocational Interest Inventory
- Career Assessment Inventory
- Temperament and Values Inventory

STRENGTH EVALUATION

TO: _____

FROM: _____

I am going through a career assessment process and thought you would be an appropriate person to ask for assistance. Would you please candidly respond to the questions below? Your comments will be given to me by the individual designated below; s/he will not reveal your name. Your comments will be used for advising purposes only. Thank you.

What are my strengths?

What weak areas might I need to improve?

In your opinion, what do I need in a job or career to make me satisfied?

Please return to: _____

C. **From yourself:** Numerous alternatives are available for you to practice redundancy. Refer to the exercises in Chapter 6 that assist you in identifying your work values, job frustrations and dissatisfactions, things you love to do, things you enjoy most about work, and your preferred interpersonal environments.

STEP 3: Project your values and preferences into the future by completing simulation and creative thinking exercises:

A. **Ten Million Dollar Exercise:** First, assume that you are given a $10,000,000 gift; now you don't have to work. Since the gift is restricted to your use only, you cannot give any part of it away. What will you do with your time! At first? Later on? Second, assume that you are given another $10,000,000, but this time you are required to give it all away. What kinds of causes, organizations, charities, etc. would you support? Complete the following form in which you answer these questions:

WHAT WILL I DO WITH
TWO $10,000,000 GIFTS?

First gift is restricted to my use only:

_____

_____

Second gift must be given away:

_____

_____

SOURCE: John C. Crystal, *"Life/Work Planning Workshop"*

B. **Obituary Exercise:** Make a list of the most important things you would like to do or accomplish before you die. Two alternatives are available for doing this. First, make a list in response to this lead-in statement: "Before I die, I want to..."

BEFORE I DIE, I WANT TO . . .

1. _____

   _____

2. _____

   _____

3. _____

   _____

4. _____

   _____

5. _____

   _____

6. _____

   _____

7. _____

   _____

8. _____

   _____

9. _____

   _____

10. _____

    _____

Second, write a newspaper article which is actually your obituary for 10 years from now. Stress your accomplishments over the coming ten year period.

MY OBITUARY

Obituary for Mr./Ms. _____ to appear in the _____ Newspaper in 2004.

_____

_____

_____

_____

_____

_____

_____

_____

_____

_____

_____

_____

_____

_____

_____

_____

C. **My Ideal Work Week:** Starting with Monday, place each day of the week as the headings of seven sheets of paper. Develop a daily calendar with 30-minute intervals, beginning at 7am and ending at midnight. Your calendar should consist of a 118-hour week. Next, beginning at 7am on Monday (sheet one), identify the *ideal activities* you would enjoy doing, or need to do for each 30-minute segment during the day. Assume you are capable of doing anything; you have no constraints except those you impose on yourself. Furthermore, assume that your work schedule consists of 40 hours per week. How will you fill your time? Be specific.

MY IDEAL WORK WEEK

Monday
am   pm

7:00 _____		4:00 _____
7:30 _____		4:30 _____
8:00 _____		5:00 _____
8:30 _____		5:30 _____
9:00 _____		6:00 _____
9:30 _____		6:30 _____
10:00 _____		7:00 _____
10:30 _____		7:30 _____
11:00 _____		8:00 _____
11:30 _____		8:30 _____
12:00 _____		9:00 _____
p.m. _____		9:30 _____
12:30 _____		10:00 _____
1:00 _____		10:30 _____
1:30 _____		11:00 _____
2:00 _____		11:30 _____
2:30 _____		12:00 _____
3:00 _____		Continue for Tuesday,
		Wednesday, Thursday,
3:30 _____		and Friday

D.   My Ideal Job Description: Develop your ideal future job.
Be sure you include:

- Specific interests you want to build into your job.
- Work responsibilities.
- Working conditions.
- Earnings and benefits.
- Interpersonal environment.
- Working circumstances, opportunities, and goals.

Use "My Ideal Job Specifications" on page 132 to outline your ideal job. After completing this exercise, synthesize the job and write a detailed paragraph which describes the kind of job you would most enjoy:

DESCRIPTION OF MY IDEAL JOB

MY IDEAL JOB SPECIFICATIONS

Job Interests	Work Responsibilities	Working Conditions	Earnings/ Benefits	Interpersonal Environment	Circumstances/ Opportunities/ Goals

STEP 4: **Test your objective against reality. Evaluate and refine it by conducting market research, a force field analysis, library research, and informational interviews.**

A. **Market Research:** Four steps are involved in conducting this research:

1. **Products or services:** Based upon all other assessment activities, make a list of what you *do* or *make*:

PRODUCTS/SERVICES I DO OR MAKE

1. _____

2. _____

3. _____

4. _____

5. _____

6. _____

7. _____

8. _____

9. _____

10. _____

2. **Market:** Identify who needs, wants, or buys what you do or make. Be specific. Include individuals, groups, and organizations. Then, identify *what* specific *needs* your products or services fill. Next, assess the *results* you achieve with your products or services.

THE MARKET FOR MY PRODUCTS/SERVICES

Individuals, groups, organizations needing me:

1. _____

2. _____

3. _____

4. _____

5. _____

Needs I fulfill:

1. _____

2. _____

3. _____

4. _____

5. _____

Results/Outcomes/Impacts of my products/services:

1. _____

2. _____

3. _____

4. _____

5. _____

3. **New Markets:** Brainstorm a list of *who else* needs your products or services. Think about ways of expanding your market. Next, list any new needs your current or new market has which you might be able to fill:

DEVELOPING NEW NEEDS

Who else needs my products/services?

1. _____

2. _____

3. _____

4. _____

5. _____

New ways to expand my market:

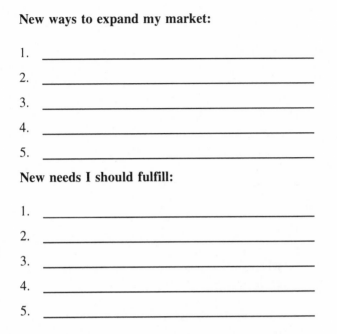

1. _____
2. _____
3. _____
4. _____
5. _____

New needs I should fulfill:

1. _____
2. _____
3. _____
4. _____
5. _____

4. **New products and/or services:** List any new products or services you can offer and any new needs you can satisfy:

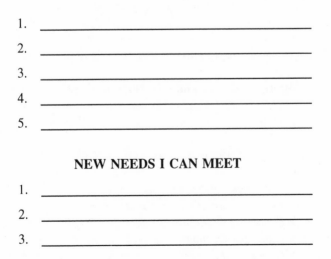

**NEW PRODUCTS/
SERVICES I CAN OFFER**

1. _____
2. _____
3. _____
4. _____
5. _____

NEW NEEDS I CAN MEET

1. _____
2. _____
3. _____

4. _____

5. _____

B.   Force Field Analysis: Once you have developed a tentative or firm objective, force field analysis can help you understand the various internal and external forces affecting the achievement of your objective. Force field analysis follows a specific sequence of activities:

- Clearly state your objective or course of action.

- List the positive and negative forces affecting your objective. Specify the internal and external forces working *for* and *against* you in terms of who, what, where, when, and how much. Estimate the impact of each force upon your objective.

- Analyze the forces. Assess the importance of each force upon your objective and its probable affect upon you. Some forces may be irrelevant to your goal. You may need additional information to make a thorough analysis.

- Maximize positive forces and minimize negative ones. Identify actions you can take to strengthen positive forces and to neutralize, overcome, or reverse negative forces. Focus on real, important, and probable key forces.

- Assess the feasibility of attaining your objective and, if necessary, modifying it in light of new information.

C.   Conduct Library and CD-ROM Research: This research should strengthen and clarify your objective. Consult various reference materials on alternative jobs and careers:

CAREER & JOB ALTERNATIVES

- *Dictionary of Occupational Titles*
- *Encyclopedia of Careers and Vocational Guidance*
- *Enhanced Guide for Occupational Exploration*
- *Guide for Occupational Exploration*
- *Occupational Outlook Handbook*

INDUSTRIAL DIRECTORIES

- *Bernard Klein's Guide to American Directories*
- *Dun and Bradstreet's Middle Market Directory*
- *Dun and Bradstreet's Million Dollar Directory*
- *Encyclopedia of Business Information Sources*
- *Geography Index*
- *Poor's Register of Corporations, Directors, and Executives*
- *Standard Directory of Advertisers*
- *The Standard Periodical Directory*
- *Standard and Poor's Industrial Index*
- *Standard Rate and Data Business Publications Directory*
- *Thomas' Register of American Manufacturers*

ASSOCIATIONS

- *Directory of Professional and Trade Associations*
- *Encyclopedia of Associations*

GOVERNMENT SOURCES

- *The Book of the States*
- *Congressional Directory*
- *Congressional Staff Directory*
- *Congressional Yellow Book*
- *Federal Directory*
- *Federal Yellow Book*
- *Municipal Yearbook*
- *Taylor's Encyclopedia of Government Officials*
- *United Nations Yearbook*
- *United States Government Manual*
- *Washington Information Directory*

NEWSPAPERS

- *The Wall Street Journal*
- Major city newspapers
- Trade newspapers
- Any city newspaper—especially the Sunday edition.

BUSINESS PUBLICATIONS

- *Barron's, Business Week, Business World, Forbes, Fortune, Harvard Business Review, Money, Time, Newsweek, U.S. News and World Report*

OTHER LIBRARY RESOURCES

- Trade journals (refer to the *Directory of Special Libraries and Information Centers* and *Subject Collections: A Guide to Specialized Libraries of Businesses, Governments, and Associations*).
- Publications of Chambers of Commerce; State Manufacturing Associations; and federal, state, and local government agencies
- Telephone books—The Yellow Pages
- Trade books on "How to get a job"

4. **Conduct Informational Interviews:** This may be the most useful way to clarify and refine your objective. We'll discuss this procedure in subsequent chapters.

After completing these steps, you will have identified what it is you *can* do (abilities and skills), enlarged your thinking to include what it is you would *like* to do (aspirations), and probed the realities of implementing your objective. Thus, setting a realistic work objective is a function of the diverse considerations represented on page 139.

Your work objective is a function of both subjective and objective information as well as idealism and realism. We believe the strongest emphasis should be placed on your competencies and should include a broad data-base. Your work objective is realistic in that it is tempered by your past experiences, accomplishments, skills, and current research. An objective formulated in this manner permits you to think beyond your past experiences.

STATE A FUNCTIONAL OBJECTIVE

Your job objective should be oriented toward skills and results or outcomes. You can begin by stating a functional job objective at two different levels: a general objective and a specific one for communicating your qualifications to employers both on resumes and in interviews. Thus,

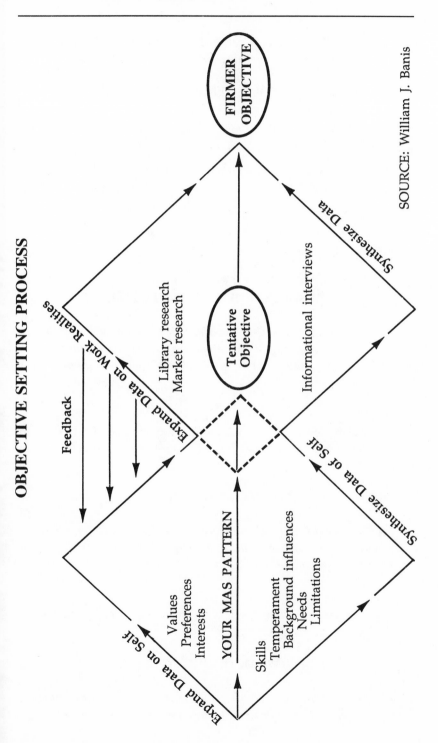

OBJECTIVE SETTING PROCESS

FIRMER OBJECTIVE

Synthesize Data

Tentative Objective

Library research
Market research

Informational interviews

Expand Data on Work Realities

Feedback

Synthesize Data of Self

YOUR MAS PATTERN

Values
Preferences
Interests

Skills
Temperament
Background influences
Needs
Limitations

Expand Data on Self

SOURCE: William J. Banis

this objective setting process sets the stage for other key job search activities. For the general objective, begin with the statement:

STATING YOUR GENERAL OBJECTIVE

I would like a job where I can use my ability to _____
which will result in _____ *.*

SOURCE: Richard Germann and Peter Arnold, *Bernard Haldane Associates Job & Career Building* (New York: Harper and Row, 1980), 54-55.

The objective in this statement is both a *skill* and an *outcome.* For example, you might state:

SKILLS-BASED AND
RESULTS-ORIENTED OBJECTIVE

I would like a job where my experience in program development, supported by innovative decision-making and systems engineering abilities, will result in an expanded clientele and a more profitable organization.

At a second level you may wish to re-write this objective in order to target it at various consulting firms. For example, on your resume it becomes:

JOB TARGETED OBJECTIVE

An increasingly responsible research position in consulting, where proven decision-making and system engineering abilities will be used for improving organizational productivity.

The following are examples of weak and strong objective statements. Various styles are also presented:

WEAK OBJECTIVES

Management position which will use business administration degree and will provide opportunities for rapid advancement.

A position in social services which will allow me to work with people in a helping capacity.

A position in Personnel Administration with a progressive firm.

Sales Representative with opportunity for advancement.

STRONG OBJECTIVES

To use computer science training in software development for designing and implementing operating systems.

A public relations position which will maximize opportunities to develop and implement programs, to organize people and events, and to communicate positive ideas and images. Effective in public speaking and in managing a publicity/promotional campaign.

A position as a General Sales Representative with a pharmaceutical house which will use chemistry background and ability to work on a self-directed basis in managing a marketing territory.

A position in data analysis where skills in mathematics, computer programming, and deductive reasoning will contribute to new systems development.

Retail Management position which will use sales/customer service experience and creative abilities for product display and merchandising. Long term goal: Progression to merchandise manager with corporate-wide responsibilities for product line.

Responsible position in investment research and analysis. Interests and skills include securities analysis, financial planning, and portfolio management. Long range goal: to become a Chartered Financial Analyst.

It is important to relate your objective to your audience. While you definitely want a good job, your audience wants to know what you can do for them. Remember, your objective should be work-centered, not self-centered.

We will return to this discussion when we examine how to develop the objective section on your resume. Your objective will become the key element for organizing all other elements on your resume. It gives meaning and direction to your job search. Your objective says something very important about how you want to make your career transition from the Army.

9

CREATE DYNAMITE RESUMES & LETTERS

Now that you know (1) what you do well, (2) what you enjoy doing, and (3) what you want to do in the future—assuming you have completed the exercises in the four previous chapters—you have the basic information necessary for communicating your qualifications to employers. But what will you do with this information? What messages do you want to send to employers about yourself? How do you plan to convey these messages—by telephone, computer, letter, or in face-to-face meetings?

USE RESUME ASSISTANCE DESIGNED FOR YOU

We realize this will be your first resume upon leaving the Army. Because it is so important to your job search, your resume needs to be expertly crafted with both your goals and employers' needs in mind. As with many other aspects of the transition process, the Army and the federal government offer free assistance to Army personnel in developing resumes, from mini-resumes appropriate for electronic databases to the traditional one- to two-page resumes appropriate for applications, networking, and job interviews. In Chapter 4 we identified several of these Army, government, and association-sponsored transition services. For example, you can attend resume writing classes available through both ACAP and JAC. Transition specialists in the JAC will review and help you refine your resume at no cost. Other organizations, like AUSA, will help you craft your resume for a minimal fee. We recommend that you take advantage of such resume guidance services and then develop the initial draft of your resume on your own. These transition specialists have a great deal of experience in working with hundreds of Army resumes. Their job is to make sure your resume best communicates your qualifications to civilian employers.

COMMUNICATING POSITIVE IMAGES

At every stage in the job search you must communicate a positive image to potential employers. The initial impression you make on an employer through applications, resumes, letters, telephone calls, or informational interviews will determine whether the employer is interested in interviewing you and offering you a position.

Developing and managing effective job search communication should play a central role in everything you do related to finding employment. While this communication will take several verbal and nonverbal forms, your first communication with employers will most likely be by letter, telephone, or in a face-to-face meeting. Job search letters often include your calling card—the resume. Essentially nonverbal forms of communication, these documents should be written and distributed with impact.

WRITING RESUMES

Resumes are important tools for communicating your purpose and capabilities to employers. While many jobs only require a completed application form, you should always prepare a resume for influencing the hiring process. Application forms do not substitute for resumes.

Many myths surround resumes and letters. Some people still believe a resume should summarize one's history. Others believe it will get them a job. And still others believe they should be mailed in response to classified ads. The reality is this: A resume advertises your qualifications to prospective employers. It is your calling card for getting interviews.

A resume advertises your qualifications to prospective employers. It is your calling card for getting interviews.

INEFFECTIVE RESUMES

Most people write ineffective resumes. Misunderstanding the purpose of resumes, they make numerous mistakes commonly associated with weak resumes and poor advertising copy. Their resumes often lack an objective, include unrelated categories of information, are too long, and appear unattractive. Other common pitfalls identified by employers include:

- Unknown military acronyms
- Poor layout
- Misspellings and punctuation errors
- Poor grammar
- Unclear purpose
- Too much jargon
- Irrelevant data
- Too long or too short
- Poorly typed and reproduced
- Unexplained time gaps
- Too boastful
- Deceptive or dishonest
- Difficult to understand or interpret

Your resume, instead, should incorporate the characteristics of strong and effective resumes:

- Clearly communicate your purpose and competencies in relation to employers' needs.
- Are concise and easy to read.

- Motivate the reader to read it in-depth.
- Tell employers that you are a responsible and purposeful individual—a doer who can solve their problems.

Employers are busy people who normally only glance at a resume for 20 or 30 seconds.

Keep in mind that most employers are busy people who normally glance at a resume for only 20 to 30 seconds. Your resume, therefore, must sufficiently catch their attention to pass the 20 to 30 second evaluation test. When writing your resume, ask yourself the same question asked by employers: "Why should I read this resume or contact this person for an interview?" Your answer should result in an attractive, interesting, unique, and skills-based resume.

TYPES OF RESUMES

You have four types of resumes to choose from: chronological, functional, combination, or resume letter. Each format has various advantages and disadvantages, depending on your background and purpose. For example, someone first entering the job market should use a functional resume. For most transitioning Army members, we recommend the combination format because it highlights your functional expertise and also shows your range of assignments. On the other hand, a person who wants to target a particular job may choose to use a resume letter. Examples of these different types of resumes are included at the end of this chapter. Further assistance in developing each section of your resume is found in the Krannichs' two comprehensive resume development books, *High Impact Resumes and Letters* and *Dynamite Resumes*.

The **chronological resume** is the standard resume used by most applicants. It comes in two forms: traditional and improved. The **traditional chronological resume** is also known as the "obituary resume," because it both "kills" your chances of getting a job and is a good source for writing your obituary. Summarizing your work history, this resume lists dates and names first and duties and responsibilities second; it includes extraneous information such as height, weight, age, marital status, sex, and hobbies. While relatively easy to write, this is the most ineffective resume you can produce. Its purpose at best is to inform people of what you have done in the past as well as where, when, and with whom. It tells employers little or nothing about what you want to do, can do, and will do for them. Unfortunately, this type of resume is often written by transitioning military personnel who don't know much about resume writing nor effective job search communication.

The **improved chronological resume** communicates directly to employers your purpose, past achievements, and probable future performance. You should use this type of resume when you have extensive experience directly related to a position you seek. This resume should include a work objective which reflects both your work experience and professional goals. The work experience section should include the names and addresses of former employers followed by a brief description of your accomplishments, skills, and responsibilities; inclusive employment dates should appear at the end. Do not begin with dates; they are the least significant element in the descriptions. Be sure to stress your *accomplishments* and *skills* rather than your formal duties and responsibilities. You want to inform your audience that you are a productive and responsible person who gets things done—a doer. Military personnel with a great deal of progressive work experience relevant to the civilian work world should use this type of resume. However, for this resume to work best, you must make sure your military experience clearly translates into the language of the civilian work world. It is *your* responsibility—not employers'—to interpret what your military work experience means in civilian language.

Functional resumes should be used by individuals making a significant career change.

Functional resumes should be used by individuals making a significant career change, first entering the work force, or re-entering the job market after a lengthy absence. This resume should stress your accomplishments and transferable skills regardless of previous work settings and job titles. This could include accomplishments as a volunteer worker, housewife, or Sunday school teacher. Names of employers and dates of employment should not appear on this resume.

Functional resumes have certain weaknesses. While they are important bridges for the inexperienced and for those making a career change, some employers dislike these resumes. Since many employers still look for names, dates, and direct job experience—where's the beef?—this resume does not meet their expectations. You should use a functional resume only if you have limited work experience or your past work experience does not strengthen your objective when making a major career change. We know few transitioning military personnel who would be best served by writing one of these resumes.

Combination resumes are a compromise between chronological and functional resumes. Having more advantages than disadvantages, this resume may be exactly what you need as you make a career change with military experience relevant to a civilian career.

Combination resumes have the potential to both *meet* and *raise* the expectations of employers. You should stress your accomplishments and skills as well as include your work history. Your work history should appear as a separate section immediately following your presentation of accomplishments and skills in the "Areas of Effectiveness" or "Experience" section. It is not necessary to include dates unless they enhance your resume. This is the perfect resume for someone with work experience who wishes to change to a job in a related career field.

Resume letters are substitutes for resumes. Appearing as a job inquiry or application letter, resume letters highlight various sections of your resume, such as work history, experience, areas of effectiveness, objective, or education, in relation to employers' needs. These letters are used when you prefer not sending your more general resume. Resume letters have one major weakness: they give employers insufficient information and thus may prematurely eliminate you from consideration.

STRUCTURING RESUME CONTENT

After choosing an appropriate resume format, you should generate the necessary information for structuring each category of your resume. You developed much of this information when you identified your motivated abilities and skills and specified your objective in Chapters 5 through 8. Include the following information on separate sheets of paper:

CONTACT INFO: name, address, and telephone number.

WORK   refer to your data in Chapter 8 on
OBJECTIVE: writing an objective.

EDUCATION: degrees, schools, dates, highlights,
                    special training.

WORK   paid, unpaid, civilian, military, and part-time
EXPERIENCE: employment. Include job titles, employers,
                    locations, dates, skills, accomplishments,
                    duties, and responsibilities. Use the func-
                    tional language in Chapters 5 and 6.

OTHER   volunteer, civic, and professional member-
EXPERIENCE: ships. Include your contributions, demonstrat-
                    ed skills, offices held, names, and dates.

SPECIAL SKILLS foreign languages, teaching, paramedical,
OR LICENSES/   etc. relevant to your objective
CERTIFICATES:

OTHER   references, expected salary, willingness
INFORMATION: to relocate/travel, availability dates

PRODUCING DRAFTS

Once you generate the basic data for constructing your resume, your next task is to reduce this data into draft resumes. If, for example, you write a combination resume, the internal organization of the resume should be as follows:

- Contact information
- Work objective
- Qualifications or functional experience
- Work history or employment
- Education

Be careful in including any other type of information on your re-sume. Other information most often is extraneous or negative information.

You should only include information designed to strengthen your objective.

While your first draft may run more than two pages, try to get everything into one or two pages for the final draft. Most employers lose interest after reading the first page. If you produce a two-page resume, one of the best formats is to attach a single supplemental page to a self-contained one-page resume.

Your final draft should conform to the following rules for creating an excellent resume:

RULES FOR EFFECTIVE RESUMES

Resume "Don'ts"

- **Don't** use military acronyms or slang.
- **Don't** use abbreviations except for your middle name.
- **Don't** make the resume cramped and crowded; it should be pleasing to the eyes.
- **Don't** make statements you can't document.
- **Don't** use the passive voice.
- **Don't** change tense of verbs.
- **Don't** use lengthy sentences and descriptions.
- **Don't** refer to yourself as "I."
- **Don't** include negative information.
- **Don't** include extraneous information.

Resume "Dos"

- **Do** use action verbs and the active voice.
- **Do** be direct, succinct, and expressive with your language.
- **Do** appear neat, well organized, and professional.
- **Do** use ample spacing and highlights (all caps, underlining, bulleting) for different emphases.
- **Do** maintain an eye pleasing balance. Try centering your contact information at the top, keeping information categories on the left in all caps, and describing the categories in the center and on the right.
- **Do** check carefully your spelling, grammar, and punctuation.
- **Do** clearly communicate your purpose and value to employers.
- **Do** communicate your strongest points first.

EVALUATING THE FINAL PRODUCT

You should subject your resume drafts to two types of evaluations. An *internal evaluation* consists of reviewing our lists of "dos" and "don'ts" to make sure your resume conforms to these rules. An *external evaluation* should be conducted by circulating your resume to three or more individuals whom you believe will give you frank, objective, and useful feedback. Avoid people who tend to flatter you. The best evaluator would be someone in a hiring position similar to one you will encounter in the actual interview. Ask these people to critique your draft resume and suggest improvements in both form and content. This will be your most important evaluation. After all, the only evaluation that counts is the one that helps get you an interview. Asking someone to critique your resume is one way to spread the word that you are job hunting. As we will see in Chapter 11, this is one method for getting invited to an interview!

FINAL PRODUCTION

Your final resume can be typed, word processed, or typeset. If you type it, be sure it looks professional. Use an electric typewriter with a carbon ribbon. Varying the typing elements and styles can produce an attractive copy. Do not use a portable typewriter with a nylon ribbon since it does not produce professional copy. Many typists will do your resume on the proper machine for $10 to $20.

If you use a word processor, be sure the final copy is printed on a letter quality printer using a carbon ribbon or on a laser printer. Dot matrix and near letter quality printers make resumes look both unprofessional and mass produced. Word processed resumes give you the greatest flexibility to custom design your resume for individual employers.

Alternatively, you can have a printer typeset your resume. This may cost anywhere from $20 to $50. The final product should look first-class. However, it may look *too* professional or *too* slick; some employers may think you had someone else write the resume for you.

Whichever method you use, be sure to proofread the final copy. Many people spend good money on production only to later find typing errors.

When reproducing the resume, you must consider the quality and color of paper as well as the number of copies you need. By all means use good quality paper. You should use watermarked 20-pound or heavier bond paper. Costing 3¢ to 7¢ per sheet, this paper can be purchased through stationery stores and printers. It is important not to cut corners at this point by purchasing cheap paper or using copy machine paper. You may save $5 on 100 copies, but you also will communicate an unprofessional image to employers.

Remember, your resume is your calling card—it should represent your best professional image.

Use one of the following paper colors: white, cream, light tan, light gray, or light blue. Avoid blue, yellow, green, pink, orange, red, or any other bright or pastel colors. Conservative, light, neutral colors are the best. Any of these colors can be complemented with black ink. In the case of light gray—our first choice—a navy blue ink looks best. Dark brown ink is especially attractive on light tan paper.

Your choices of paper quality and color say something about your personality and professional style. They communicate nonverbally your potential strengths and weaknesses. Employers will use these as indicators for screening you in or out of an interview. At the same time, these choices may make your resume stand out from the crowd of standard black-on-white resumes.

You have two choices in reproducing your resume: a copy machine or an offset process. Many of the newer copy machines give good reproductions on the quality paper you need—nearly the same quality as the offset process. You should be able to make such copies for 10-20¢ per page. The offset process produces the best quality because it uses a printing plate. It also is relatively inexpensive—5 to 10¢ per copy with a minimum run of 100 copies. The cost per copy decreases with large runs of 300, 500, or 1000. In the end, you should be able to have your resume typed and 100 copies reproduced on high quality colored bond paper for less than $25. If you have it typeset, the same number of copies may cost you $50.

Whatever your choices, do not try to cut costs when it comes to producing your resume. It simply is not worth it. Remember, your resume is your calling card—it should represent your best professional image. Put your best foot forward at this stage. Go in style; spend a few dollars on producing a first-class resume.

JOB SEARCH LETTERS

Resumes sent through the mail are normally accompanied by a cover letter. After interviewing for information or a position, you should send a thank-you letter. Other occasions will arise when it is both proper and necessary for you to write different types of job search letters. Examples of these letters are presented in the Krannichs' *High Impact Resumes and Letters, Dynamite Cover Letters,* and *Job Search Letters That Get Results.*

Your letter writing should follow the principles of good resume and business writing. Job hunting letters are like resumes—they advertise you for interviews. Like good advertisements, these letters should follow four basic principles for effectiveness:

1. Catch the reader's attention.
2. Persuade the reader of your benefits or value.
3. Convince the reader with evidence.
4. Move the reader to acquire the product.

BASIC PREPARATION RULES

Before you begin writing a job search letter, ask yourself several questions to clarify the content of your letter:

- What is the *purpose* of the letter?
- What are the *needs* of my audience?
- What *benefits* will my audience gain from me?
- What is a good opening sentence or paragraph for grabbing the *attention* of my audience?
- How can I maintain the *interests* of my audience?
- How can I best end the letter so that the audience will be *persuaded* to contact me?
- If a resume is enclosed, how can my letter best *advertise the resume*?
- Have I spent enough *time* revising and proofreading the letter?
- Does the letter represent my *best professional effort*?

Since your letters are a form of business communication, they should conform to the rules of good business correspondence:

PRINCIPLES OF GOOD BUSINESS
COMMUNICATION

- Plan and organize what you will say by outlining the content of your letter.
- Know your purpose and structure your letter accordingly.
- Communicate your message in a logical and sequential manner.
- State your purpose immediately in the first sentence and paragraph; main ideas always go first.
- End by stating what your reader can expect next from you.
- Use short paragraphs and sentences; avoid complex sentences.
- Punctuate properly and use correct grammar and spelling.
- Use simple and straight-forward language; avoid jargon.
- Communicate your message as directly and briefly as possible.

The rules stress how to both *organize and communicate* your message with impact. At the same time, you should always have a specific purpose in mind as well as know the needs of your audience.

Approach letters should get employers to engage in the 5R's of informational interviewing.

TYPES OF LETTERS

Cover letters provide cover for your resume. You should avoid overwhelming a one-page resume with a two-page letter or repeating the contents of the resume in the letter. A short and succinct one-page letter which highlights one or two points in your resume is sufficient. Three paragraphs will suffice. The first paragraph should state your interests and purposes for writing. The second paragraph should highlight your possible value to the employer. The third paragraph should state that you will call the individual at a particular time to schedule an interview.

However, do not expect great results from cover letters. Many professional job search firms use word processing equipment and mailing lists to flood the job market with resumes and cover letters. Other job seekers use "canned" job search letters produced by computer software programs designed to generate model letters. As a result, employers are increasingly suspicious of the authenticity of such letters.

Approach letters are written for the purpose of developing job contacts, leads, or information as well as for organizing networks and getting interviews—the subjects of Chapter 11. Your primary purposes should be to get employers to engage in the 5R's of informational interviewing:

- *Reveal* useful information and advice.
- *Refer* you to others.
- *Read* your resume.
- *Revise* your resume.
- *Remember* you for future reference.

These letters help you gain access to the hidden job market by making important networking contacts that lead to those all-important informational interviews.

Approach letters can be sent out en masse to uncover job leads, or they can target particular individuals or organizations. It is best to target these letters since they have maximum impact when personalized in reference to particular positions.

The structure of approach letters is similar to other letters. The first paragraph states your purpose. In so doing, you may want to use a personal statement for openers, such as "Mary Tillis recommended that I write to you..." or "I am familiar with your..." State your purpose, but do not suggest that you are asking for a job—only career advice or information. In your final paragraph, request a meeting and indicate you will call to schedule such a meeting at a mutually convenient time.

Thank you letters may well become your most effective job search letters. They especially communicate your thoughtfulness. These letters come in different forms and are written for various occasions. The most common thank you letter is written after receiving assistance, such as job search information or a critique of your resume. Other occasions include:

- **Immediately following an interview:** Thank the interviewer for the opportunity to interview for the position. Repeat your interest in the position.

- **Receive a job offer:** Thank the employer for his or her faith in you and express your appreciation.

- **Rejected for a job:** Thank the employer for giving you the "opportunity" to interview for the job. Ask to be remembered for future reference.

- **Terminate employment:** Thank the employer for the experience and ask to be remembered for future reference.

- **Begin a new job:** Thank the employer for giving you this new opportunity and express your confidence in producing the value he or she is expecting from you.

Examples of these letters are included at the end of this chapter.

Several of these thank you letters are unusual, but they all have the same goal in mind—to be remembered by potential employers in a positive light. In a job search, being remembered by employers is the closest thing to being invited to an interview and offered a job. A thank you letter is a powerful way to get remembered in a job search.

DISTRIBUTION AND MANAGEMENT

The only good resumes are the ones that get read, remembered, referred, and result in a job interview. Therefore, after completing a first-rate resume, you must decide what to do with it. Are you planning to only respond to classified ads with a standard mailing piece consisting of your resume and a formal cover letter? What other creative distribution methods might you use, such as sending it to friends, relatives, and former employers? Do you want to submit it to an electronic resume database such as DORS, Job Bank USA, Connexion, kiNexus, or the Career Placement Registry? Do you plan to contact executive search firms, attend job fairs, and go to professional conferences with your resume? What is the best way to proceed?

RESPONDING TO CLASSIFIED ADS

Most of your writing activities should focus on the hidden job market. At the same time, you should respond to job listings in newspapers, magazines, and personnel offices. While this is largely a numbers game, you can increase your odds by the way you respond to the listings.

You should be selective in your responses. Since you know what you want to do, you will be looking for only certain types of positions. Once you identify them, your response entails little expenditure of time and effort—an envelope, letter, stamp, resume, and maybe 20 minutes of your time. You have little to lose. While you have the potential to gain by sending a letter and resume in response to an ad, remember the odds are usually against you.

It is difficult to interpret job listings. Some employers place blind ads with P.O. Box numbers in order to collect resumes for future reference. Others wish to avoid aggressive applicants who telephone or "drop-in" for interviews. Many employers work through professional recruiters who place these ads. While you may try to second guess the rationale behind such ads, respond to them as you would to ads with an employer's name, address, or telephone number. Assume there is a real job behind the ad.

Most ads request a copy of your resume. You should respond with a cover letter and resume as soon as you see the ad. Depending on how much information about the position is revealed in the ad, your letter should be tailored to emphasize your qualifications vis-a-vis the ad. Examine the ad carefully. Underline any words or phrases which relate to your qualifications. In your cover letter, you should use similar terminology in emphasizing your qualifications. Keep the letter brief and to the point.

If the ad asks you to state your salary history or salary requirements, state "negotiable" or "open." Alternatively, you can include a figure by stating a salary range 30 to 40 percent above your present military base pay. For example, if your base pay is $30,000 a year, figure your military benefits to be another 25 to 30 percent or $7,500 to $9,000; therefore, your total Army compensation, or salary history, at present is closer to $40,000 a year. When you state a salary range, figure 30 to 40 percent above your base pay or 10 to 20 percent above your total compensation. Based on your total compensation figure, your salary range should be $45,000 to $50,000. If your base pay is $50,000, figure another $13,000 for benefits to arrive at a total compensation figure of $63,000. Your salary requirements should be in the $70,000 to $75,000 range.

Use your own judgment in addressing the salary question. There is no hard and fast rule on stating a figure or range. A figure helps the employer screen-out individuals with too high a salary expectation. However, most people prefer to keep salary considerations to the end of the interview—after you have demonstrated your value and have more information about the position. We'll return to this question again in Chapter 13 when we address the salary and compensation question for military personnel.

You may be able to increase your odds by sending a second copy of your letter and resume two or three weeks after your initial response.

Most applicants normally reply to an ad during the seven day period immediately after it appears in print. Since employers often are swamped with responses, your letter and resume may get lost in the crowd. If you send a second copy of your application two or three weeks later, the employer will have more time to give you special attention. By then, he or she also will have a better basis on which to compare you to the others.

Keep in mind that your cover letter and resume may be screened among 400 other resumes and letters. Thus, you want your cover letter to be eye catching and easy to read. Keep it brief and concise and highlight your qualifications as stated in the employer's ad. Don't spend a great deal of time responding to an ad or waiting anxiously at your mailbox or telephone for a reply. Keep moving on to other job search activities. Your goal should be to contact as many employers as possible because uncovering fruitful job leads is a numbers game.

Keep your letter brief and concise and highlight your qualifications as stated in the employer's ad.

SELF-INITIATED METHODS

Your letters and resumes can be distributed and managed in various ways. Many people shotgun hundreds of cover letters and resumes to prospective employers. This is a form of gambling where the odds are against you. For every 100 people you contact in this manner, expect one or two who might be interested in you. After all, successful direct-mail experts at best expect only a 2 percent return on their mass mailings!

If you choose to use the shotgun methods, you can increase your odds by using the *telephone*. Call the prospective employer within a week after he or she receives your letter. This technique will probably increase your effectiveness rate from 1 to 5 percent.

However, many people are shotgunning their resumes today. As more resumes and letters descend on employers with the increased use of word processing equipment, the effectiveness rates may be even lower. This also can be an expensive marketing method.

Your best distribution strategy will be your own modification of the following procedure:

1. Selectively identify whom you would be interested in working for.

2. Send an approach letter.

3. Follow up with a telephone call seeking an appointment for an interview.

In more than 50 percent of the cases, you will get an interview. It is best not to include a copy of your resume with the approach letter. Keep your resume for the end of the interview. Chapter 11 outlines the procedures for conducting this informational interview.

ELECTRONIC RESUME DATABASES

One of the newest approaches to resume distribution involves participation in an electronic resume database. Individuals pay an annual membership fee for getting their resume into an electronic database; employers pay either an annual fee and/or a per-search fee to use the database for accessing resumes in response to their hiring needs. Using sophisticated search and retrieval software to "match" individuals' resumes to employers' vacancy requirements, these electronic database firms are quickly becoming part of today's much touted "information highway" for job seekers. They offer an important avenue for marketing your resume on a nationwide basis to hundreds of potential employers.

Numerous organizations offer these electronic database services. Within the military, the DORS program (Defense Outplacement Referral System) operates an electronic resume database for service personnel. For Army personnel, the DORS program is integrated into the ACAP program. DORS is designed for active duty personnel, their spouses, and those separated up to six months who can use this service free of charge. For information on both the ACAP and DORS programs, contact your nearest ACAP office which is listed in Chapter 4. You also can call the DORS program directly by dialing 1-800-727-3677. They will send you information on how to participate in their electronic database.

Several private firms also operate electronic databases for job seekers. These firms charge annual membership fees. The largest and best known firms are Job Bank USA, kiNexus, Connexion, Career Placement

Registry, and Internet. For more information on these resume distribution services, see Chapter 17—"Computer Pathways to Career Fitness."

For more information on the use of electronic resume databases, we recommend two new books:

Joyce Lain Kennedy and Thomas J. Morrow, *Resume Revolution* (New York: Wiley, 1994)

Peter D. Weddle, *Electronic Resumes for the New Job Market: Resumes That Work for You 24 Hours a Day* (Manassas Park, VA: Impact Publications, 1994)

Both books go into great detail on how to write a resume appropriate for electronic databases as well as identify various firms that offer electronic resume distribution services.

RECORDKEEPING

Once you begin distributing letters and resumes, you also will need to keep good records for managing your job search writing campaign. Purchase file folders for your correspondence and notes. Be sure to make copies of all letters you write since you may need to refer to them over the telephone or before interviews. Record your activities with each employer—letters, resumes, telephone calls, interviews—on a 4x6 card and file it according to the name of the organization or individual. These files will help you quickly access information and evaluate your job search progress.

Always remember the purpose of resumes and letters—*advertise you for interviews.* They do not get jobs. Since most employers know nothing about you, *you must effectively communicate your value in writing prior to the critical interview.* While you should not overestimate the importance of this written communication, neither should you underestimate it.

RESUME AND LETTER EXAMPLES

The following set of resume and letter examples incorporates many of the writing principles outlined in this chapter as well as relates to the job search strategies specified in other chapters. The six resume examples on pages 164-177 were chosen as a representative sample of resumes by transitioning Army members. We have organized these resumes by the following rank categories:

- **Field Grade Officer:** John C. Dillon on pages 164-165

- **Company Grade Officer:** Terry Harper on pages 166-167 and Lynn Jones on pages 168-169

- **Senior NCO:** Chris Thomas on pages 170-171

- **Junior NCO:** Joseph A. Martinez on pages 172-173

- **Junior Enlisted:** Jennifer R. Joel on pages 174-177

We've included two resume examples for each individual. Each example represents one of two major resume formats—chronological and combination—the formats most relevant to experienced Army personnel. You will find on pages 162 and 163 outlines for structuring the major elements in these two resume formats. We have not included examples of the functional format because we believe such resumes do not best represent the experience, skills, and goals of our audience.

Please note that our chronological examples stress *positions and skills* rather than names and dates. We have purposefully de-emphasized work dates by placing them *after* positions, employers, and locations. Following our previous discussion on placement of resume elements, we always put the most important and eye-catching information first.

Our letter examples represent the most common situations for writing different types of job search letters. The Resume Letter example on page 178 substitutes for a formal resume; on certain occasions you may find this resume/letter combination serves you best. If you want to be most effective in your job search, you should write several other letters as represented on pages 179-185. These letters follow the job search principles and strategies outlined in this and subsequent chapters, especially Chapters 11, 12, and 13 on networking, job interviews, and negotiations.

Our examples are not meant to represent Army personnel as a whole. Rather, they are presented as instructional devic2es to assist you in creating your own effective resumes and letters based on a solid understanding of the job search principles outlined in this book. We believe the most important element on the resume is the objective statement. That simple two or three line statement represents a great deal of self-assessment work that should result in a clear vision of what each individual wants to do with the next stage of his or her life. Providing a central focus, the objective is closely related to all other elements on the resume.

CHRONOLOGICAL (IMPROVED) RESUME FORMAT

JOHN E. SOLDIER
2821 Patriot Drive
Killeen, TX 90641
H: (501) 960-0186 / W: (501) 805-4831

OBJECTIVE

- Give a clear and concise statement of desired position.

QUALIFICATION SUMMARY (*Optional*)

- Short, concise list of your major qualifications. Bullet key points.

EXPERIENCE

- List each assignment, starting with your most recent one. Include organization name, job title, location, and assignment dates.

- For each assignment, *highlight your accomplishments* using the language outlines in Chapter 5. Do not state job descriptions. Prospective employers want to know *what* you can do for them.

EDUCATION

- List relevant degrees, certificates, and long training courses, starting with the most recent.

PERSONAL DATA (*include only data relevant to the position desired*)

- Security clearance (important to many defense-related firms).

- Professional associations (e.g., AUSA).

- Professional licenses (e.g., Professional Engineer).

- Publications or papers you authored.

- Foreign languages (only if fluent).

COMBINATION RESUME FORMAT

JOHN E. SOLDIER
2821 Patriot Drive
Killeen, TX 90641
H: (501) 960-0186 / W: (501) 805-4831

OBJECTIVE

- Give a clear and concise statement of desired position.

ACCOMPLISHMENTS

- Highlight three or four major functional skills you possess.

- For each skill, describe your qualifications — stress accomplishments; quantify results of your work.

EXPERIENCE OR WORK HISTORY

- List assignments in reverse chronological order (most recent first).

- State, position, organization, location, assignment dates.

EDUCATION

- List relevant degrees, certificates, and long training courses, starting with the most recent.

PERSONAL DATA (*include only data relevant to the position desired*)

- Security clearance (important to many defense-related firms).

- Professional associations (e.g., AUSA).

- Professional licenses (e.g., Professional Engineer).

- Publications or papers you authored.

- Foreign languages (only if fluent).

JOHN C. DILLON
2913 West Broad St.
Philadelphia, PA 19199
555-999-2121 (H) / 555-999-1212 (W)

OBJECTIVE: A financial services position where strong communication and leadership skills will result in increased sales.

EDUCATION: **University of Michigan, Ann Arbor, MI**
M.S. in Business Administration, 1987

United States Military Academy, West Point, NY
B.S. in General Engineering, 1979

EXPERIENCE: **Assistant Athletic Director, Administration**, U.S. Military Academy, West Point, NY (6/88-6/92). Personnel Staff Officer in Intercollegiate Athletic Department. Assisted in developing a $12 million annual budget for a department of 180 employees. Introduced new cost-cutting measures that resulted in savings of $500,000 during FY 1991.

Division Aviation Staff Officer (11/85-5/88). Coordinated aviation training for the Third Armored Division, Frankfurt, Germany (17,000 soldiers, 360 armored vehicles, and 120 helicopters). Implemented a new unit training system for the division. System rated the best and most innovative in Germany; adopted by all units in Germany.

Aviation Company Commander, Fort Rucker, AL (5/83-10/85). Led an Attack Helicopter Company (11 helicopters and 33 crewmen); raised training rating from worst to best of six companies on two evaluations; received a Zero Aircraft Accident Safety Award; and raised aircraft readiness rate to 85%, which was 15% above standard.

Infantry and Aviation Officer (2/79-4/83). Held various leadership and staff positions that included Platoon Leader, Personnel Staff Officer, and Executive Officer. Commended as Personnel Staff Officer during Annual Inspection on all six areas inspected. Commended as an Executive Officer on annual training evaluation for management of vehicle maintenance.

MILITARY TRAINING: Participated in a variety of training programs: Command and General Staff College, Aviation Officers' Advanced Course, Personnel Management Staff Officers' Course, Army Flight School, Ranger School, Airborne School, and Infantry Officers' Basic Course.

FIELD GRADE OFFICER—Combination Format

JOHN C. DILLON
2913 West Broad St.
Philadelphia, PA 19199
555-999-2121 (H) / 555-999-1212 (W)

OBJECTIVE: A financial services position where strong communication and leadership skills will result in increased sales.

ACCOMPLISHMENTS:

Financial Management   Assisted in developing a $12 million annual budget for a department of 180 employees. Introduced new cost-cutting measures that resulted in saving $500,000 in a single year.

Leadership   Held various leadership and staff positions (Platoon Leader, Company Commander, Executive Officer, Personnel Staff Officer) while serving in the U.S. Army. Received three commendations for quality of performance.

Communication   Coordinated aviation training for the Third Armored Division, Frankfurt, Germany (17,000 soldiers, 360 armored vehicles, and 120 helicopters). Implemented a new unit training system for the division. System rated the best and most innovative in Germany.

Training   Raised training ratings from the worst to the best for six helicopter attack companies on two evaluations. Received a Zero Aircraft Accident Safety Award, and raised aircraft readiness rate to 85% which was 15% above the standard.

WORK HISTORY: **Assistant Athletic Director, Administration**, U.S. Military Academy, 1988-1992.

Division Aviation Staff Officer, Third Armored Division, Germany, 1985-1987.

Aviation Company Commander, 111th Helicopter Company, Fort Rucker, AL, 1983-1984

Infantry and Aviation Officer, Fort Benning, GA, 1979-1982.

EDUCATION: **University of Michigan, Ann Arbor, MI**
M.S. in Business Administration, 1987

United States Military Academy, West Point, NY
B.S. in General Engineering, 1979

MILITARY TRAINING: Participated in a variety of training programs: Command and General Staff College, Aviation Officers' Advanced Course, Personnel Management Staff Officers' Course, Army Flight School, Ranger School, Airborne School, and Infantry Officers' Basic Course.

TERRY HARPER
139 Georgia Avenue
Denver, CO 80808
499-217-3219 (H) or 499-217-9123 (W)

OBJECTIVE: An industrial engineering position with a broad-based manufacturing firm.

EXPERIENCE: **Operations Research and Systems Analyst**. U.S. Total Army Personnel Command, Alexandria, VA (1990 to present). Direct a four person analytical team developing, evaluating, and recommending personnel reduction policies mandated by Congress.
- Developed mainframe-based computer forecasting models to predict an individual's risk for selection by a separation board.
- Created a marketing plan encouraging those at risk to leave resulting in 700 fewer force outs.
- Designed computer programs that resulted in removing 2,000 erroneous records.
- Created and implemented a system acceptance testing plan for a $3 million out-sourced optimization model. Resulted in four critical design enhancements and an 8.2% reporting accuracy increase.

Consultant. Massachusetts Department of Public Works, Wellesley, MA (1988-1989). Developed a PC-based pavement management decision support system.
- Saved $200,000 in first six months through quantitative decision analysis.
- Conducted user needs analysis, established test methodology, collected and analyzed data, authored detailed report, and presented results to senior management.

Personnel Officer. US Army, 3rd Support Command, Giessen, Germany (1986-1987). Managing human resource matters for a 750 employee organization including compensation and benefits, education, legal support, performance appraisals, reassignments, and personnel strength.
- Automated typewriter-based office environment reducing administrative processing time by 35%
- Received Army Commendation Medal for improvements.

General Manager. US Army, 32d Army Air Defense Command, Sweinfurt, Germany (1984-1986). Supervised 180 employees with 34 different specialty skills performing maintenance and supply operations. Managed a 24-hour repair and warehouse facility servicing 13 retail customers' vehicles, missiles, and communications equipment valued at $2.1 million.
- Reduced annual operating expenses from $1.5 million to $1.3 million in first year of operation while increasing customer maintenance support levels 7.2%.
- Decreased maintenance backlog by 92.4% in three months through production control policy changes.
- Relocated $20.3 million supply stockage increasing on-hand inventory accountability by 7.8%

EDUCATION: **University of Massachusetts**, Amherst, MA.
M.S. in Industrial Engineering and Operations Research, 1991.

Louisiana State University, Baton Rouge, LA.
B.S. in Industrial Engineering, 1994, Deans List.

TERRY HARPER
139 Georgia Avenue
Denver, CO 80808
499-217-3219 (H) or 499-217-9123 (W)

OBJECTIVE: An industrial engineering position with a broad-based manufacturing firm.

EXPERIENCE:

Systems Analysis
- Developed mainframe-based computer forecasting models to predict an individual's risk for selection by a separation board.
- Designed computer programs that resulted in removing 2,000 erroneous records.
- Created and implemented a system acceptance testing plan for a $3 million out-sourced optimization model resulting in four critical design enhancements and an 8.2% reporting accuracy increase.

Data Automation
- Developed a PC-based pavement management decision support system; saved $200,000 in first six months through quantitative decision analysis.
- Automated typewriter-based office environment reducing administrative processing time by 35%

Personnel Management
- Managing human resource matters for a 750 employee organization including compensation and benefits, education, legal support, performance appraisals, reassignments, and personnel strength.

Management
- Supervised 180 employees with 34 different specialty skills performing maintenance and supply operations.
- Managed a 24-hour repair and warehouse facility servicing 13 retail customers' vehicles, missile, and communications equipment valued at $2.1 million.

WORK HISTORY:
- **Operations Research and Systems Analyst**, US Total Army Personnel Command, Alexandria, VA, 1990-present.

- **Consultant**, Massachusetts Department of Public Works, Wellesley, 1988-1989.

- **Personnel Officer**, US Army, 3rd Support Command, Giessen, Germany, 1987-1987.

- **General Manager**, US Army, 32d Army Air Defense Commands, Sweinfurt, Germany, 1984-1986.

EDUCATION: **University of Massachusetts**, Amherst, MA.
M.S. in Industrial Engineering and Operations Research, 1991.

Louisiana State University, Baton Rouge, LA.
B.S. in Industrial Engineering, 1994, Deans List.

LYNN JONES

1229 East York Ave.
New Livery, CT 09558
(Home) 913-558-9877; (Work) 913-487-8993

OBJECTIVE

A product management position in a fast growing cellular communication company where organization, leadership, and communication experience will be used for improving product quality and innovation.

WORK EXPERIENCE

Communication Staff Officer, 12th Signal Brigade, Fort Lewis, WA, 1991-1992. Designed and coordinated communications for Pacific Command Joint Training Exercises. Organized and chaired engineering conferences. Presented decision briefings and prepared staff action papers for a variety of communication-related issues of considerable importance to the command. Served as Watch Officer during operations and exercises.

Communications Company Commander, C Company, 430th Signal Battalion, Mainz, West Germany, 1989-1990. Installed, operated, and maintained satellite, switching, cable, and message communications in support of numerous U.S. Army units distributed throughout central Germany. Led 110 soldiers in performing all assigned communications missions. Total responsibility for the training, morale, welfare and discipline of all the soldiers under my command.

Platoon Leader, B Company, 17th Signal Battalion, Hoechst, West Germany, 1986-1988. Planned and supervised installation of telecommunication systems of V Corps exercises. Maintained and accounted for vehicle and communications equipment valued at approximately $1.5 million. Planned and conducted individual and collective training in technical skills and general military subjects. Supervised, trained, and led 23 personnel.

EDUCATION AND TRAINING

- U.S. Army Directory of Information Management Course, Fort Gordon, GA, 1991

- U.S. Army Signal Officer Advanced Course, Fort Gordon, GA, 1990

- U.S. Army Airborne School, Fort Benning, GA, 1985

- U.S. Army Signal Officer Basic Course, Fort Gordon, GA, 1985

- B.A., Psychology, Brigham Young University, Salt Lake City, UT, 1981-1985

LYNN JONES
1229 East York Ave.
New Livery, CT 09558
(Home) 913-558-9877; (Work) 913-487-8993

OBJECTIVE: A product management position in a fast growing cellular communication company where organization, leadership, and communication experience will be used for improving product quality and innovation.

EXPERIENCE:

Organization Designed and coordinated communications for Pacific Command Joint Training Exercises. Organized and chaired engineering conferences. Presented decision briefings and prepared staff action papers for a variety of communication-related issues of considerable importance to the command. Served as Watch Officer during operations and exercises.

Leadership Installed, operated, and maintained satellite, switching, cable, and message communications in support of numerous U.S. Army units distributed throughout central Germany. Led 110 soldiers in performing all assigned communications missions. Total responsibility for the training, morale, welfare and discipline of all the soldiers under my command.

Communication Planned and supervised installation of telecommunication systems of V Corps exercises. Maintained and accounted for vehicle and communications equipment valued at approximately $1.5 million. Planned and conducted individual and collective training in technical skills and general military subjects. Supervised, trained, and led 23 personnel.

WORK HISTORY: Communication Staff Officer, 12th Signal Brigade, Fort Lewis, Washington, 1991-1992.

Communications Company Commander, C Company, 430th Signal Battalion, Mainz, West Germany, 1989-1990.

Platoon Leader, B Company, 17th Signal Battalion, Hoechst, West Germany, 1986-1988.

EDUCATION & TRAINING:
- U.S. Army Directory of Information Management Course, Fort Gordon, GA, 1991
- U.S. Army Signal Officer Advanced Course, Fort Gordon, GA, 1990
- U.S. Army Airborne School, Fort Benning, GA, 1985
- U.S. Army Signal Officer Basic Course, Fort Gordon, GA, 1985
- B.A., Psychology, Brigham Young University, Salt Lake City, UT, 1981-1985

CHRIS THOMAS
2480 Davis Circle
Washington, DC 29036
(299) 521-4832

OBJECTIVE

An organizational development position with a security company requiring leadership and management expertise.

SUMMARY OF EXPERIENCE

Fourteen years of leadership and training experience. Responsible for organizing, motivating, and directing soldiers in accomplishing assigned missions.

WORK HISTORY

Platoon Sergeant, 24th Division, Fort Stewart, GA (1991-present).
Responsible for the well-being, discipline, morale, and readiness of a 30-member unit. Set and enforced high standards in the areas of personal appearance, physical fitness, and weapons qualifications. Demonstrated essential leadership, supervision, management, and team building skills for accomplishing the platoon's mission.

Training NCO, 5th Infantry Division, Fort Polk, LA (1987-1990).
Assisted in developing weekly training plans for the company. Helped establish and conduct training programs in the areas of nuclear biological and chemical protection, physical fitness, land navigation, weapons qualifications, and equipment maintenance.

Infantry Squad Leader, 3rd US Infantry, Fort Myer, VA (1983-1985).
Organized and led a 10-member team through numerous missions. Planned team work schedules and training for accomplishing mission objectives. Set and enforced high standards of performance.

Team Leader, 197th Infantry Brigade, Fort Benning, GA (1981-1982).
First line supervisor responsible for the productivity of a four-man team. Organized training, planned daily activities, and supervised team members.

EDUCATION AND TRAINING

- Infantry Advanced Noncommissioned Officers Course, 1986
- Infantry Basic Noncommissioned Officers Course, 1984
- Leadership Development Course, Noncommissioned Officers Academy, 1982
- Infantry Basic Training, 1980

CHRIS THOMAS
2480 Davis Circle
Washington, DC 29036
(299) 521-4832

OBJECTIVE   An organizational development position with a security company requiring leadership and management expertise.

SUMMARY   Fourteen years of increasingly responsible leadership and training experience. Responsible for organizing, motivating, and directing soldiers in accomplishing assigned missions.

EXPERIENCE   **Leadership**. Responsible for the well-being, discipline, morale, and readiness of a 30-member unit. Set and enforced high standards in the areas of personal appearance, physical fitness, and weapons qualifications. Demonstrated essential leadership, supervision, management, and team building skills for accomplishing the platoon's mission.

Training. Assisted in developing weekly training plans for the company. Helped establish and conduct training programs in the areas of nuclear biological and chemical protection, physical fitness, land navigation, weapons qualifications, and equipment maintenance.

Management. Organized and led a 10-member team through numerous missions. Planned team work schedules and training for accomplishing mission objectives. Set and enforced high standards of performance.

Supervision. First line supervisor responsible for the productivity of a four-man team. Organized training, planned daily activities, and supervised team members.

WORK
HISTORY   **Platoon Sergeant**, 24th Division, Fort Stewart, GA (1991-present).

Training NCO, 5th Infantry Division, Fort Polk, LA (1987-1990).

Infantry Squad Leader, 3rd US Infantry, Fort Myer, VA (1983-1985).

Team Leader, 197th Infantry Brigade, Fort Benning, GA (1981-1982).

EDUCATION
- Infantry Advanced Noncommissioned Officers Course, 1986
- Infantry Basic Noncommissioned Officers Course, 1984
- Leadership Development Course, Noncommissioned Officers Academy, 1982
- Infantry Basic Training, 1980

JOSEPH A. MARTINEZ
95 Colgate Drive, Apt. 131
Eureka, TX 45886
(Home) 399-887-1256
(Work) 399-990-5667

OBJECTIVE: Become a police officer in a diversified, bilingual community where leadership and communication skills will be used for improving community relations.

WORK
EXPERIENCE: **Training NCO, 75th Infantry Battalion, 82nd Airborne Division, Fort Bragg, NC, 1990-1992.** Provided the Battalion's soldiers with training in Infantry tactics, land navigation, physical fitness, marksmanship, weaponry, leadership, and drill and ceremonies. Raised overall proficiency level from 75% to 90%.

Squad Leader, 82nd Airborne Division, Fort Bragg, NC, 1989. Served as an Infantry squad leader responsible for the discipline, morale, and training of ten soldiers. Counseled and motivated soldiers in all aspects of military training.

Infantry Scout, 82nd Airborne Division, Fort Bragg, NC, 1987-1988. Developed proficiency in light weapon systems. Became the recognized expert in land navigation. Received award for Best Soldier of the Quarter.

EDUCATION:
- Air Assault School, 1991

- Primary Leadership Development Course, Fort Benning, GA, 1990

- Airborne School, 1987

- Basic Infantry Course, 1987

- High School Diploma, Freedom High, Tallahassee, FL, 1986

PERSONAL: Secret security clearance

JOSEPH A. MARTINEZ
95 Colgate Drive, Apt. 131
Eureka, TX 45886
(Home) 399-887-1256
(Work) 399-990-5667

OBJECTIVE

Become a police officer in a diversified, bilingual community where leadership and communication skills will be used for improving community relations.

EXPERIENCE

Training: Provided the Battalion's soldiers with training in Infantry tactics, land navigation, physical fitness, marksmanship, weaponry, leadership, and drill and ceremonies. Raised overall proficiency level from 75% to 90%.

Leadership: Served as an Infantry squad leader responsible for the discipline, morale, and training of ten soldiers. Counseled and motivated soldiers in all aspects of military training.

Weapons Proficiency: Developed proficiency in light weapon systems. Became the recognized expert in land navigation. Received award for Best Soldier of the Quarter.

WORK HISTORY

Training NCO, 75th Infantry Battalion, 82nd Airborne Division, Fort Bragg, NC, 1990-1992.

Squad Leader, 82nd Airborne Division, Fort Bragg, NC, 1989.

Infantry Scout, 82nd Airborne Division, Fort Bragg, NC, 1987-1988.

EDUCATION

- Air Assault School, 1991
- Primary Leadership Development Course, Fort Benning, GA, 1990
- Airborne School, 1987
- Basic Infantry Course, 1987
- High School Diploma, Freedom High, Tallahassee, FL, 1986

PERSONAL

Secret security clearance

JENNIFER R. JOEL
112 Oleander Road
Mystic, UT 85220

Home: (801) 795-1467   Work: (801) 775-1988

OBJECTIVE

A technical position with a dynamite telecommunication firm specializing in the design, development, and fielding of local area networks.

HIGHLIGHTS OF QUALIFICATIONS

- Five years experience with microcomputers, desktop applications, and local area networks (LANs).
- Installed cable and connected associated LAN/WAN hardware.
- Skilled in recognizing and troubleshooting problems with network and computer systems.
- Committed to patient, observant, and personable interaction with users and their problems.

RELEVANT EXPERIENCE

Network Administrator, Fort Stewart, GA, 1992-present

- Loaded software for 100 terminals.
- Skilled in troubleshooting Ethernet networks.
- Added, deleted, and updated users and mail groups for a 100 terminal, 200 user 3Com Network.
- Analyzed networks using Network General's Sniffer protocol analyzer.
- Tested new software for LAN compatibility.
- Coordinated System Trouble Reports.

Instructor, Fort Lee, VA, 1991

- Trained users to be self-sufficient on a 100 terminal, 200 user LAN:
  — Introduced the Macintosh operating system;
  — Introduced the 3+Share network operating system;
  — Taught the 3+Mail E-mail program;
  — Taught the application, Microsoft Works.
- Taught advanced word processing and desktop publishing using Microsoft Word, version 4.0 for the Macintosh.
- Received an Army Achievement medal for exceptional computer training while stationed in Fort Lewis, WA.

Computer Operator, Fort Lee, VA, 1990

- Developed and maintained a large tape and disk library.
- Made RS-232 connectors for twisted pair cables and installed cabling.
- Installed Etherlink cards.
- Installed math co-processors in 40 PCs.
- Prepared color graphics and color slide presentations.
- Designed and edited the unit newsletter.

ADDITIONAL EXPERIENCE

- Knowledge and experience with Unix and DEC VAX VMS operating systems.
- Knowledge and experience with MS-DOS and Macintosh operating systems.
- Knowledge and experience with the following IBM PC applications: MS Works, MS Word, MacDraw II, MacDraw Pro, MacPaint, SuperPaint, MS Excel, and Aldus Pagemaker.

WORK HISTORY

Served in the U.S. Army from 1990 to the present. Held positions of increasing responsibility in the areas of local area networks and microcomputer-based systems. Trained military personnel in a variety of desktop software applications. Assigned to bases in Panama and at Ft. Sill, Oklahoma and Fort Lewis, Washington.

EDUCATION AND TRAINING

Education
- Completing a B.S. in Computer Information Systems, University of Washington, Seattle, WA.

Training
- 3Com 3+Network Installation and Administration.
- 3Com Network Architectures, Standards, and Protocols.
- Network General's Introduction to LAN Technology and Analysis.
- Network General's Ethernet Network Analysis and Troubleshooting.
- U.S. Army Ultrix/Unix Systems Operations.

JENNIFER R. JOEL
112 Oleander Road
Mystic, UT 85220

Home: (801) 795-1467   Work: (801) 775-1988

OBJECTIVE

A technical position with a dynamite telecommunication firm specializing in the design, development, and fielding of local area networks.

HIGHLIGHTS OF QUALIFICATIONS

- Five years experience with microcomputers, desktop applications, and local area networks (LANs).
- Installed cable and connected associated LAN/WAN hardware.
- Skilled in recognizing and troubleshooting problems with network and computer systems.
- Committed to patient, observant, and personable interaction with users and their problems.

RELEVANT EXPERIENCE

Network Administrator

- Loaded software for 100 terminals.
- Skilled in troubleshooting Ethernet networks.
- Added, deleted, and updated users and mail groups for a 100 terminal, 200 user 3Com Network.
- Analyzed networks using Network General's Sniffer protocol analyzer.
- Tested new software for LAN compatibility.
- Coordinated System Trouble Reports.

Software Instructor

- Trained users to be self-sufficient on a 100 terminal, 200 user LAN:
  — Introduced the Macintosh operating system;
  — Introduced the 3+Share network operating system;
  — Taught the 3+Mail E-mail program;
  — Taught the application, Microsoft Works.
- Taught advanced word processing and desktop publishing using Microsoft Word, version 4.0 for the Macintosh.
- Received an Army Achievement medal for exceptional computer training while stationed in Fort Lewis, WA.

Computer Operator

- Developed and maintained a large tape and disk library.
- Made RS-232 connectors for twisted pair cables and installed cabling.
- Installed Etherlink cards.
- Installed math co-processors in 40 PCs.
- Prepared color graphics and color slide presentations.
- Designed and edited the unit newsletter.

ADDITIONAL TECHNICAL EXPERIENCE

- Knowledge and experience with Unix and DEC VAX VMS operating systems.
- Knowledge and experience with MS-DOS and Macintosh operating systems.
- Knowledge and experience with the following IBM PC applications: MS Works, MS Word, MacDraw II, MacDraw Pro, MacPaint, SuperPaint, MS Excel, and Aldus Pagemaker.

WORK HISTORY

Served in the U.S. Army from 1990 to the present. Held positions of increasing responsibility in the areas of local area networks and microcomputer-based systems. Trained military personnel in a variety of desktop software applications. Assigned to bases in Panama and at Ft. Sill, Oklahoma and Fort Lewis, Washington. Acquired experience in the following positions:

- **Network Administrator**, Fort Stewart, GA, 1992-present
- **Instructor, Fort Lee, VA**, 1991
- **Computer Operator**, Fort Lee, VA, 1990

EDUCATION AND TRAINING

Education
- Completing a B.S. in Computer Information Systems, University of Washington, Seattle, WA.

Training
- 3Com 3+Network Installation and Administration.
- 3Com Network Architectures, Standards, and Protocols.
- Network General's Introduction to LAN Technology and Analysis.
- Network General's Ethernet Network Analysis and Troubleshooting.
- U.S. Army Ultrix/Unix Systems Operations.

RESUME LETTER

4921 Tyler Drive
Washington, DC 20011
March 15, 19____

Doris Stevens
STR Corporation
179 South Trail
Rockville, Maryland 21101

Dear Ms. Stevens:

STR Corporation is one of the most dynamic computer companies in the nation. In addition to being a leader in the field of small business computers, STR has a progressive employee training and development program which could very well become a model for other organizations. This is the type of organization I am interested in joining.

I am seeking a training position with a computer firm which would utilize my administrative, communication, and planning abilities to develop effective training and counseling programs. My experience includes:

Administration: Supervised the activity of four team leaders. Coordinated the administrative and resource management functions for the organization.

Communication: Provided daily computer-based training to 20 individuals. Ensured training was effective by testing selected individuals on a periodic basis.

Planning: Planned and developed PC-based training courses for the organization. Organized and directed a staff of four instructors. Established course loads and dates of instruction.

In addition, I am completing my Bachelor's Degree in industrial psychology with emphasis on developing training and counseling programs for technical personnel.

Could we meet to discuss your program as well as how my experience might relate to your needs? I will call your office on Tuesday morning, March 23, to arrange a convenient time to meet with you.

Sincerely yours,

James T. Inger

COVER LETTER

2842 South Plaza
Chicago, Illinois 60228
March 12, 19__

David C. Johnson
Director of Personnel
Bank of Chicago
490 Michigan Avenue
Chicago, Illinois 60222

Dear Mr. Johnson:

The accompanying resume is in response to your listing in the Chicago Tribune for a security officer.

I am especially interested in this position because my experience as an Infantry Noncommissioned Officer has prepared me for understanding the need for a disciplined, secure working environment and the problems associated with unexpected events. I wish to use this experience to protect a growing and community-conscious bank such as yours.

I would appreciate an opportunity to meet with you to discuss how my experience will best meet your needs. My ideas on how to improve your bank's security posture may be of particular interest to you. Therefore, I will call your office on the morning of March 17 to inquire if a meeting can be scheduled at a convenient time.

I look forward to meeting you.

Sincerely yours,

Joyce Peterson

APPROACH LETTER
Referral

> 821 Stevens Points
> Boston, MA 01990
> April 14, 19__

Terri Fulton
Director of Personnel
TRS Corporation
6311 W. Dover
Boston, MA 01991

Dear Ms. Fulton:

Alice O'Brien suggested that I contact you about my interest in personnel management. She said you are one of the best people to talk to in regard to careers in personnel.

I am leaving the U.S. Army after seven years of experience in personnel administration. Because of my positive Army experience, I would like to continue working in a large organization. However, before I venture further into the civilian job market, I would like to benefit from the experience and knowledge of others in the field who might advise me on opportunities for someone with my qualifications.

Perhaps we could meet briefly sometime during the next two weeks to discuss my career plans. I have several questions which I believe you could help clarify. I will call your office on Tuesday, April 22, to schedule a meeting time.

I look forward to discussing my plans with you.

> Sincerely yours,

> Kristine Kellerman

APPROACH LETTER
Cold Turkey

2189 West Church Street
New York, NY 10011
May 3, 19__

Patricia Dotson, Director
Northeast Association for
 the Disabled
9930 Jefferson Street
New York, NY 10013

Dear Ms. Dotson:

I have been impressed with your work with the disabled. Your organization takes a community perspective in trying to integrate the concerns of the disabled with those of other community groups. Perhaps other organizations will soon follow your lead.

While serving in the U.S. Army, I had the distinct privilege of volunteering to work with Army soldiers who had become disabled as a result of service in our nation's armed conflicts. Based on my experience and knowledge in assisting such individuals on a part-time basis, I have decided that I would like to pursue this vocation full-time.

However, before I pursue my interest further, I need to talk to people with civilian experience in working with disabled individuals. In particular, I would like to know how my background might fit in this field.

I am hoping you can assist me in this matter. I would like to meet with you briefly at your convenience. I will call next week to see if your schedule permits such a meeting.

I look forward to meeting you.

Sincerely,

Carol Timmons

THANK YOU LETTER
Post-Informational Interview

9910 Thompson Drive
Cleveland, Ohio 43382
June 21, 19___

Jane Evans, Director
Evans Finance Corporation
2122 Forman Street
Cleveland, Ohio 43380

Dear Ms. Evans:

Your advice was most helpful in clarifying my questions on careers in finance. I am now reworking my resume and have included many of your thoughtful suggestions. I will send you a copy next week.

Thanks so much for taking time from your busy schedule to see me. I will keep in contact and follow through on your suggestion to see Sarah Cook about opportunities with the Cleveland-Akron Finance Company.

Sincerely,

Daryl Haines

THANK YOU LETTER
Post-Job Interview

2962 Forrest Drive
Denver, Colorado 82171
May 28, 19___

Thomas F. Harris
Director, Personnel Department
Coastal Products Incorporated
7229 Lakewood Drive
Denver, Colorado 82170

Dear Mr. Harris:

Thank you again for the opportunity to interview for the marketing position. I appreciated your hospitality and enjoyed meeting you and members of your staff.

The interview convinced me of how compatible my background, interest, and skills are with the goals of Coastal Products Incorporated. As I mentioned during our conversation, my experience as an Army recruiter has prepared me well for direct sales opportunities both in the U.S. and Germany. I am confident my work for you will result in increased profits within the first two years.

For more information on my success as a recruiter, please call Lieutenant Colonel Dave Garrett at 202/726-0132. I talked to Dave this morning and mentioned your interest in his program.

I look forward to meeting you again.

Sincerely,

Thomas Potman

THANK YOU LETTER
Job Rejection

564 Court Street
St. Louis, MO 53167
April 29, 19___

Ralph Ullman, President
S.T. Ayer Corporation
6921 Southern Blvd.
St. Louis, MO 53163

Dear Mr. Ullman:

I appreciated your consideration for the Research Associate position. While I am disappointed in not being selected, I learned a great deal about your corporation, and I enjoyed meeting with you and your staff. I felt particularly good about the professional manner in which you conducted the interview.

Please keep me in mind for future consideration. I have a strong interest in your company. I believe we would work well together. I will be closely following the progress of your company over the coming months. Perhaps we will be in touch at some later date.

Best wishes.

Sincerely,

Martin Tollins

THANK YOU LETTER
Job Offer Acceptance

7694 James Court
San Francisco, CA 94826
June 7, 19___

Judith Greene
Vice President
West Coast Airlines
2400 Van Ness
San Francisco, CA 94829

Dear Ms. Greene:

I am pleased to accept your offer, and I am looking forward to joining you and your staff next month.

The customer relations position is ideally suited to my background and interests. I assure you I will give you my best effort in making this an effective position within your company.

I understand I will begin work on July 7, 19___. If, in the meantime, I need to complete any paperwork or take care of any other matters, please contact me at (303) 777-1234.

I enjoyed meeting with you and your staff and appreciated the professional manner in which the hiring was conducted.

Sincerely,

Joan Kilmer

10

CONDUCT RESEARCH IN KEY AREAS

*T*he old adage that "knowledge is power" is especially true when conducting a job search. Your job search is only as good as the knowledge you acquire and use for finding the job you want.

Gathering, processing, and using information is the lifeblood of any job search. Research integrates the individual job search activities and provides feedback for adapting strategies to the realities of the job market. Given the numerous individuals and organizations involved in your job search, you must develop an information gathering strategy that will help you gain knowledge about, as well as access to, those individuals and organizations that will play the most important role in your job search.

USE YOUR BASE RESOURCES

Since this may be the first time you've looked for a civilian job, you need to properly research the job market by acquainting yourself with the right career resources. In addition to using the resources available through the ACAP program and the Job Assistance Centers for research purposes, we strongly recommend using two other very important resources available to Army personnel for conducting research—your base library and your Army Community Service (ACS) center. Many base libraries have put together excellent collections of career resources, from key directories to job search books—many of which are identified in this chapter and Chapter 18—for your use. Also, check with your Army Community Service center. During the past four years these centers have received budgets for acquiring career resources. They have been very active in putting together excellent career resource collections to assist service personnel and their spouses. Many have key directories, job search books, videos, and computer software for conducting job searches. Many personnel operating the base library and the Army Community Service center are very knowledgeable about career transition and job search resources. You may be surprised at what you find.

RESEARCH PURPOSES

Research is the key to gathering, processing, and using information in your job search. It is a skill that will point you in fruitful directions for minimizing job search frustrations and maximizing successes. Be sure to make research one of your top priorities.

However, most people are reluctant to initiate a research campaign which involves using libraries, computers, and telephoning and meeting new people. Such reluctance is due in part to the lack of knowledge on how to conduct research and where to find resources, and in part to a certain cultural shyness which inhibits individuals from initiating contacts with strangers. However, research is not a difficult process. After all, most people conduct research daily as they read and converse with others about problems. This daily research process needs to be specified and focused on your job search campaign.

Research serves several purposes when adapted to your job search. First, knowing the who, what, when, and where of organizations and individuals is essential for targeting your resume and conducting informational and job interviews. Second, the research component should broaden your perspective on the job market in relationship to your motivated abilities and skills and job objective. Since there are over 13,000 different job titles as well as several million job markets, even a full-time research campaign will uncover only a small segment of the job market relevant to your interests and skills.

A third purpose of research is to better understand how to relate your motivated abilities and skills to specific jobs and work environments. Once you research and understand the critical requirements of a given job in a specific work environment, you can assess the appropriateness of that job for you vis-a-vis your pattern of motivated abilities and skills (MAS).

Fourth, researching organizations and individuals should result in systematically uncovering a set of contacts for developing your job search network. One of your major research goals should be to compile names, addresses, and telephone numbers of individuals who may become important resources in your new network of job contacts.

A fifth purpose of research is to learn the *languages* of alternative jobs and careers. This is especially important if you are leaving the Army after many years of military service. You can learn to better converse in these languages by reading trade journals, annual reports, pamphlets, and other organizational literature as well as talking with people in various occupational fields. Knowing these languages—especially asking and answering intelligent questions in the language of the employer—is important for conducting successful referral and job interviews.

Finally, research should result in bringing some degree of structure, coherence, and understanding to the inherently decentralized, fragmented, and chaotic job market. Without research, you place yourself at the mercy of chance and luck; thus, you become a subject of your environment. Research best enables you to take control of your situation. It is power.

Your research activities should focus on four major targets: occupational alternatives, organizations, individuals, and communities. If you give equal time to all four, you will be well on your way to getting job interviews and offers.

INVESTIGATE ALTERNATIVE JOBS AND CAREERS

Your initial research should help familiarize you with *job and career alternatives*. For example, the U.S. Department of Labor identifies approximately 13,000 job titles. Most individuals are occupationally illiterate and unaware of the vast array of available jobs and careers. Therefore, it is essential to investigate occupational alternatives in order to broaden your perspective on the job market. As a member of the

Army, it is especially important for you to discover how your Army job skills and titles best correspond to specific civilian job skills and titles. You can do this by conducting basic job market research.

You should start your research by examining several key directories that provide information on alternative jobs and careers:

- *The Occupational Outlook Handbook*
- *Dictionary of Occupational Titles*
- *Encyclopedia of Careers and Vocational Guidance*
- *Enhanced Guide to Occupational Exploration*
- *Guide to Occupational Exploration*

You will also find several books that focus on alternative jobs and careers. National Textbook Company, for example, publishes one of the most comprehensive series of books on alternative jobs and careers. Their books now address 145 different job and career fields. Representative titles in their *"Opportunities in..."* series include:

- *Opportunities in Advertising*
- *Opportunities in Banking*
- *Opportunities in Business Management*
- *Opportunities in Electrical Trades*
- *Opportunities in Eye Care*
- *Opportunities in Interior Design*
- *Opportunities in Laser Technology*
- *Opportunities in Microelectronics*
- *Opportunities in Optometry*
- *Opportunities in Pharmacy*
- *Opportunities in Public Relations*
- *Opportunities in Robotics*
- *Opportunities in Sports and Athletics*
- *Opportunities in Telecommunications*

National Textbook also publishes two other useful sets of books in a *"Careers in..."* and a *"Careers for You"* series. The titles in the *"Careers in..."* series consist of

- *Careers in Accounting*
- *Careers in Advertising*
- *Careers in Business*
- *Careers in Communications*
- *Careers in Computers*

- *Careers in Education*
- *Careers in Engineering*
- *Careers in Finance*
- *Careers in Health Care*
- *Careers in High Tech*
- *Careers in Law*
- *Careers in Marketing*
- *Careers in Medicine*
- *Careers in Science*
- *Careers in Social and Rehabilitation Services*

Books in National Textbook's *"Careers for You"* series include:

- *Careers for Animal Lovers*
- *Careers for Bookworms*
- *Careers for Computer Buffs*
- *Careers for Crafty People*
- *Careers for Culture Lovers*
- *Careers for Environmental Types*
- *Careers for Film Buffs*
- *Careers for Foreign Language Aficionados*
- *Careers for Good Samaritans*
- *Careers for Gourmets*
- *Careers for Nature Lovers*
- *Careers for Numbers Crunchers*
- *Careers for Sports Nuts*
- *Careers for Travel Buffs*

Also look for fifteen volumes in the *"Career Directory"* series published by Visible Ink Press (Gale Research):

- *Advertising Career Directory*
- *Book Publishing Career Directory*
- *Business and Finance Career Directory*
- *Computing and Software Design Career Directory*
- *Environmental Career Directory*
- *Magazine Publishing Career Directory*
- *Marketing and Sales Career Directory*
- *Mental Health and Social Work Career Directory*
- *Newspaper Publishing Career Directory*
- *Nurses and Physicians Career Directory*
- *Public Relations Career Directory*

- *Radio and Television Career Directory*
- *Technologists and Technicians Career Directory*
- *Therapists and Allied Health Professionals Career Directory*
- *Travel and Hospitality Career Directory*

Peterson's publishes a *"Careers Without College"* series of books. They currently have ten books in this growing series:

- *Cars*
- *Computers*
- *Emergencies*
- *Fashion*
- *Fitness*
- *Health Care*
- *Kids*
- *Music*
- *Sports*
- *Travel*

Facts on File publishes a few books on alternative jobs and careers in the communication and entertainment industries:

- *Career Opportunities in Advertising and Public Relations*
- *Career Opportunities in Art*
- *Career Opportunities in the Music Industry*
- *Career Opportunities in the Sports Industry*
- *Career Opportunities in Television, Cable, and Video*
- *Career Opportunities in Theater and Performing Arts*
- *Career Opportunities in Writing*

Impact Publications publishes nine volumes on international and public service careers:

- *Almanac of American Government Jobs and Careers*
- *Almanac of International Jobs and Careers*
- *Complete Guide to International Jobs and Careers*
- *Complete Guide to Public Employment*
- *Find a Federal Job Fast!*
- *Guide to Careers in World Affairs*
- *Jobs for People Who Love Travel*
- *Jobs in Russia and the Newly Independent States*
- *The Right SF 171 Writer*

Many other books examine a wide range of jobs and careers. Some are annual or biannual reviews of today's most popular jobs. You should find several of these books particularly helpful:

- *101 Careers,* Michael Harkavy (Wiley)
- *American Almanac of Jobs and Salaries,* John W. Wright (Avon)
- *Best Jobs for the 1990s and Into the 21st Century,* Ron and Caryl Krannich (Impact)
- *The Best Jobs for the 1990s and Beyond,* Carol Kleiman (Dearborn)
- *Bob Adams Job Almanac 1994* (Bob Adams)
- *Careers Encyclopedia,* Craig T. Norback ed. (National Textbook)
- *Great Careers,* Devon Cottrell Smith, ed. (Garrett Park Press)
- *Jobs! What They Are, Where They Are, What They Pay,* Robert and Anne Snelling (Simon and Schuster)
- *Jobs 1994,* Ross and Kathryne Petras (Simon and Schuster)
- *The Jobs Rated Almanac,* Les Krantz (St. Martin's Press)
- *Occupational Outlook Handbook,* U.S. Department of Labor (U.S. Government Printing Office)
- *Top Professions,* Nicholas Basta (Peterson's)

A new CD-ROM program, produced by JIST Works, incorporates the *Occupational Outlook Handbook* into an easy-to-use interactive program complete with color photos, sound, and job matching options: *America's Top Jobs.* On-screen graphics include color photos of 250 occupations. Users select the occupational cluster that interests them, and the program leads them to specific jobs. Users can look up just one element of a job description such as earnings, working conditions, or training required, or view the complete *Occupational Outlook Handbook* text for each job. The program also allows you to print out one or more descriptions.

If you are unable to find these books and CD-ROM in your local library or bookstore, they can be ordered directly from Impact Publications. Order information is found at the end of this book. You may also want to request a copy of their free catalog of over 2,700 annotated job and career resources which includes these titles.

TARGET ORGANIZATIONS

After completing research on occupational alternatives, you should identify specific organizations which you are interested in learning more about. Next compile lists of names, addresses, and telephone numbers of important individuals in each organization. Also, write and telephone the organizations for information, such as an annual report and recruiting literature. The most important information you should be gathering concerns the organizations' goals, structures, functions, problems, and projected future opportunities and development. Since you invest part of your life in such organizations, treat them as you would a stock market investment. Compare and evaluate different organizations.

Several directories will assist you in researching organizations. Most are available in the reference sections of libraries:

- *America's Corporate Families and International Affiliates*
- *Companies and Their Brands*
- *Consultants and Consulting Organizations Directory*
- *Corporate Technology Directory*
- *Directory of American Firms Operating in Foreign Countries*
- *The Directory of Corporate Affiliations: Who Owns Whom*
- *Dun & Bradstreet's Billion Dollar Directory*
- *Dun & Bradstreet's Middle Market Directory*
- *Dun & Bradstreet's Million Dollar Directory*
- *Dun & Bradstreet's Reference Book of Corporate Managements*
- *Dun's Career Guide*
- *Encyclopedia of Business Information Sources*
- *Encyclopedia of Information Services and Agencies*
- *Fitch's Corporation Reports*
- *MacRae's Blue Book*
- *Moody's Manuals*
- *The Multinational Marketing and Employment Directory*
- *National Directory of Addresses and Telephone Numbers*
- *National Directory of Minority-Owned Business Firms*
- *National Directory of Non-Profit Organizations*
- *National Directory of Women-Owned Business Firms*
- *O'Dwyer's Directory of Corporate Communications*
- *Standard & Poor's Industrial Index*
- *Standard Rate and Data Business Publications Directory*
- *Thomas' Register of American Manufacturers*
- *Ward's Business Directory of U.S. Private & Public Companies*
- *World Business Directory*

Peterson's Guides publishes two annual directories in their new *"Job Opps"* series that are the definitive guides to organizations that hire business, engineering, environment, and health care specialists:

- *Job Opportunities in Business*
- *Job Opportunities in Engineering and Technology*
- *Job Opportunities in Environment*
- *Job Opportunities in Health Care*

The following trade books identify organizations that are considered to be some of the best to work for today:

- *100 Best Companies to Work for in America*
- *150 Best Companies for Liberal Arts Graduates*
- *America's Fastest Growing Employers*
- *Best Companies for Minorities*
- *Companies That Care*
- *Job Seekers Guide to 1000 Top Employers*

If you are interested in jobs with a particular organization, you should contact the personnel office for information on the types of jobs offered within the organization. You may be able to examine vacancy announcements which describe the duties and responsibilities of specific jobs. If you are interested in working for federal, state, or local governments, each agency will have a personnel office which can supply you with descriptions of their jobs. While gathering such information, be sure to ask people about their jobs.

Many directories and information services can now be accessed by computer using diskettes, CD-ROM, or a variety of on-line services as outlined in Chapter 17. Unfortunately, the costs of most such services on diskettes and CD-ROM are prohibitive for most individuals. It's best to check with your local public library or college and university library for information on these directories and information services. Ask about the following:

- *Business and Company Profile* (CD-ROM)
- *Business America on CD-ROM*
- *Business Dateline Ondisc, UMI* (CD-ROM)
- *Business Periodicals Index* (CD-ROM)
- *Career Search* (diskettes)
- *Companies International* (CD-ROM)
- *CompuServe* (on-line)
- *Corporate America* (CD-ROM)
- *Corporate Jobs Outlook!*

- *CorpTech*
- *Dow Jones News/Retrieval* (on-line)
- *Duns Million Dollar Disc* (CD-ROM)
- *Encyclopedia of Associations* (CD-ROM)
- *General BusinessFile, Public Edition* (CD-ROM)
- *Hoover's Handbooks* (CD-ROM)
- *Investext on InfoTrac*
- *Lexis/Nexis* (on-line)
- *Moody's Bank & Finance Disc* (CD-ROM)
- *Moody's Industrial Disc* (CD-ROM)
- *S&P Corporations* (CD-ROM)
- *Ultimate Job Finder* (diskettes)

You will find it's much easier to access company information in these forms than by using paper directories. Computerized versions of directories enable you to quickly search and retrieve specific information on companies. In addition, since most of these information services periodically update their files on a monthly or quarterly basis, the information is more current than found in annual or biannual directories.

For more information on these and other electronic databases, we recommend a new book on this subject, Joyce Lain Kennedy and Thomas J. Morrow, *Electronic Job Search Revolution* (New York: Wiley, 1994).

CONTACT INDIVIDUALS

While examining directories and reading books on alternative jobs and careers will provide you with useful job search information, much of this material may be too general for specifying the right job for you. In the end, the best information will come directly from people in specific jobs in specific organizations. To get this information you must interview people. You especially want to learn more about the people who make the hiring decisions.

You might begin your investigations by contacting various professional and trade associations for detailed information on jobs and careers relevant to their members. For names, addresses, and telephone numbers of such associations, consult the following key directories which are available in most libraries:

- *The Encyclopedia of Associations* (Gale Research)
- *National Trade and Professional Associations* (Columbia Books)

One of your most useful resources should be a new directory published by Gale Research: *Personnel Executives Contactbook* (Cindy Spomer, ed.). This one-stop resource contains essential information to help job seekers quickly locate the right person to contact for employment opportunities. It includes complete contact information for key personnel officers at 30,000 companies across the United States. Arranged alphabetically, each listing includes company name, address, and phone number; SIC code; number of employees; annual revenues; the name of the key personnel executive; and names of other human resource staff.

Your most productive research activity will be talking to people. Informal, word-of-mouth communication is still the most effective channel of job search information. In contrast to reading books, people have more current, detailed, and accurate information. Ask them about:

- Occupational fields
- Job requirements and training
- Interpersonal environments
- Performance expectations
- Their problems
- Salaries
- Advancement opportunities
- Future growth potential of the organization
- How best to acquire more information and contacts in a particular field

You may be surprised how willingly friends, acquaintances, and strangers will give you useful information. But before you talk to people, do your library research so that you are better able to ask thoughtful questions.

ASK THE RIGHT QUESTIONS

The quality of your research will only be as good as the questions you ask. Therefore, you should focus on a few key questions that will yield useful information for guiding your job search. Answers to these questions will help make important job search decisions relevant to informational and job interviews.

Who Has the Power to Hire?

Finding out who has the power to hire may take some research effort on your part. Keep in mind that personnel offices normally do not have the power to hire. They handle much of the paper work involved in announcing vacancies, taking applications, testing candidates, screening credentials, and placing new employees on the payroll. In other words, personnel offices tend to perform auxiliary support functions for those who do the actual hiring—usually individuals in operating units.

If you want to learn who really has the power to hire, you need to conduct research on the particular organization that interests you. You should ask specific questions concerning who normally is responsible for various parts of the hiring process:

- Who describes the positions?
- Who announces vacancies?
- Who receives applications?
- Who administers tests?
- Who selects eligible candidates?
- Who chooses whom to interview?
- Who offers the jobs?

If you ask these questions about a specific position you will quickly identify who has what powers to hire. Chances are the power to hire is *shared* between the personnel office and the operating unit. You should not neglect the personnel office, and in some cases it will play a powerful role in all aspects of the hiring. Your research will reveal to what degree the hiring function has been centralized, decentralized, or fragmented within a particular organization.

How Does Organization X Operate?

It's best to know something about the internal operation of an organization before joining it. Your research may uncover information that would convince you that a particular organization is not one in which you wish to invest your time and effort. You may learn, for example, that Company X has a history of terminating employees before they become vested in the company retirement system. Or Company X may be experiencing serious financial problems. Or advancement within Company X may be very political and company politics are vicious and debilitating.

You can get financial information about most companies by examining their annual reports as well as by talking to individuals who know the organization well. Information on the internal operations, especially company politics and power, must come from individuals who work within the organization. Ask them: "Is this a good organization to work for?" and let them expand on specific areas you wish to probe—advancement opportunities, working conditions, relationships among co-workers and supervisors, growth patterns, internal politics, management styles, work values, opportunities for taking initiative.

What Do I Need to Do To Get A Job With Organization X?

The best way to find how to get a job in a particular organization is to follow the advice in the next chapter on prospecting, networking, and informational interviewing. This question can only be answered by talking to people who know both the formal and informal hiring practices.

You can get information on the formal hiring system by contacting the personnel office. A telephone call should be sufficient to get this information.

But you must go beyond the formal system and personnel office in order to learn how best to conduct your job search. This means contacting people who know how one really gets hired in the organization, which may or may not follow the formal procedures. The best sources of information will be individuals who play a major role in the hiring process.

LOCATE JOB VACANCIES

While most people tend to look to the classified section of the newspaper for job listings, be sure to investigate other sources for vacancy announcements. Your local state employment office, for example, should have a comprehensive list of current vacancies for positions paying in the $15,000 to $35,000 range. Many of these offices also have access to America's Job Bank, a national computerized job listing database. Many of the job openings will give veterans preference. Government offices and many private companies routinely post vacancy announcements through their personnel offices. Be sure to contact these offices for job information. And don't overlook trade and professional associations, many of which have placement offices and publications which routinely list vacancies appropriate for their members.

Four of the best sources of information on where to find vacancy announcements are Daniel Lauber's three books and one computer program:

- *The Government Job Finder* (book)
- *The Nonprofit's Job Finder* (book)
- *The Professional's Private Sector Job Finder* (book)
- *The Ultimate Job Finder* (computer software)

Each book is a goldmine of information on various publications, associations, and databases offering job information and vacancy information unknown to most job seekers. The computer program enables users to quickly find information available in the three books. The books are published by Planning/Communication and the software program is produced by InfoBusiness; all of these products also are available through Impact Publications.

Once you locate appropriate vacancy announcements, be sure to respond to them in a timely and intelligent manner. We recommend consulting Kenneth Elderkin's book, *How to Get Interviews from Classified Job Ads,* for tips and strategies on how to best respond to classified ads and vacancy announcements.

IDENTIFY THE RIGHT COMMUNITY

Your final research target is central to all other research targets and it may occur at any stage in your research. As you separate from the Army, identifying the geographical area where you would like to work will be one of your most important career decisions. Once you make this decision, other job search decisions and activities become easier. For example, if you separate in a small town, you may need to move to a larger community which offers more opportunities for career changers. If you are a member of a two-career family, opportunities for both you and your spouse will be greater in a growing metropolitan area. As you plan to relocate to another community, you will need to develop a long-distance job search campaign which has different characteristics from a local campaign. It involves writing letters, making long-distance phone calls, and visiting a community for strategic one to two-week periods during your vacations.

Deciding where you want to live involves researching various communities and comparing advantages and disadvantages of each. In addition to identifying specific job alternatives, organizations, and individuals in the community, you need to do research on other aspects of the community. After all, you will live in the community, buy or rent a residence, perhaps send children to school, and participate in community organizations and events. Often these environmental factors are just as important to your happiness and well-being as the particular job you accept. For example, you may be leaving a $40,000 a year Army job for a position in your favorite community—San Francisco. But you may quickly find you are worse off with your new $47,000 a year job, because you must pay $300,000 for a house in San Francisco that is nearly identical to the $110,000 house you owned in your last community. Your situation will even be worse if you lived on base in previous assignments but now live on the local economy; your cost of living may increase significantly. Consequently, it would be foolish for you to take a new job without first researching several facets of the community other than job opportunities.

Research on different communities can be initiated from your local library. While most of this research will be historical in nature, several resources will provide you with a current profile of various communities. Statistical overviews and comparisons of states and cities are found in the *U.S. Census Data, The Book for the States,* and the *Municipal Yearbook.* Many libraries have a reference section of telephone books on various cities. If this section is weak or absent in your local library, contact your local telephone company. They have a relatively comprehensive library of telephone books. In addition to giving you names, addresses, and telephone numbers, the Yellow Pages are invaluable sources of information on the specialized structures of the public and private sectors of individual communities. The library may also have state and community directories as well as subscriptions to some state and community magazines and city newspapers. Research magazine, journal, and newspaper articles on different communities by consulting references in the *Reader's Guide to Periodical Literature,* the *Social Science and Humanities Index,* the *New York Times Index,* and the *Wall Street Journal Index.*

If you are trying to determine the best place to live, you should start with the latest edition of David Savageau's and Richard Boyer's *Places Rated Almanac* (Simon & Schuster). This book ranks cities by various indicators. The new *Moving and Relocation Sourcebook* (Omnigraphics) profiles the 100 largest metropolitan areas with information on population, education, recreation, arts, media, health care, taxes, transportation, and per capita income. If you are planning to live and work abroad, you should consult *Craighead's International Business, Travel, and Relocation Guide to 71 Countries* (Gale Research).

An excellent resource for identifying employers by region and state is Dorgan and Mast's (eds.) *Job Seeker's Guide to Private and Public Companies* (Gale Research). Published in four volumes, these directories profile nearly 15,000 companies in the West, Midwest, Northeast, and

South. Each volume tells job seekers whom to contact and how to approach companies regarding potential employment. Each volume includes company names, addresses, and phone numbers; business descriptions; human resources contacts; application procedures; company histories; parent companies and branch officers; corporate officers; benefits offered, and revenue and income figures.

You should also consult several city job banks that will give you contact information on specific employers in major metropolitan communities. Bob Adams, Inc. annually publishes *The National JobBank* and *The JobBank Guide to Employment Services* as well as twenty annual job bank guides:

- *The Atlanta JobBank*
- *The Boston JobBank*
- *The Carolina JobBank*
- *The Chicago JobBank*
- *The Dallas/Fort Worth JobBank*
- *The Denver JobBank*
- *The Detroit JobBank*
- *The Florida JobBank*
- *The Houston JobBank*
- *The Los Angeles JobBank*
- *The Minneapolis/St. Paul JobBank*
- *The New York JobBank*
- *The Ohio JobBank*
- *The Philadelphia JobBank*
- *The Phoenix JobBank*
- *The San Francisco Bay Area JobBank*
- *The Seattle JobBank*
- *The St. Louis JobBank*
- *The Tennessee JobBank*
- *The Metro Washington D.C. JobBank*

Surrey Books also publishes a similar job bank series for ten major metropolitan areas:

- *How to Get a Job in Atlanta*
- *How to Get a Job in Boston*
- *How to Get a Job in Chicago*
- *How to Get a Job in Dallas/Ft. Worth*
- *How to Get a Job in Houston*
- *How to Get a Job in Los Angeles/San Diego*

- *How to Get a Job in New York*
- *How to Get a Job in San Francisco*
- *How to Get a Job in Seattle/Portland*
- *How to Get a Job in Washington, DC*

Another series, published by NET Research, provides information on employment agencies and executive search firms in major regions, states, and cities throughout the country:

- *Boston and New England Job Seekers Sourcebook*
- *Chicago and Illinois Job Seekers Sourcebook*
- *Los Angeles and Southern California Job Seekers Sourcebook*
- *Mid-Atlantic Job Seekers Sourcebook*
- *Mountain States Job Seekers Sourcebook*
- *New York and New Jersey Job Seekers Sourcebook*
- *Northern Great Lakes Job Seekers Sourcebook*
- *Ohio Valley Job Seekers Sourcebook*
- *Pacific Northwest Job Seekers Sourcebook*
- *Plains States Job Seekers Sourcebook*
- *Southern Atlantic Coast Job Seekers Sourcebook*
- *Southern California Job Seekers Sourcebook*
- *Southern States Job Seekers Sourcebook*
- *Southwest Job Seekers Sourcebook*

Since you may be interested in relocating to a community with nearby military facilities you will want to use, you should consult Dan Cragg's latest edition of *Guide to Military Installations* (Mechanicsburg, PA: Stackpole Books). This is a comprehensive guide to U.S. Army, Navy, Air Force, and Marine Corps installations both stateside and overseas. It details all base facilities, services, and attractions.

After narrowing the number of communities that interest you, further research them in depth. Ask fellow service personnel, relatives, friends, and acquaintances for contacts in the particular community; they may know people whom you can write or telephone for information and referrals. Remember, fellow service personnel are like family—many will go out of their way to help you establish contacts and give you job leads. Once you have decided to focus on one community, if your current assignment situation permits, visit it in order to establish personal contacts with key reference points, such as the local Chamber of Commerce, real estate firms, schools, libraries, churches, Forty-Plus Club (if appropriate), government agencies, and business firms and associations. Begin developing personal networks based upon the research and referral strategies in the next chapter. Subscribe to the local newspaper and to any community magazines which help profile the community. Follow the help-wanted, society, financial, and real estate sections of the newspaper—especially the Sunday edition. Keep a list of names of individuals who appear to hold influential community positions; you may want to contact these people for referrals. Write letters to set up informational interviews with key people; give yourself two months of lead time to complete your letter writing campaign. Your overall community research should focus on developing personal contacts which may assist you in both your job search and your move to the community.

KNOW WHAT'S IMPORTANT

Reviewing published resources can be extremely time consuming if taken to the extreme. While you should examine several of them, do not spend an inordinate amount of time reading and taking notes. Your time will be best spent in gathering information through meetings and conversations with key people. Your primary goals in conducting research should be identifying people to contact, setting appointments, and asking the right questions which lead to more information and contacts. If you engage in these activities you will know what is important when conducting research.

As you get further into your job search, networking for information, advice, and referrals will become an important element in your overall job search strategy. At that time you will come into closer contact with potential employers who can provide you with detailed information on their organizations and specific jobs. If you have a well defined MAS, specific job objectives, and a clearly focused resume, you should be in a good position to make networking pay off with useful information, advice, and referrals. You will quickly discover that the process of linking your MAS and objectives to specific jobs is an ongoing one involving several steps in your job search.

11

NETWORK YOUR WAY TO CAREER SUCCESS

*N*ow that you have identified your skills, specified your objective, written your resume, and conducted research, what should you do next? At this point let's examine where you are going so you don't get preoccupied with the trees and thus lose sight of the larger forest. Let's identify the most effective methods for linking your previous job search activities to job interviews and offers.

FOCUS ON GETTING INTERVIEWS

Everything you do up to this point in your job search should be aimed at *getting a job interview*. The skills you identified, the goals you set, the resume you wrote, and the information you gathered are carefully related to one another so you will have maximum impact for communicating your qualifications to employers who, in turn, will decide to invite you to a job interview.

But there are secrets to getting a job interview you should know before continuing further with your job search. The most important secret is the *informational interview*—a type of interview which yields useful job search information and *may* lead to job interviews and offers. Based on prospecting and networking techniques, these interviews minimize rejections and competition as well as quickly open the doors to organizations and employers. If you want a job interview, you first need to understand the informational interview and how to initiate and use it for maximum impact.

PROSPECTING AND NETWORKING

What do you do after you complete your resume? Most people send cover letters and resumes in response to job listings; they then wait to be called for a job interview. Viewing the job search as basically a direct-mail operation, many are disappointed in discovering the realities of direct-mail—a 5 percent response rate is considered outstanding!

Successful job seekers break out of this relatively passive job search role by orienting themselves toward face-to-face action. Being proactive, they develop interpersonal strategies in which the resume plays a *supportive* rather than a central role in the job search. They first present themselves to employers; the resume appears only at the end of a face-to-face conversation.

Throughout the job search you will acquire useful names and addresses as well as meet people who will assist you in contacting potential employers. Such information and contacts become key building blocks for generating job interviews and offers.

Since the best and most numerous jobs are found on the hidden job market, you must use methods appropriate for this job market. Indeed, research and experience clearly show the most effective means of communication are face-to-face and word-of-mouth. The informal, interpersonal system of communication is the central nervous system of the hidden job market. Your goal should be to penetrate this job market with proven methods for success. Appropriate methods for making important job contacts are *prospecting and networking*. Appropriate methods for getting these contacts to provide you with useful job information are *informational and referral interviews*.

COMMUNICATE YOUR QUALIFICATIONS

Taken together, these interpersonal methods help you *communicate your qualifications to employers*. Although many job seekers may be reluctant to use this informal communication system, they greatly limit their potential for success if they do not.

Put yourself in the position of the employer for a moment. You have a job vacancy to fill. If you advertise the position, you may be bombarded with hundreds of resumes, applications, phone calls, faxes, and walkins. While you do want to hire the best qualified individual for the job, you simply don't have time or patience to review scores of applications. Even if you use a P.O. Box number, the paperwork may quickly overwhelm you. Furthermore, with limited information from application forms, cover letters, and resumes, you find it hard to identify the best qualified individuals to invite for an interview; many look the same on paper.

So what do you do? You might hire a professional job search firm or use the services of a temporary employment agency to take on all of this additional work. On the other hand, you may want to better control the hiring process, especially since it appears to be filled with uncertainty and headaches. You want to minimize your risks and time so you can get back to what you do best—accomplishing the external goals of the organization. Like many other employers, you begin by calling your friends, acquaintances, and other business associates and ask if they or someone else might know of any good candidates for the position. If they can't help, you ask them to give you a call should they learn of anyone qualified for your vacancy. You, in effect, create your own hidden job market—an informal information network for locating desirable candidates. Your trusted contacts initially screen the candidates in the process of referring them to you. This both saves you time and minimizes your risks in hiring a stranger.

Based on this understanding of the employer's perspective, what should you do to best improve your chances of getting an interview and job offer? Networking for information, advice, and referrals should play a central role in your overall job search. Remember, employers need to solve personnel problems. By conducting *informational interviews and networking* you help employers identify their needs, limit their alternatives, and thus make decisions and save money. Most important, such networking activities help relieve their anxiety of hiring a career changer.

At the same time, you gain several advantages by conducting these interviews:

1. You are less likely to encounter rejections since you are not asking for a job—only information, advice, and referrals.

2. You go after high level positions.

3. You encounter little competition.

4. You go directly to the people who have the power to hire.

5. You are likely to be invited to job interviews based upon the referrals you receive.

Most employers want more information on candidates to supplement the "paper qualifications" represented in application forms, resumes, and letters. Studies show that employers in general seek candidates who have these skills: communication, problem solving, analytical, assessment, and planning. Surprising to many job seekers, technical expertise ranks third or fourth in employers' lists of most desired skills. These findings support a frequent observation made by employers: the major problems with employees relate to communication, problem solving, and analysis; individuals get fired because of political and interpersonal conflicts rather than technical incompetence.

Employers seek individuals they *like* both personally and professionally. Therefore, communicating your qualifications to employers entails more than just informing them of your technical competence. You must communicate that you have the requisite personal *and* professional skills for performing the job. Informal prospecting, networking, and informational interviewing activities are the best methods for communicating your "qualifications" to employers.

DEVELOP NETWORKS

Networking is the process of purposefully developing relations with others. Networking in the job search involves connecting and interacting with other individuals who can be helpful to you. Your network consists of you interacting with others. The more you develop, maintain, and expand your networks, the more successful should be your job search.

Your network is your interpersonal environment. While you know and interact with hundreds of people, on a day-to-day basis you may encounter no more than 20 people. You frequently contact these people in face-to-face situations. Some people are more *important* to you than others. You *like* some more than others. And some will be more *helpful* to you in your job search than others.

As a member of the Army, you already have an extensive network in place. Based on your many moves and the scores of people you have come in contact with through your military service, you should be well positioned to take advantage of this important employment avenue. It's now time to begin networking your way to career transition success.

Your most important network may be your military contacts—both those still in the military and those who have retired. This is not the time to be bashful. You need to let your military colleagues know that you are actively searching for a job. You will be pleasantly surprised as to the positive response you will receive. Indeed, the Army tends to be a close knit family that looks out for each other. Military friends who have already transitioned to the private sector can be especially helpful for they know "first hand" where the hidden jobs are within their organization. You might want to begin by referring to your Christmas card list or by using the Army worldwide locator service (call 317/542-4211) to identify where all of your old friends and colleagues are now located. You also should join various Army and military associations (see Chapter 4 and Appendix) where you can make important professional contacts.

Your basic network will encompass the following individuals and groups: friends, acquaintances, immediate family, distant relatives, professional colleagues, spouse, supervisor, fellow workers, close friends and colleagues, and local businessmen and professionals, such as your banker, lawyer, doctor, minister, and insurance agent. You should contact many of these individuals for advice relating to your job search.

You need to *identify everyone in your network* who might help you with your job search. You first need to expand your basic network to include individuals you know and have interacted with over the past 10 or more years. Make a list of at least 200 people you know. Include friends and relatives from your Christmas card list, past and present neighbors, former classmates, politicians, business persons, previous employers, professional associates, ministers, insurance agents, lawyers, bankers, doctors, dentists, accountants, and social acquaintances.

After identifying your extended network, you should try to *link your network to others' networks.* The figure on page 209 illustrates this linkage principle. Individuals in these other networks also have job information and contacts. Ask people in your basic network for referrals. This approach should greatly enlarge your basic job search network.

What do you do if individuals in your immediate and extended network cannot provide you with certain job information and contacts? While it

LINKING YOUR NETWORKS TO OTHERS

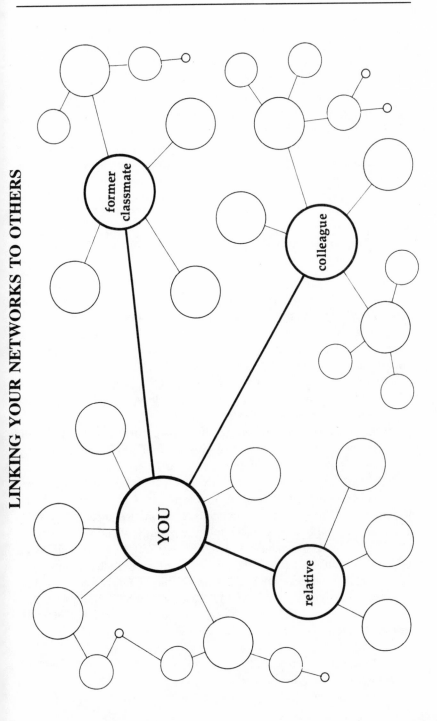

is much easier and more effective to meet new people through personal contacts, on occasion you may need to *approach strangers without prior contacts*. In this situation, try the "cold turkey" approach. Write a letter to someone you feel may be useful to your job search. Research this individual so you are acquainted with their background and accomplishments. In the letter, refer to their accomplishments, mention your need for job information, and specify a date and time you will call to schedule a meeting. Another approach is to introduce yourself to someone by telephone and request a meeting and/or job information. While you may experience rejections in using these approaches, you also will experience successes. And those successes should lead to further expansion of your job search network.

PROSPECT FOR LEADS

The key to successful networking is an active and routine *prospecting campaign*. Salespersons in insurance, real estate, Amway, Shaklee, and other direct-sales businesses understand the importance and principles of prospecting; indeed, many have turned the art of prospecting into a science! The basic operating principle is *probability*: the number of sales you make is a direct function of the amount of effort you put into developing new contacts and following-through. Expect no more than a 10 percent acceptance rate: for every 10 people you meet, 9 will reject you and 1 will accept you. Therefore, the more people you contact, the more acceptances you will receive. If you want to be successful, you must collect many more "nos" than "yeses." In a 10 percent probability situation, you need to contact 100 people for 10 successes.

These prospecting principles are extremely useful for making a career change. Like sales situations, the job search is a highly ego-involved activity often characterized by numerous rejections accompanied by a few acceptances. While no one wants to be rejected, few people are willing and able to handle more than a few rejections. They take a "no" as a sign of personal failure—and quit prematurely. If they persisted longer, they would achieve success after a few more "nos." Furthermore, if their prospecting activities were focused on gathering information rather than making sales, they would considerably minimize the number of rejections. Therefore, you should do the following:

- Prospect for job leads.
- Accept rejections as part of the game.
- Link prospecting to informational interviewing.

- Keep prospecting for more information and "yeses" which will eventually translate into job interviews and offers.

The job search is a highly ego-involved activity often characterized by numerous rejections accompanied by a few acceptances.

A good prospecting pace as you start your search is to make two new contacts each day. Start by contacting people in your immediate network. Let them know you are conducting a job search, but emphasize that you are only doing research. Ask for a few moments of their time to discuss your information needs. You are only seeking *information and advice* at this time—not a job.

It should take you about 20 minutes to make a contact by letter or telephone. If you make two contacts each day, by the end of the first week you will have 10 new contacts for a total investment of less than seven hours. By the second week you may want to increase your prospecting pace to four new contacts each day or 20 each week. The more contacts you make, the more useful information, advice, and job leads you will receive. If your job search bogs down, you probably need to increase your prospecting activities.

Expect each contact to refer you to two or three others who will also refer you to others. Consequently, your contacts should multiply considerably within only a few weeks.

HANDLE AND MINIMIZE REJECTIONS

These prospecting and networking methods are effective. While they are responsible for building, maintaining, and expanding multi-million dollar businesses, they work extremely well for job hunters. But they only work if you are patient and persist. *The key to networking success is to focus on gathering information while also learning to handle rejections.* Learn from rejections, forget them, and go on to more productive networking activities. The major reason direct-sales people fail is because they don't persist. The reason they don't persist is because they either can't take, or get tired of taking, rejections.

Rejections are no fun, especially in such an ego-involved activity as a job search. But you will encounter rejections as you travel on the road toward job search success. This road is strewn with individuals who quit prematurely because they were rejected four or five times. Don't be one of them!

Our prospecting and networking techniques differ from sales approaches in one major respect: we have special techniques for minimizing the number of rejections. If handled properly, at least 50 percent—maybe as many as 90 percent—of your prospects will turn into "yeses" rather than "nos." The reason for this unusually high acceptance rate is how you introduce and handle yourself before your prospects. Many insurance agents and direct distributors expect a 90 percent rejection rate, because they are trying to sell specific products potential clients may or may not need. Most people don't like to be put on the spot—especially when it is in their own home or office—to make a decision to buy a product.

BE HONEST AND SINCERE

The principles of selling yourself in the job market are similar. People don't want to be put on the spot. They feel uncomfortable if they think you expect them to give you a job. Thus, you should never introduce yourself to a prospect by asking them for a job or a job lead. You should do just the opposite: relieve their anxiety by mentioning that you are not looking for a job from them—only job information and advice. You must be honest and sincere in communicating these intentions to your contact. The biggest turn-off for individuals targeted for informational interviews is insincere job seekers who try to use this as a mechanism to get a job.

Your approach to prospects must be subtle, honest, and professional. You are seeking *information, advice, and referrals* relating to several subjects: job opportunities, your job search approach, your resume, and contacts who may have similar information, advice, and referrals. Most people gladly volunteer such information. They generally like to talk about themselves, their careers, and others. They like to give advice. This approach flatters individuals by placing them in the role of the expert-advisor. Who doesn't want to be recognized as an expert-advisor, especially on such a critical topic as one's employment?

This approach should yield a great deal of information, advice, and referrals from your prospects. One other important outcome should result from using this approach: people will *remember* you as the person who made them feel at ease and who received their valuable advice. If they hear of job opportunities for someone with your qualifications, chances are they will contact you with the information. After contacting 100 prospects, you will have created 100 sets of eyes and ears to help you in your job search!

The best way to get a job is to ask for job information, advice, and referrals; never ask for a job.

PRACTICE THE 5R's OF INFORMATIONAL INTERVIEWING

The guiding principle behind prospecting, networking, and informational interviews is this: the best way to get a job is to ask for job information, advice, and referrals; never ask for a job. Remember, you want your prospects to engage in the 5R's of informational interviewing:

- *Reveal* useful information and advice.
- *Refer* you to others.
- *Read* your resume.
- *Revise* your resume.
- *Remember* you for future reference.

If you follow this principle, you should join the ranks of thousands of successful job seekers who paid a great deal of money learning it from highly-paid professionals.

APPROACH KEY PEOPLE

Whom should you contact within an organization for an informational interview? Contact people who are busy, who have the power to hire, and who are knowledgeable about the organization. The least likely candidate will be someone in the personnel department. Most often the heads of operating units are the most busy, powerful, and knowledgeable individuals in the organization. However, getting access to such individuals may be difficult. Some people at the top may appear to be informed and powerful, but they may lack information on the day-to-day personnel changes or their influence is limited in the hiring process. It is difficult to give one best answer to this question.

Therefore, we recommend contacting several types of people. Aim for the busy, powerful, and informed, but be prepared to settle for less. Secretaries, receptionists, and the person you want to meet may refer you to others. From a practical standpoint, you may have to take whomever you can schedule an appointment with. Sometimes people who are less powerful can be helpful. Talk to a secretary or receptionist sometime about their boss or working in the organization. You may be surprised with what you learn!

Nonetheless, you will conduct informational interviews with different types of people. Some will be friends, relatives, or acquaintances. Others will be referrals or new contacts. You will gain the easiest access to people you already know. This can usually be done informally by telephone. You might meet at their home or office or at a restaurant.

You should use a more formal approach to gain access to referrals and new contacts. The best way to initiate a contact with a prospective employer is to *send an approach letter* and follow it up with a phone call. Examples of approach letters are found at the end of Chapter 9. This letter should include the following elements:

OPENERS   If you have a referral, tell the individual you are considering a career in _____. His or her name was given to you by _____who suggested he or she might be a good person to give you useful information about careers in _____. Should you lack a referral to the individual and thus must use a "cold turkey" approach to making this contact, you might begin your letter by stating that you are aware he or she has been at the forefront of _____ business—or whatever is both truthful and appropriate for the situation. A subtle form of flattery will be helpful at this stage.

REQUEST   Demonstrate your thoughtfulness and courtesy rather than aggressiveness by mentioning that you know he or she is busy. You hope to schedule a mutually convenient time for a brief meeting to discuss your questions and career plans. Most people will be flattered by such a request and happy to talk with you about their work—if they have time and are interested in you.

CLOSINGS In closing the letter, mention that you will call the person to see if an appointment can be arranged. Be specific by stating the time and day you will call—for example, Thursday at 2pm. You must take initiative to follow-up the letter with a definite contact time. If you don't, you cannot expect to hear from the person. It is *your* responsibility to make the telephone call to schedule a meeting.

ENCLOSURE Do *not* enclose your resume with this approach letter. You should take your resume to the interview and present it as a topic of discussion near the end of your meeting. If you send it with the approach letter, you communicate a mixed and contradictory message. Remember your purpose for this interview: to gather information and advice. You are not—and never should be—asking for a job. A resume accompanying a letter appears to be an application or a job request.

Many people will meet with you, assuming you are sincere in your approach. On the other hand, many people also are very busy and simply don't have the time to meet with you. If the person puts you off when you telephone for an appointment, clearly state your purpose and emphasize that you are not looking for a job with this person—only information and advice. If the person insists on putting you off, make the best of the situation: try to conduct the informational interview over the telephone. Alternatively, write a nice thank you letter in which you again state your intended purpose; mention your disappointment in not being able to learn from the person's experience; and ask to be remembered for future reference. Enclose your resume with this letter.

While you are ostensibly seeking information and advice, treat this meeting as an important preliminary interview. You need to communicate your qualifications—that you are competent, intelligent, honest, and likeable. These are the same qualities you should communicate in a formal job interview. Hence, follow the same advice given for conducting a formal interview and dressing appropriately for a face-to-face meeting (Chapter 12).

CONDUCT THE INTERVIEW WELL

An informational interview will be relatively unstructured compared to a formal job interview. Since you want the interviewer to advise you, you reverse roles by asking questions which should give you useful information. You, in effect, become the interviewer. You should structure this interview with a particular sequence of questions. Most questions should be open-ended, requiring the individual to give specific answers based upon his or her experience.

The structure and dialogue for the informational interview might go something like this. You plan to take no more than 45 minutes for this interview. The first three to five minutes will be devoted to small talk—the weather, traffic, the office, mutual acquaintances, or an interesting or humorous observation. Since these are the most critical moments in the interview, be especially careful how you communicate nonverbally. Begin your interview by stating your appreciation for the individual's time:

> *"I want to thank you again for scheduling this meeting with me. I know you're busy. I appreciate the special arrangements you made to see me on a subject which is very important to my future."*

Your next comment should be a statement reiterating your purpose as stated in your letter:

> *"As you know, I am exploring job and career alternatives. I know what I do well and what I want to do. But before I commit myself to a new job, I need to know more about various career options. I thought you would be able to provide me with some insights into career opportunities, job requirements, and possible problems or promising directions in the field of _____."*

This statement normally will get a positive reaction from the individual who may want to know more about what it is you want to do. Be sure to clearly communicate your job objective. If you can't, you may communicate that you are lost, indecisive, or uncertain about yourself. The person may feel you are wasting his or her time.

Your next line of questioning should focus on "how" and "what" questions centering on (1) specific jobs and (2) the job search process. Begin by asking about various aspects of specific jobs:

- Duties and responsibilities
- Knowledge, skills, and abilities required
- Work environment relating to fellow employees, work flows, deadlines, stress, initiative
- Advantages and disadvantages
- Advancement opportunities and outlook
- Salary ranges

Your informer will probably take a great deal of time talking about his or her experience in each area. Be a good listener, but make sure you move along with the questions.

Your next line of questioning should focus on your job search activities. You need as much information as possible on how to:

- Acquire the necessary skills
- Best find a job in this field
- Overcome any objections employers may have to you
- Uncover job vacancies which may be advertised
- Develop job leads
- Approach prospective employers

Your final line of questioning should focus on your resume. Do not show your resume until you focus on this last set of questions. The purpose of these questions is to: (1) get the individual to read your resume in-depth, (2) acquire useful advice on how to strengthen it, (3) refer you to prospective employers, and (4) be remembered. With the resume in front of you and your interviewee, ask the following questions:

- Is this an appropriate type of resume for the jobs I have outlined?
- If an employer received this resume in the mail, how do you think he or she would react to it?
- What do you see as possible weaknesses or areas that need to be improved?
- What should I do with this resume? Shotgun it to hundreds of employers with a cover letter? Use resume letters instead?
- What about the length, paper quality and color, layout, and typing? Are they appropriate?
- How might I improve the form and content of the resume?

You should receive useful advice on how to strengthen both the content and use of your resume. Most important, these questions force the individual to *read* your resume which, in turn, may be *remembered* for future reference.

Your last question is especially important in this interview. You want to be both *remembered* and *referred.* Some variation of the following question should help:

> *"I really appreciate all this advice. It is very helpful and it should improve my job search considerably. Could I ask you one more favor? Do you know two or three other people who could help me with my job search? I want to conduct as much research as possible, and their advice might be helpful also."*

Before you leave, mention one more important item:

> *"During the next few months, should you hear of any job oppor-tunities for someone with my interests and qualifications, I would appreciate being kept in mind. And please feel free to pass my name on to others."*

Send a nice thank you letter within 48 hours of completing this informational interview. Express your genuine gratitude for the individual's time and advice. Reiterate your interests, and ask to be remembered and referred to others.

Follow-up on any useful advice you receive, particularly referrals. Approach referrals in the same manner you approached the person who gave you the referral. Write a letter requesting a meeting. Begin the letter by mentioning:

> *"Mr./Ms. _____ suggested that I contact you concerning my research on careers in _____."*

If you continue prospecting, networking, and conducting informational interviews, soon you will be busy conducting interviews and receiving job offers. While 100 informational interviews over a two-month period should lead to several formal job interviews and offers, the pay-offs are uncertain because job vacancies are unpredictable. We know cases where the first referral turned into a formal interview and job offer. More typical cases require constant prospecting, networking, and informational interviewing activities. The telephone call or letter inviting you to a job interview can come at any time. While the timing may be unpredictable, your persistent job search activities will be largely responsible for the final outcome.

TELEPHONE FOR JOB LEADS

Telephone communication should play an important role in prospecting, networking, and informational interviews. However, controversy centers around how and when to use the telephone for generating job leads and scheduling interviews. Some people recommend writing a letter and waiting for a written or telephone reply. Others suggest writing a letter and following it with a telephone call. Still others argue you should use the telephone exclusively rather than write letters.

How you use the telephone will indicate what type of job search you are conducting. Exclusive reliance on the telephone is a technique used by highly formalized job clubs which operate phone banks for generating job leads. Using the Yellow Pages as the guide to employers, a job club member may call as many as 50 employers a day to schedule job interviews. A rather aggressive yet typical telephone dialogue goes something like this:

"Hello, my name is Jim Morgan. I would like to speak to the head of the training department. By the way, what is the name of the training director?"

"You want to talk to Ms. Stevens. Her number is 723-8191 or I can connect you directly."

"Hello, Ms. Stevens. My name is Jim Morgan. I have several years of training experience in Army communication systems. In addition to providing training to Army soldiers for over seven years, I also worked with GTE in developing the training materials. I'd like to meet with you to discuss possible openings in your department for someone with my qualifications. Would it be possible to see you on Friday?"

Not surprising, this telephone approach generates many "nos." If you have a hard time handling rejections, this telephone approach will help you confront your anxieties. The principle behind this approach is *probability*: for every 25 telephone "nos" you receive, you will probably get one or two "yeses." Success is just 25 telephone calls away! If you start calling prospective employers at 9am and finish your 25 calls by 12 noon, you should generate at least one or two interviews. That's not bad for three hours of job search work. It beats a direct-mail approach.

While the telephone is more efficient than writing letters, its effectiveness is questionable. When you use the telephone in this manner, you are basically asking for a job. You are asking the employer: "Do you have a job for me?" There is nothing subtle or particularly professional about this approach. It is effective in uncovering particular types of job leads for particular types of individuals. If you need a job in a hurry, this is one of the most efficient ways of finding employment. However, if you seek a job that is right for you—a job you do well and enjoy doing, one that is fit for you—this telephone approach is inappropriate.

You must use your own judgment in determining when and how to use the telephone in your job search. There are appropriate times and methods for using the telephone, and there are subtler telephone techniques and scripts you can use which yield good results. These are revealed in the Krannichs' new book, *Dynamite Tele-Search.*

We prefer the more conventional approach of writing a letter requesting an informational interview and following it up with a telephone call. While you take the initiative in scheduling an appointment, you do not put the individual on the spot by asking for a job. You are only seeking information and advice. This low-keyed approach results in numerous acceptances and has a higher probability of paying off with interviews than the aggressive telephone request. You should be trying to uncover jobs that are right for you rather than any job that happens to pop up from a telephoning blitz.

USE JOB CLUBS AND SUPPORT GROUPS

The techniques outlined thus far are designed for individuals conducting a self-directed job search. Job clubs and support groups are two important alternatives to these techniques. Check with the ACAP and JAC programs on your base to see if support groups have been formed and how you can join one. If none have been formed, organize one yourself.

Job clubs are designed to provide a group structure and support system to individuals seeking employment. These groups consist of about 12 individuals who are led by a trained counselor and supported with telephones, copying machines, and a resource center.

Highly formalized job clubs, such as the 40-Plus Club, organize job search activities for both the advertised and hidden job markets. As outlined by Azrin and Besalel in their book *Job Club Counselor's Manual*, job club activities include:

- Signing commitment agreements to achieve specific job search goals and targets.
- Contacting friends, relatives, and acquaintances for job leads.
- Completing activity forms.
- Using telephones, typewriters, photocopy machines, postage, and other equipment and supplies.
- Meeting with fellow participants to discuss job search progress.
- Telephoning to uncover job leads.
- Researching newspapers, telephone books, and directories.
- Developing research, telephone, interview, and social skills.
- Writing letters and resumes.
- Responding to want ads.
- Completing employment applications.

In other words, the job club formalizes many of the prospecting, networking, and informational interviewing activities within a group context and interjects the role of the telephone as the key communication device for developing and expanding networks.

Job clubs place excessive reliance on using the telephone for uncovering job leads. Members call prospective employers and ask about job openings. The Yellow Pages become the job hunting bible. During a two-week period, a job club member might spend most of his or her mornings telephoning for job leads and scheduling interviews. Afternoons are normally devoted to job interviewing.

We do not recommend joining such job clubs for obvious reasons. Most job club methods are designed for the hardcore unemployed or for individuals who need a job—any job—quickly. Individuals try to fit into available vacancies; their objectives and skills are of secondary concern. We recommend conducting your own job search or forming a support group which adapts some job club methods to our central concept of finding a job fit for you—one appropriate to your objective and in line with your particular mix of skills, abilities, and interests.

Support groups, which may be sponsored by JAC and ACAP, are a useful alternative to job clubs. They have one major advantage: they may cut your job search time in half. Forming or joining one of these groups can help direct as well as enhance your individual job search activities.

Your support group should consist of three or more individuals who are job hunting. Try to schedule regular meetings with specific purposes in mind. While the group may be highly social, especially if it involves close friends, it also should be *task-oriented*. Meet at least once a week and include your spouse. At each meeting set *performance goals* for the week. For example, your goal can be to make 20 new contacts and conduct five informational interviews. The contacts can be made by telephone, letter, or in person. Share your experiences and job information with each other. *Critique* each other's progress, make suggestions for improving the job search, and develop new strategies together. By doing this, you will be gaining valuable information and feedback which is normally difficult to gain on one's own. This group should provide important psychological supports to help you through your job search. After all, job hunting can be a lonely, frustrating, and exasperating experience. By sharing your experiences with others, you will find you are not alone. You will quickly learn that rejections are part of the game. The group will encourage you, and you will feel good about helping others achieve their goals. Try building small incentives into the group, such as the individual who receives the most job interviews for the month will be treated to dinner by other members of the group.

EXPLORE ELECTRONIC NETWORKING

Networking is increasingly taking on new communication forms in today's high-tech electronic revolution. As outlined in Chapters 4, 9, and 17, job seekers can now take advantage of several electronic databases for conducting a job search, from gathering information on the job market to disseminating resumes to employers. The electronic revolution also allows job seekers to network for information, advice, and job leads. If you belong to one of the online computer information systems, such as Prodigy, CompuServe, or America OnLine, you can use electronic bulletin boards, e-mail systems, and the Internet system to gather job information and make contacts with potential employers. Through e-mail systems you may even make a personal contact which gives you job leads for further networking via computer or through the more traditional networking methods outlined in this chapter.

We expect these electronic communication systems will play an increasingly important role in conducting job searches. They offer new networking options for individuals who are literate in today's computer technology and telecommunication systems. If you have access to any of the online telecommunications systems, we recommend exploring their electronic bulletin board, e-mail, and job vacancy ("career corner") options. Within just a few minutes of electronic networking you may pick up important job information, advice, and leads that could turn into a real job. For more information on their electronic networks, see Chapter 17.

12

INTERVIEW FOR THE RIGHT JOB

*M*ake no mistake—the job interview is *the* most important step in the job search process. All previous job search activities lead to this one. Put simply, no interview, no job offer; no job offer, no negotiations, no salary, and no job.

Your previous job search activities have assisted you in getting this far, but the interview itself will determine whether you will be invited to a second interview and offered a position. How you approach the interview will make a difference in the outcome of the interview. Therefore, you need to know what best to do and not to do in order to make a good impression on your prospective employer.

INTERVIEWING FOR THE JOB

Nearly 95 percent of all organizations require job interviews prior to hiring employees. In fact, employers consider an effective interview to be

223

the most important hiring criteria—outranking grade point average, related work experience, and recommendations.

While the job interview is the most important job search activity, it also is the most stressful job search experience. Your application, resume, and letters may get you to the interview, but you must perform well in person in order to get a job offer. Knowing the stakes are high, most people face interviews with dry throats and sweaty palms; it is a time of great stress. You will be on stage, and you are expected to put on a good performance.

How do you prepare for the interview? First, you need to understand the nature and purpose of the interview. Second, you must prepare to respond to the interview situation and the interviewer. Make sure whomever assists you in preparing for the interview evaluates your performance. Practice the whole interviewing scenario, from the time you enter the door until you leave. You should sharpen your nonverbal communication skills and be prepared to give positive answers to questions as well as ask intelligent questions. The more you practice, the better prepared you will be for the real job interview.

COMMUNICATION

An interview is a two-way communication exchange between an interviewer and interviewee. It involves both verbal and nonverbal communication. While we tend to concentrate on the content of what we say, research shows that approximately 65 percent of all communication is nonverbal. Furthermore, we tend to give more credibility to nonverbal than to verbal messages. Regardless of what you say, how you dress, sit, stand, use your hands, move your head and eyes, and listen communicates both positive and negative messages.

Job interviews can occur in many different settings and under various circumstances. You will write job interview letters, schedule interviews by telephone, be interviewed over the phone, and encounter one-on-one as well as panel, group, and series interviews. Each situation requires a different set of communication behaviors. For example, while telephone communication is efficient, it may be ineffective for interview purposes. Only certain types of information can be effectively communicated over the telephone because this medium limits nonverbal behavior. Honesty, intelligence, and likability—three of the most important values you want to communicate to employers—are primarily communicated nonverbally. Therefore, you should be very careful of telephone interviews—whether giving or receiving them.

Job interviews have different purposes and can be negative in many ways. From your perspective, the purpose of an initial job interview is to get a second interview, and the purpose of the second interview is to get a job offer. However, for many employers, the purpose of the interview is to eliminate you from a second interview or job offer. The interviewer wants to know why he or she should *not* hire you. The interviewer tries to do this by identifying your weaknesses. These differing purposes can create an adversarial relationship and contribute to the overall interviewing stress experienced by both the applicant and the interviewer.

Since the interviewer wants to identify your weaknesses, you must counter by *communicating your strengths* to lessen the interviewer's fears of hiring you. Recognizing that you are an unknown quantity to the employer, you must raise the interviewer's expectations of you.

ANSWERING QUESTIONS

Hopefully your prospecting, networking, informational interviewing, and resume and letter writing activities result in several invitations to interview for jobs appropriate to your objective. Once you receive an invitation to interview, you should do a great deal of work in preparation for your meeting. You should prepare for the interview as if it were a $1,000,000 prize. After all, that may be what you earn during your employment.

You should prepare for the interview
as if it were a $1,000,000 prize.

The invitation to interview will most likely come by telephone. In some cases, a preliminary interview will be conducted by telephone. The employer may want to shorten the list of eligible candidates from ten to three. By calling each individual, the employer can quickly eliminate marginal candidates as well as up-date the job status of each individual. When you get such a telephone call, you have no time to prepare. You may be dripping wet as you step from the shower or you may have a splitting headache as you pick up the phone. Telephone interviews always seem to occur at bad times. Whatever your situation, put your best foot forward based upon your thorough preparation for an interview. You may want to keep a list of questions near the telephone just in case you receive such a telephone call.

Telephone interviews often result in a face-to-face interview at the employer's office. Once you confirm an interview time and place, you should do as much research on the organization and employer as possible. Learn to lessen your anxiety and stress levels by practicing the interview situation. *Preparation and practice* are the keys to doing your best.

During the interview, you want to impress upon the interviewer your knowledge of the organization by asking excellent questions and giving intelligent answers. Your library research and networking activities (Chapters 10 and 11) should yield useful information on the organization and employer. Be sure you know something about the organization. Interviewers are normally impressed by interviewees who demonstrate knowledge and interest in their organization.

You should practice the actual interview by mentally addressing several questions most interviewers ask. Most of these questions will relate to your educational background, work experience, career goals, personality, and related concerns. Some of the most frequently asked questions include:

Education

- Describe your educational background.
- How have you improved your education while in the Army?
- Have you started work on an associate's or bachelor's degree? If not, why not?
- What military training courses did you take? How did you do in these courses? How are they relevant to this job?
- Did you take any correspondence courses? What were they?
- Why did you attend _____ University (College or School)?
- Why did you major in _____?
- What was your grade point average?
- What subjects did you enjoy the most? The least? Why?
- What leadership positions did you hold?
- How did you finance your education?
- If you started all over, what would you change about your education?
- Why were your grades so low? So high?
- Did you do the best you could in school? If not, why not?
- What additional education/training did you receive in the Army?

- What plans do you have to continue your education?
- What new skills do you hope to acquire through education and training during the next five years?

Work Experience

- How many different jobs have you held?
- What were your major achievements in each of your past jobs?
- What did you do in the Army?
- How does your Army experience relate to this job?
- What did you enjoy the most about your Army career? The least?
- What is your typical work day like?
- What functions do you enjoy doing the most?
- What did you like about your boss? Dislike?
- Which job did you enjoy the most? Why? Which job did you enjoy the least? Why?
- Have you ever been fired? Why?

Career Goals

- Why did you decide to leave the Army?
- Why do you want to join our organization?
- Why do you think you are qualified for this position?
- Why are you looking for another job?
- Why do you want to make a career change?
- What ideally would you like to do?
- Why should we hire you?
- How would you improve our operations?
- What do you want to be doing five years from now?
- How much do you want to be making five years from now?
- What are your short-range and long-range career goals?
- If you could choose your job and organization, where would you go?
- What other jobs and companies are you considering?
- When will you be ready to begin work?
- How do you feel about relocating, traveling, working over-time, and spending weekends in the office?
- What attracted you to our organization?

Personality and Other Concerns

- Tell me about yourself.
- What are your major weaknesses? Your major strengths?
- What causes you to lose your temper?
- What do you do in your spare time? Any hobbies?
- What types of books do you read?
- What role does your family play in your career?
- How well do you work under pressure? In meeting deadlines?
- Tell me about your management philosophy.
- How much initiative do you take?
- What types of people do you prefer working with?
- How _____(creative, analytical, tactful, etc.) are you?
- If you could change your life, what would you do differently?

HANDLE OBJECTIONS AND NEGATIVES WITH EASE

Interviewers must have a healthy skepticism of job candidates. They expect people to exaggerate their competencies and overstate what they will do for the employer. They sometimes encounter dishonest applicants, and many people they hire fail to meet their expectations. Being realists who have made poor hiring decisions before, they want to know why they should *not* hire you. Although they do not always ask you these questions, they think about them nonetheless:

- Why should I hire you?
- What do you really want?
- What can you really do for me?
- What are your weaknesses?
- What problems will I have with you?

Underlying these questions are specific employers' objections to hiring you:

- You're not as good as you say you are; you probably hyped your resume or lied about yourself.
- I'm not sure someone with Army experience will fit in here.
- All you want is a job, a paycheck, and security.
- You have weaknesses like the rest of us. Is it alcohol, sex, drugs, finances, shiftlessness, petty politics?

- You'll probably want my job in another 5 months.
- You won't stay long with us. You'll probably join the competition or become the competition.

As noted in Chapter 2 (Myth 18 on pages 22-24), some employers have specific objections to hiring ex-military personnel. Employers raise such suspicions and objections because it is difficult to trust strangers in the employment game; many have been "burned" before by excellent "role playing" applicants—those who write excellent resumes and perform well in the job interview but then disappoint employers on the job. Indeed, there is an alarming rise in the number of individuals lying on their resumes or falsifying their credentials.

How can you best handle employers' objections? You must first recognize their biases and stereotypes and then *raise* their expectations. You do this by stressing your strengths and avoiding your weaknesses. You must be impeccably honest in doing so.

Your answers to employers' questions should be positive and emphasize your *strengths*. Remember, the interviewer wants to know what's wrong with you—your *weaknesses*. When answering questions, both the *substance* and *form* of your answers should be positive. For example, such words as "couldn't," "can't," "won't," and "don't" may create a negative tone and distract from the positive and enthusiastic image you are trying to create. While you cannot eliminate all negative words, at least recognize that the type of words you use makes a difference and therefore word choice should be better managed. Compare your reactions to the following interview answers:

QUESTION: **Why do you want to leave your present job?**

ANSWER 1:   *After serving in the Army for twenty years, I'm burned out. Morale isn't good and promotions are slow. I really don't like soldiering any more.*

ANSWER 2:   *After serving in the Army for twenty years, I've learned a great deal about leadership and teamwork. I have been given lots of responsibility for someone my age and demonstrated that I could handle it, even under high stress situations. While I'm very proud of my military service, it's time for me to return to the civilian world and apply my skills and experience in that*

> *environment. I'm ready to take on more respon-*
> *sibilities as part my professional growth.*

Which one has the greatest impact in terms of projecting positives and strengths? The first answer communicates too many negatives. The second answer is positive and upbeat in its orientation toward skills, accomplishments, and the future.

In addition to choosing positive words, select *content information* which is positive and *adds* to the interviewer's knowledge about you. Avoid simplistic "yes/no" answers; they say nothing about you. Instead, provide information which explains your reasons and motivations behind specific events or activities. For example, how do you react to these two factual answers?

QUESTION: **I see from your resume that you've been in the Army for twelve years. Are you one of those being affected by the Army's recent downsizing?**

ANSWER 1:   *Yes, that's correct.*

ANSWER 2:   *The Army's downsizing has given me the oppor-tunity to leave the military while I'm young. Although I've enjoyed the time I have served in the Army, I believe that now is the right time to take advantage of the skills I have learned and apply my knowledge in a civilian setting. I'm excited about starting a new career.*

Let's try another question reflecting possible objections to hiring you:

QUESTION: **Your background bothers me somewhat. You've been with the Army over 10 years. We are a profit-oriented organization. Why should I hire you?**

ANSWER 1:   *I can understand that.*

ANSWER 2:   *I understand your hesitation in hiring someone with my background. I would too, if I were you. Yes, many people don't do well in different*

> *occupational settings. But I don't believe I have that problem. As a member of the Army, I'm used to working with people. I work until the job gets done, which often means long hours and on weekends. I'm very concerned with achieving results. But most important, I've done a great deal of thinking about my goals. I've researched your organization as well as many others. From what I have learned, this is exactly what I want to do, and your organization is the one I'm most interested in joining. I know I will do a good job, as I have always done in the past.*

The first answer is incomplete. It misses an important opportunity to give evidence that you have resolved this issue in a positive manner which is clearly reflected in the second response.

The most difficult challenge to your positive strategy comes when the interviewer asks you to describe your negatives or weaknesses:

QUESTION: **We all have our negatives and weaknesses. What are some of yours?**

You can handle this question in any of five different ways, yet still give positive information on yourself:

STRATEGIES FOR HANDLING NEGATIVES

1. **Discuss a negative which is not related to the job being considered:**

   I don't enjoy accounting. I know it's important, but I find it boring. Even at home my wife takes care of our books. Marketing is what I like to do. Other people are much better at bookkeeping than I am. I'm glad this job doesn't involve any accounting!

2. **Discuss a negative which the interviewer already knows:**

   Since I spent a great deal of time working in the Army and pursuing advanced degrees, I lack extensive civilian work experience. However, I believe my experience and education have prepared me well for this job. My leadership experience in the Army taught me how to work with people, organize, and solve problems. I write well and quickly. My research experience helped me analyze, synthesize, and develop strategies.

3. Discuss a negative which you have improved upon:

I used to get over-committed and miss important deadlines. But then I read a book on time management and learned what I was doing wrong. Within three weeks I reorganized my use of time and found I could meet my deadlines with little difficulty. The quality of my work also improved. Now I have time to work out at the gym each day. I'm doing more and feeling better at the same time.

4. Discuss a "negative" which can also be a positive:

I'm somewhat of a workaholic. I love my work, but I sometime neglect my family because of it. I've been going into the office seven days a week, and I often put in 12 hour days. I'm now learning to better manage my time.

5. Discuss a negative outside yourself:

I don't feel that there is anything seriously wrong with me. Like most people, I have my ups and downs. But overall I have a positive outlook, feel good about myself and what I've accomplished so far in my life. However, I am somewhat concerned how you might view my wanting to change careers. I want to assure you that I'm not making this change on a whim. I've taken my time in thinking through the issues and taking a hard look at what I do well and enjoy doing. Like a lot of young people, I guess I didn't have much life experience when I started my Army career ten years ago. However, as I got more experience and had opportunities to become a squad/platoon/company leader, my interest in management training developed. I found that I not only enjoyed those activities, but that I had some natural talent for them. While I've enjoyed my years in the Army, I am committed to finding work that will enable me to build on these experience.

All of these examples stress the basic point about effective interviewing. Your single best strategy for managing the interview is to *emphasize your strengths and positives.* Questions come in several forms. Anticipate these questions, especially the negative ones, and practice positive responses in order to project your best self in an interview situation.

ILLEGAL QUESTIONS

Other questions are illegal, but some employers ask them nonetheless. Consider how you would respond to these questions:

- Are you married, divorced, separated, or single?
- How old are you?
- Do you go to church regularly?
- Do you have many debts?
- Do you own or rent your home?
- What social and political organizations do you belong to?
- What does your spouse think about your career?
- Are you living with anyone?
- Are you practicing birth control?
- Were you ever arrested?
- How much insurance do you have?
- How much do you weigh?
- How tall are you?

Don't get upset and say "That's an illegal question...I refuse to answer it!" While you may be perfectly right in saying so, this response lacks tact, which may be what the employer is looking for. For example, if you are divorced and the interviewer asks about your divorce, you might respond with "Does a divorce have a direct bearing on the responsibilities of this position?" Some employers may ask such questions just to see how you react under stress. Others may do so out of ignorance of the law. Whatever the case, be prepared to tactfully handle these questions.

ASKING QUESTIONS

Interviewers expect candidates to ask intelligent questions concerning the organization and the nature of the work. Moreover, you need information and should indicate your interest in the employer by asking questions. Try to avoid asking self-centered questions which indicate you are primarily interested in knowing about salaries, benefits, perks, and advancement opportunities. Keep your questions employer- and job-centered. Consider asking some of these questions if they haven't been answered early in the interview:

- Please tell me about the duties and responsibilities of this job.
- How long has this position been in the organization?
- How does this position relate to other positions within this organization?
- What would be the ideal type of person for this position? Skills? Personality? Working style? Background?
- Can you tell me about the people who have been in this position before? Backgrounds? Promotions? Terminations?
- Whom would I be working with in this position?
- Who would be my first and second level managers and what are their positions?
- Please tell me something about these people? Strengths? Weaknesses? Performance expectations?
- What am I expected to accomplish during the first year?
- How will I be evaluated?
- Are promotions and raises usually tied to performance criteria?
- Are there other ways people get promoted and advance in this organization?
- Please tell me how this operates?
- What is the normal salary range for such a position?
- Based on your experience, what type of problems would someone new in this position likely encounter?
- I'm interested in your career with this organization. When did you start? What are your plans for the future?
- What is particularly unique about working in this organization?
- What does the future look like for this organization?

You may want to write your questions on a 3 x 5 card and take them with you to the interview. While it is best to memorize the jist of your questions, you may need to refer to your list when the interviewer asks you if you have any questions. You might do this by saying: "Yes, I jotted down a few questions which I want to make sure I ask you before leaving." Then pull out your card and refer to the questions.

DRESS APPROPRIATELY

Appearance is the first thing you communicate to others. Before you have a chance to speak, others notice how you dress and accordingly draw certain conclusions about your personality and competence. Indeed, research shows that appearance makes the greatest difference when an evaluator has little information about the other person. This is precisely the situation you find yourself in at the start of the interview.

Many people object to having their capabilities evaluated on the basis of their appearance and manner of dress. "But that is not fair," they argue. "People should be hired on the basis of their ability to do the job—not on how they look." But debating the lack of merit or complaining about the unfairness of such behavior does not alter reality. Like it or not, people do make initial judgments about others based on their appearance. Since you cannot alter this fact and bemoaning it will get you nowhere, it is best to learn to use it to your advantage. If you learn to effectively manage your image, you can convey marvelous messages regarding your authority, credibility, and competence.

Some estimates indicate that as much as 65 percent of the hiring decision may be based on the nonverbal aspects of the interview! Employers sometimes refer to this phenomenon with such terms as "chemistry," "body warmth," or that "gut feeling" the individual is right for the job. This correlates with findings of communication studies that approximately 65 percent of a message is communicated nonverbally. The remaining 35 percent is communicated verbally.

Rules of the Game

You know how important proper appearance is for success in the Army. You are accustomed to projecting a "spit and polish" image and wearing uniforms. However, this is not the same image and dress required in the civilian world where different style, color, and accessorized suits rather than uniforms constitute proper dress. In fact, since many Army members are not familiar with the nuances of civilian dress and appearance, many face difficulties in selecting the proper colors, fabrics, and materials as well as in choosing the right suits, shirts, ties, blouses, skirts, and accessories for putting together a professional wardrobe. If inappropriately selected, your wardrobe could send the wrong messages during the job interview. You want to project a positive, professional image of success.

Knowing how to dress appropriately for the interview requires knowing important rules of the game. Like it or not, employers play by these rules. Once you know the rules, you at least can make a conscious choice whether or not you want to play. If you decide to play, you will stand a better chance of winning by using the often unwritten rules to your advantage.

Much has been written on how to dress professionally, especially since John Molloy first wrote his books on dress for success in the 1970s. While this approach has been criticized for promoting a "cookie cutter" or "carbon copy" image, it is still valid for most interview situations. The degree to which employers adhere to these rules, however, will depend on particular individuals and situations. Your job is to know when, where, and to what extent the rules apply to you. When in doubt, follow our general advice on looking professional.

Knowing and playing by the rules does not imply incompetent people get jobs simply by dressing the part. Rather, it means qualified and competent job applicants can gain an extra edge over a field of other qualified, competent individuals by dressing to convey positive professional images.

Winning the Game

Much advice has been written about how to dress for success—some of it excellent. However, there is a major flaw in most of the advice you encounter. Researchers on the subject have looked at how people in positions of power view certain colors for professional attire. Few have gone beyond this to note that colors do different things on different people. Various shades or clarities of a color or combinations of contrast between light and dark colors when worn together may be unenhancing to some individuals and actually diminish that person's "power look."

If you combine the results of research done by John Molloy on how colors relate to one's power look and that done by JoAnne Nicholson and Judy Lewis-Crum as explained in their book *Color Wonderful* (New York: Bantam) on how colors relate to people as unique individuals, you can achieve a win-win situation. You can retain your individuality and look your most enhanced while, at the same time, achieving a look of success, power, and competence.

Your Winning Appearance

The key to effective dressing is to know how to relate the clothing you put on your body to your own natural coloring. Once you know how to do this, most other dress and appearance decisions are relatively easy to make. Into which category does your coloring fit? Let's find out where you belong in terms of color type:

- **Contrast coloring:** If you are a contrast color type, you have a definite dark-light appearance. You have very dark brown or black hair and light to medium ivory or olive toned skin. Black men and women in this category will have clear light to dark skin tones and dark hair.

- **Light-bright coloring:** If you are of this color type, you have golden tones in your skin and golden tones in your blond or light to medium brown hair. Most of you had blond or light brown hair as children. Black men and women in this category will have clear golden skin in their face and dark hair.

- **Muted coloring:** If you are a muted color type, you have a definite brown-on-brown or red-on-brown appearance. Your skin tone is an ivory-beige, brown-beige, or golden-beige tone—that is, you have a beige skin with a golden-brown cast. Your hair could be red or light to dark brown with camel, bronze, or red highlights. Black men and women in this category will have golden or brown skin tones and dark hair.

- **Gentle coloring:** If you are of this color type, you have a soft, gentle looking appearance. Your skin tone is a light ivory or pink-beige tone and your hair is ash blond or ash brown. You probably had blond or ash brown hair as a child. Black men and women in this category will have pink tones in their skin and dark hair.

There are also some individuals who may be a combination of two color types. If your skin tone falls in one category and your hair color in another, you are a combination color type.

However, if you are not certain which hair or skin tone is yours and are hence undecided as to which color type category you belong to, you may wish to contact Color 1 Associates by calling 1/800-523-8496 (2211 Washington Circle, NW, Washington, DC 20037). In addition, the *Color Wonderful* book includes a listing of professionally trained associates located nearest you.

A Color 1 associate can provide you with an individualized color chart that allows you to wear every color in the spectrum, but in your best *shade* and *clarity* as well as written material telling you how you can combine your colors for the best amounts of contrast for your natural coloring (color type).

The color chart is an excellent one-time investment considering the costs of buying the wrong colored suit, shirt, or blouse. It will more than pay for itself if it contributes to an effective interview as you wear your suit in your best shade and put your clothing together to work with, rather than against, your natural coloring. It can help you convey positive images during those crucial initial minutes of the interview—as well as over a lifetime.

Images of Success

John Molloy has conducted extensive research on how individuals can dress effectively. Aimed at individuals already working in professional positions who want to communicate a success image, his advice is just as relevant for someone interviewing for a job.

Basic attire for men or women interviewing for a position is a suit. Let's look at appropriate suits in terms of color, fabric, and style. The suit color can make a difference in creating an image of authority and competence. The suit colors that make the strongest positive statements for you are *your shade* of gray in a medium to charcoal depth or *your shade* of blue in a medium to navy depth of color. However, you may choose a less authoritative look for some interview settings. Camel or beige are also considered proper colors for men's suits and women have an even greater color range. Generally even women should select fairly conservative colors for a job interview unless you are interviewing for a job in a field where non-conformity is considered a plus.

When selecting your suit, choose a shade that appears enhancing to you. Should you wear a blue-gray, a taupe-gray, or a shade in-between? Do you look better in a somewhat bright navy or a more toned-down navy; a blue navy or a black navy; a navy with a purple or a yellow base to it?

In general, most people will look better in somewhat blue grays than in grays that are closer to the taupe side of the spectrum. Most people will be enhanced by a navy that is not too bright or contain so much black that it is difficult to distinguish whether the color is navy or black. When selecting a beige or a camel, select a tone that complements your skin color. If your skin has pink tones, avoid beiges and camels that contain gold hues and select pink based beiges/camels that enhance your skin color. Similarly, those of you who have gold/olive tones to your skin should avoid the pink based camel and beiges.

Your suit(s) should be made of a natural fiber. A good blend of a natural fiber with some synthetic is acceptable as long as it has the "look" of the natural fiber. The very best suit fabrics are wool, wool blends, or fabrics that look like them. Even for the warmer summer months, men can find summer weight wool suits that are comfortable and look marvelous. They are your best buy. For really hot climates, a linen/silk fabric can work well. Normally a linen will have to be blended with another fiber, often a synthetic, in order to retain a pressed, neat look. The major disadvantage of pure linen is that it wrinkles. Women's suits also should be made of a natural fiber or have the "look" of a natural fiber. The very best winter-weight suit fabrics are wool or wool blends. For the warmer climates or the summer months, women will find few, if any, summer weight wool suits made for them. Hence linen, blended with a synthetic so it will not look as if it needs constant pressing or a good silk or silk blend are good choices. At present a lot of women's warm weather suits are made of rayon crepe blend. In good quality these can look fine, but buy carefully—inexpensive rayon suits can cheapen your image.

The style of your suit should be classic. It should be well-tailored and well-styled. Avoid suits that appear "trendy" unless you are applying for a job in a field such as arts or perhaps advertising. A conservative suit that has a timeless classic styling and also looks up-to-date will serve you best not only for the interview, but it will give you several years wear once you land the job.

Men should select a shirt color that is lighter than the color of their suit. Ken Karpinski's new book, *Red Socks Don't Work! Messages From the Real World About Men's Clothing* (filled with wonderful tips—all men can wear pleats; you should upgrade the color, design, and quality of your socks; select the right tie), and John Molloy's book on appearance and dress for men, *John Molloy's New Dress for Success*, go into great detail on shirts, ties, and practically everything you might wear or carry with you. We recommend both books over others because they are based on research rather than personal opinion and promotional fads.

When deciding on your professional wardrobe, always buy clothes to last and buy quality. For women, quality means buying silk blouses if you can afford them. Keep in mind not only the price of the blouse itself, but the cleaning bill. There are many blouse fabrics that have the look and feel of silk. Silk or a fabric that has the look and feel of silk are the fabrics for blouses to go with your suits. Choose your blouses in your most flattering shades and clarity of color. Although somewhat dated, John Molloy's book on appearance and dress for women, *The Woman's Dress for Success Book*, goes into great detail on almost anything you might wear or carry with you to the interview or on the job.

A popular look for women today combines a plaid suit jacket with a solid skirt of one of the jacket colors. Although a bit less powerful than the matched jacket and skirt, it can be a great look for the applicant and a refreshing change for an employer used to seeing similar outfits on all the applicants. Try putting the plaid jacket over a solid matching color blouse and skirt. The matched solid blouse and skirt form a base for the plaid jacket that conveys both a flattering and professional look.

Always buy clothes to last and buy quality.

Give your outfit a more "finished and polished" look by accessorizing it effectively. Collect silk scarves and necklaces of semiprecious stones in your suit colors. Wear scarves and necklaces with your suits and blouses in such a way that they repeat the color of the suit. For example, a woman wearing a navy suit and a red silk blouse could accent the look by wearing a necklace of navy sodalite beads or a silk scarf that has navy as a predominate color. If you form a base by wearing a matching solid color blouse and skirt with a plaid suit jacket, you have a choice of accessorizing with a gold or silver necklace or a necklace or solid color scarf using one of the jacket colors.

APPEAR LIKABLE

Remember, most people invited to a job interview have already been "screened in." They supposedly possess the basic qualifications for the job, such as education and work experience. At this point employers will look for several qualities in the candidates—honesty, credibility, intelligence, competence, enthusiasm, spontaneity, friendliness, and likability. Much of the message communicating these qualities will be conveyed through your dress as well as through other nonverbal behaviors.

In the end, employers hire people they *like* and who will interact well on an interpersonal basis with the rest of the staff. Therefore, you should communicate that you are a likable candidate who can get along well with others. You can communicate these messages by engaging in several nonverbal behaviors. Four of the most important ones include:

1. **Sit with a very slight forward lean toward the interviewer.**
   It should be so slight as to be almost imperceptible. If not
   overdone, it communicates your interest in what the interviewer
   is saying.

2. **Make eye contact frequently, but don't overdo it.** Good eye
   contact establishes rapport with the interviewer. You will be
   perceived as more trustworthy if you will look at the interviewer as you ask and answer questions. To say someone has "shifty
   eyes" or cannot "look us in the eye" is to imply they may not
   be completely honest. To have a direct, though moderate eye
   gaze, conveys interest, as well as trustworthiness.

3. **A moderate amount of smiling will also help reinforce your
   positive image.** You should smile enough to convey your
   positive attitude, but not so much that you will not be taken
   seriously. Some people naturally smile often and others hardly
   ever smile. Monitor your behavior or ask a friend to give you
   frank feedback.

4. **Try to convey interest and enthusiasm through your vocal
   inflections.** Your tone of voice can say a lot about you and how
   interested you are in the interviewer and organization.

CLOSE THE INTERVIEW

Be prepared to end the interview. Many people don't know when or how
to close interviews. They go on and on until someone breaks an uneasy
moment of silence with an indication that it is time to go.

Interviewers normally will initiate the close by standing, shaking
hands, and thanking you for coming to the interview. Don't end by
saying "Goodbye and thank you." You should summarize the interview
in terms of your interests, strengths, and goals. Briefly restate your
qualifications and continuing interest in working with the employer. At
this point it is proper to ask the interviewer about selection plans:

"When do you anticipate making your final decision?"

Follow this question with your final one:

"May I call you next week (or whatever is appropriate in

response to your question about timing of the final decision) to
inquire about my status?"

By taking the initiative in this manner, the employer will be prompted to
clarify your status soon, and you will have an opportunity to talk to her
further.

Many interviewers will ask you for a list of references. Be sure to
prepare such a list prior to the interview. Include the names, addresses,
and phone numbers of four individuals who will give you positive
professional and personal recommendations.

REMEMBER TO FOLLOW-UP

Once you have been interviewed, be sure to follow through to get nearer
to the job offer. One of the best follow-up methods is the thank you
letter; you will find examples of these letters at the end of Chapter
9. After talking to the employer over the telephone or in a face-to-face
interview, send a thank you letter. This letter should be typed on good
quality bond paper. In this letter express your gratitude for the opportunity to interview. Re-state your interest in the position and highlight any
particularly noteworthy points made in your conversation or anything you
wish to further clarify. Close the letter by mentioning that you will call
in a few days to inquire about the employer's decision. When you do
this, the employer should remember you as a thoughtful person.

If you call and the employer has not yet made a decision, follow
through with another phone call in a few days. Send any additional
information to the employer which may enhance your application. You
might also want to ask one of your references to call the employer to
further recommend you for the position. However, don't engage in
overkill by making a pest of yourself. You want to tactfully communicate
two things to the employer at this point: (1) you are interested in the job,
and (2) you will do a good job.

A good way to keep on top of your interviews is to maintain a record
of each interview. We recommend developing an interview tracking form,
similar to the example on page 243.

For more information on developing interviewing skills, including
follow-up and thank you letters, look for the Krannichs' *Interview for
Success, Dynamite Answers to Interview Questions, Dynamite Tele-
Search, Dynamite Salary Negotiations,* and *Job Search Letters That Get
Results.* These books go into great detail on all aspects of job interviews.

Firm's Name	Date Contacted	POC's Name	POC's Phone	Date Resume Mailed	Date of First Interview	Suit Worn	Date of Thank You Letter

13 | NEGOTIATE SALARY & BENEFITS

*T*hroughout your job search you need to seriously consider several questions about your financial value and future income. What, for example, are you worth? How much is your total Army compensation worth in equivalent civilian pay? How much should you be paid for your work? How can you demonstrate your value to an employer? What dollar value will employers assign to you? What are you willing to accept?

After impressing upon the employer that you are the right person for the job, the bottom line becomes money—your talent and labor in exchange for the employer's cash and benefits. How, then, will you deal with these questions in order to get more than employers initially offer?

You think you are worth a lot in the civilian work world—more than you have been getting paid in the Army. But when it comes to questions of compensation, you must go beyond wishful thinking. As we will see in this chapter, you need to know how to value both the job and your skills and then translate these values into specific dollar figures.

APPROACH SALARIES AS NEGOTIABLE

If you've always worked for the Army, your salary has been determined by your rank and years of service rather than by your negotiating skills. This situation is about to change as you enter the corporate world where rank and years of service are less important than your performance.

Salary is one of the most important yet least understood considerations in the job search. Many individuals do well in handling all interview questions except the salary question. They are either too shy to talk about money or they believe you must take what you are offered—because salary is predetermined by employers. As a result, many applicants may be paid much less than they are worth. Over the years, they will lose thousands of dollars by having failed to properly negotiate their salaries. Indeed, most employees are probably underpaid by $2,000 to $5,000 because they failed to properly negotiate their initial salaries.

Salary is seldom predetermined. Most employers have some flexibility to negotiate salary. While most employers do not try to exploit applicants, neither do they want to pay applicants more than what they are willing to accept.

Salaries are usually assigned to positions or jobs rather than to individuals. But not everyone is of equal value in performing the job; some are more productive than others. Since individual performance differs, you should attempt to establish your value in the eyes of the employer rather than accept a salary figure for the job. The art of salary negotiation will help you do this.

LOOK TO YOUR FINANCIAL FUTURE

We all have financial needs which our salary helps to meet. But salary has other significance too. It is an indicator of our worth to others. It also influences our future income. Therefore, it should be treated as one of the most serious considerations in the job interview.

The salary you receive today will influence your future earnings. Yearly salary increments will most likely be figured as a percentage of your base salary rather than reflect your actual job performance. Expect employers to offer you a salary similar to the one you earned in your last job. Once they learn what you made in your previous job, they will probably offer you no more than a 10% to 15% increase. If you hope to improve your income in the long run, then you must be willing to negotiate your salary from a position of strength.

MILITARY PAY AND CIVILIAN SALARY PARITY

Members of the military often undervalue themselves in the civilian work world because they tend to equate salary with base pay rates. If you've received base housing or a housing allowance, you know this benefit can be considerable; it translates into a specific dollar figure which should be added to your base salary. For example, if your base pay as an NCO is $30,000 a year, you should include another 20 percent in benefits to arrive at a total compensation figure that would be equivalent to a civilian salary—around $36,000. Commissioned officers making $50,000 a year in base pay should figure their total compensation to be near $60,000. If you only use your base pay as your current salary figure, you may undervalue yourself to civilian employers.

Always include your military benefits when figuring your total Army compensation, but don't overvalue. When asked about your current salary, you need to respond with a total compensation figure. If you forget to do this, you may undersell yourself by at least 20 percent.

PREPARE FOR THE SALARY QUESTION

You should be well prepared to deal with the question of salary anytime during your job search but especially during the job interview. Based on your library research (Chapter 12) as well as salary information gained from your networking activities (Chapter 13), you should know the approximate salary range for the position you are seeking. If you fail to gather this salary information prior to the screening or job interview, you may do yourself a disservice by accepting too low a figure or pricing yourself out of consideration. It is always best to be informed so you will be in better control to negotiate salary and benefits.

KEEP SALARY ISSUES TO THE VERY END

The question of salary may be raised anytime during the job search. Employers may want you to state a salary expectation figure on an application form, in a cover letter, or over the telephone. Most frequently, however, employers will talk about salary during the employment interview. If at all possible, keep the salary question open until the very last, and remember, you always talk about your total Army compensation rather than your base pay. Even with application forms, cover letters, and telephone screening interviews, try to delay the discussion of salary by stating "open" or "negotiable." After all, the ultimate purpose of your job search activities is to demonstrate your *value* to employers. You should not attempt to translate your value into dollar figures until you have had a chance to convince the employer of your worth. This is best done near the end of the job interview.

Salary should be the last major item you discuss with the employer.

Although employers will have a salary figure or range in mind when they interview you, they still want to know your salary expectations. How much will you cost them? Will it be more or less than the job is worth? Employers preferably want to hire individuals for the least amount possible. You, on the other hand, want to be hired for as much as possible. Obviously, there is room for disagreement and unhappiness as well as negotiation and compromise.

One easy way employers screen you in or out of consideration is to raise the salary question early in the interview. A standard question is: "What are your salary requirements?" When asked, don't answer with a specific dollar figure. You should aim at establishing your value in the eyes of the employer prior to talking about a figure. If you give the employer a salary figure at this stage, you are likely to lock yourself into it, regardless of how much you impress the employer or what you find out about the duties and responsibilities of the job. Therefore, salary should be the last major item you discuss with the employer.

You should never ask about salary prior to being offered the job. Let the employer initiate the salary question. And when he or she does, take your time. Don't appear too anxious. While you may know—based on your previous research—approximately what the employer will offer, try to get the employer to state a figure first. If you do this, you will be in a stronger negotiating position.

HANDLE THE SALARY QUESTION WITH TACT

When the salary question arises, assuming you cannot or do not want to put it off until later, your first step should be to clearly summarize the job responsibilities/duties as you understand them. At this point you are attempting to do three things:

1. Seek clarification from the interviewer as to the actual job and all it involves.

2. Emphasize the level of skills required in the most positive way. In other words, you emphasize the value and worth of this position to the organization and subtly this may help support the actual salary figure that the interviewer or you later provide.

3. Focus attention on your value in relation to the requirements of the position—the critical linkage for negotiating salary from a position of strength.

You might do this, for example, by saying,

> *As I understand it, I would report directly to the vice-president in charge of marketing and I would have full authority for marketing decisions that involved expenditures of up to $50,000. I would have a staff of five people—a secretary, two copywriters, and two marketing assistants.*

Such a summary statement establishes for both you and the interviewer that (1) this position reports to the highest levels of authority; (2) this position is responsible for decision-making involving fairly large sums of money; and (3) this position involves supervision of staff.

Although you may not explicitly draw the connection, you are emphasizing the value of this position to the organization. This position should be worth a lot more than one in which the hiree will report to the marketing manager, be required to get approval for all expenditures over $100, and has no staff—just access to the secretarial pool! By doing this you will focus the salary question (that you have not yet responded to) around the exact work you must perform on the job in exchange for salary and benefits. You have also seized the opportunity to focus on the value of the person who will be selected to fill this vacancy.

Your conversation might go something like this. The employer poses the question:

What are your salary requirements?

Your first response should be to summarize the responsibilities of the position. You might begin with a summary statement followed by a question:

> *Let me see if I understand all that is involved with this position and job. I would be expected to _____. Have I covered everything or are there some other responsibilities I should know about?*

This response focuses the salary question around the value of the position in relation to you. After the interviewer responds to your final question, answer the initial salary expectation question in this manner:

> *What is the normal salary range in your company for a position such as this?*

This question establishes the value as well as the range for the position or job—two important pieces of information you need before proceeding further into the salary negotiation stage. The employer normally will give you the requested salary range. Once he or she does, depending on how you feel about the figure, you can follow up with one more question.

> *What would be the normal salary range for someone with my qualifications?*

This question further establishes the value for the individual versus the position. This line of questioning will yield the salary expectations of the employer without revealing your desired salary figure or range. It also will indicate whether the employer distinguishes between individuals and positions when establishing salary figures.

REACH COMMON GROUND AND AGREEMENT

After finding out what the employer is prepared to offer, you have several choices. First, you can indicate that his or her figure is acceptable to you and thus conclude your final interview. Second, you can haggle for more money in the hope of reaching an acceptable compromise. Third, you can delay final action by asking for more time to consider the figure. Finally, you can tell the employer the figure is unacceptable and leave.

The first and the last options indicate you are either too eager or playing hard-to-get. We recommend the second and third options. If you decide to reach agreement on salary in this interview, haggle in a professional manner. You can do this best by establishing a salary range from which to bargain in relation to the employer's salary range. For example, if the employer indicates that he or she is prepared to offer $30,000 to $35,000, you should establish common ground for negotiation by placing your salary range into the employer's range. Your response to the employer's $30,000 to $35,000 range might be:

> *Yes, that does come near what I was expecting. I was thinking more in terms of $35,000 to $40,000.*

You, in effect, place the top of the employer's range into the bottom of your range. At this point you should be able to negotiate a salary of $37,000 to $38,000, depending on how much flexibility the employer has with salaries. Most employers have more flexibility than they admit.

Once you have placed your expectations at the top of the employer's salary range, you need to emphasize your value with *supports,* such as examples, illustrations, descriptions, definitions, statistics, comparisons, or testimonials. It is not enough to simply state you were "thinking" in a certain range; you must state why you believe you are worth what you want. Using statistics and comparisons as your supports, you might say, for example:

> *The salary surveys I have studied indicate that for the position of* _____ *in this industry and region the salary is between $60,000 and $65,000. Since, as we have discussed, I have extensive experience in all the areas you outlined, I would not need training in the job duties themselves—just a brief orientation to the operating procedures you use here at* _____ *. I'm sure I could be up and running in this job within a week or two. Taking everything in consideration—especially my skills and experience and what I see as my future contributions here—I really feel a salary of $65,000 is fair compensation. Is this possible here at* _____ *?*

Another option is to ask the employer for time to think about the salary offer. You want to sleep on it for a day or two. A common professional courtesy is to give you at least 48 hours to consider an offer. During this time, you may want to carefully examine the job. Is it worth what you are being offered? Can you do better? What are other employers offering for comparable positions? If one or two other employers are considering you for a job, let this employer know his or her job is not the only one under consideration. Let the employer know you may be in demand elsewhere. This should give you a better bargaining position. Contact the other employers and let them know you have a job offer and that you would like to have your application status with them clarified before you make any decisions with the other employer. Depending on how much flexibility an employer may have to accelerate a hiring decision, you may be able to go back to the first employer with another job offer. With a second job offer in hand, you should greatly enhance your bargaining position.

In both recommended options, you need to keep in mind that you should always negotiate from a position of knowledge and strength—not because of need or greed. Learn about salaries for your occupation, establish your value, discover what the employer is willing to pay, and negotiate in a professional manner. For how you negotiate your salary will affect your future relations with the employer. In general, applicants who negotiate well will be treated well on the job.

How you negotiate your salary will affect your future relations with the employer.

TREAT BENEFITS AS STANDARD

Many employer will try to impress candidates with the benefits offered by the company. These might include retirement, bonuses, stock options, medical and life insurance, and cost of living adjustments. If the employer includes these benefits in the salary negotiations, do not be overly impressed. Most benefits are standard—they come with the job. In addition, you may already receive certain benefits from the Army which you don't need duplicated; this puts you in an even stronger negotiating position, especially if you already receive medical benefits through the Army. An employer should be willing to give you a higher salary if you decline certain standard benefits. For example, medical benefits can cost a civilian employer $400.00 per month per employee. When negotiating salary, it is best to talk about a specific dollar figure rather than lump benefits into a total compensation figure.

On the other hand, if the salary offered by the employer does not meet your expectations, but you still want the job, you might try to negotiate for some benefits which are not considered standard. These might include longer paid vacations, some flextime, and profit sharing.

OFFER A RENEGOTIATION OPTION

You should make sure your future salary reflects your value. One approach to doing this is to reach an agreement to renegotiate your salary at a later date, perhaps in another six to eight months. Use this technique especially when you feel the final salary offer is less than what you are worth, but you want to accept the job. Employers often will agree to this provision since they have nothing to lose and much to gain if you are as productive as you tell them.

However, be prepared to renegotiate in both directions—up and down. If the employer does not want to give you the salary figure you want, you can create good will by proposing to negotiate the higher salary figure down after six months, if your performance does not meet the employer's expectations. On the other hand, you may accept this lower figure with the provision that the two of you will negotiate your salary up after six months, if you exceed the employer's expectations. It is preferable to start out high and negotiate down rather than start low and negotiate up.

Renegotiation provisions stress one very important point: you want to be paid on the basis of your performance. You demonstrate your professionalism, self-confidence, and competence by negotiating in this manner. More important, you ensure that the question of your monetary value will not be closed in the future. As you negotiate the present, you also negotiate your future with this as well as other employers.

TAKE TIME BEFORE ACCEPTING

You should accept an offer only after reaching a salary agreement. If you jump at an offer, you may appear needy. Take time to consider your options. Remember, you are committing your time and effort in exchange for money and status. Is this the job you really want? Take some time to think about the offer before giving the employer a definite answer. But don't play hard-to-get and thereby create ill-will with your new employer.

While considering the offer, ask yourself several of the same questions you asked at the beginning of your job search:

- What do I want to be doing five years from now?

- How will this job affect my personal life?

- Do I want to travel?

- Do I know enough about the employer and the future of this organization?

- How have previous occupants of this position fared? Why did they have problems?

- Are there other jobs I'm considering which would better meet my goals?

Accepting a job is serious business. If you make a mistake, you could be locked into a very unhappy situation for a long time.

If you receive one job offer while considering another, you will be able to compare relative advantages and disadvantages. You also will have some external leverage for negotiating salary and benefits. While you should not play games, let the employer know you have alternative job offers. This communicates that you are in demand, others also know your value, and the employer's price is not the only one in town. Use this leverage to negotiate your salary, benefits, and job responsibilities.

If you get a job offer but you are considering other employers, let the others know you have a job offer. Telephone them to inquire about your status as well as inform them of the job offer. Sometimes this will prompt employers to make a hiring decision sooner than anticipated. In addition you will be informing them that you are in demand; they should seriously consider you before you get away!

Some job seekers play a bluffing game by telling employers they have alternative job offers even though they don't. Some candidates do this and get away with it. We don't recommend this approach. Not only is it dishonest, it will work to your disadvantage if the employer learns that you were lying. But more important, you should be selling yourself on the basis of your strengths rather than your deceit and greed. If you can't sell yourself honestly, don't expect to get along well on the job. When you compromise your integrity, you demean your value to others and yourself.

Your job search is not over with the job offer and acceptance. You need to set the stage. Be thoughtful by sending your new employer a nice thank-you letter. As outlined at the end of Chapter 9, this is one of the most effective letters to write for getting your new job off on the right foot. The employer will remember you as a thoughtful individual whom he looks forward to working with.

The whole point of our job search methods is to clearly communicate to employers that you are competent and worthy of being paid top dollar. If you follow our advice, you should do very well with employers in interviews and negotiating your salary as well as working on the job.

TRANSLATE YOUR VALUE
INTO PRODUCTIVITY FOR OTHERS

One final word of advice. Many job seekers have unrealistic salary expectations and exaggerated notions of their worth to potential employers. Furthermore, some occupational groups appear overpaid for the type of skills they use and the quality of the work they produce. In recent years several unions began renegotiating contracts in a new direction—downwards. Unions gave back salary increases and benefits won in previous years in order to maintain job security in the face of deepening recessions. Workers in many industries were not in a position to further increase their salaries. Many employers believed salaries had become extremely inflated in relation to profits. Such salaries, in turn, created even more inflated salary expectations among job hunters.

Given the declining power of unions, turbulent economic conditions, the increased prevalence of "give-back" schemes, and greater emphasis on productivity and performance in the work place, many employers are reluctant to negotiate salaries upwards prior to seeing you perform in their organization. Especially in a tight job market, many employers feel they can maintain their ground on salary offers. After all, as more well qualified candidates glut the job market, many job seekers are willing to take lower salaries.

Given this situation, you may find it increasingly difficult to negotiate better salaries with employers. You will need to stress your value more than ever. For example, if you think you are worth $40,000 a year in salary, will you be productive enough to generate $300,000 of business for the company to justify that amount? If you can't translate your salary expectations into dollars and cents profits for the employer, you simply are not prepared to negotiate from strength. The employer will have the advantage because you failed to communicate what you and the job are worth. If you invest a few hours in following the salary negotiation strategies outlined in this chapter, you will probably be rewarded with thousands of dollars in additional income in the coming years.

14

RELOCATE TO THE RIGHT COMMUNITY

*R*elocation is nothing new to you. You've probably relocated several times already, courtesy of the U.S. Army. If you are still in the Army, your last Army-sponsored relocation may be your most important one. Hopefully, this move will be to a place where you will begin a new and exciting career.

Indeed, most people change residences as frequently as they change jobs. One in every five families changes residences each year; the average person changes addresses eleven times during their life. Each year approximately 7 million Americans move to another state. As you well know from military transfers, relocation also means changing jobs and lifestyles. What's different this time is that you have greater freedom to choose where you want to live and work. So let's do it right!

255

MILITARY BASES, BENEFITS, AND RELOCATION OPTIONS

Many separating Army members choose to relocate to areas where they will have access to military facilities. Since you may be eligible to use such facilities, you probably want access to the commissary, post exchange, hospital, and recreational facilities. In addition, you may prefer living in communities where you can associate with other Army members. If these are important relocation concerns, make sure you research the present base closure and alignment situation. Many military bases are closing and thus shutting down facilities for military retirees. For a good overview of current bases, we recommend getting a copy of Dan Cragg's *Guide to Military Installations* (Mechanicsburg, PA: Stackpole Books). This comprehensive guide to Army, Navy, Air Force, and Marine Corps installations in the United States and overseas includes detailed information on facilities, services, and attractions.

Keep in mind that many military installations are found in small communities that offer few job opportunities; thus, you may pay a high price in lost income just to exercise your military base privileges. Taking a job that pays $30,000 less so you can gain $5,000 in base benefits may not be to your long-term career nor financial benefit. Therefore, you may want to focus your job search on large metropolitan communities, such as Washington, DC, Los Angeles, San Diego, San Francisco, Honolulu, Seattle, Las Vegas, Phoenix, Denver, San Antonio, Omaha, St. Louis, Chicago, Memphis, Miami, and Norfolk, which offer excellent base facilities as well as good paying job opportunities.

RELOCATE TO A NEW CAREER

Where will you be working and living next year, five years, or ten years from today? If you had the freedom to pick up and move today, where would you love to live? Choosing where you want to live can be just as important as choosing what you want to do. Such a choice involves making career and lifestyle changes.

When you conduct a job search, you do so by targeting specific employers in particular communities. In most cases, individuals will conduct their job search in the same community in which they live. For other people, moving to another community is desirable for career and lifestyle purposes. And for others, staying in their present community is preferable to taking any job in another community.

Whatever your choices, you should weigh the relative costs and benefits of relocating to a new community where job opportunities for someone with your skills may be plentiful. If you live in a declining community or one experiencing little economic growth, job and career opportunities for you may be very limited. You should consider whether it would be better for you to examine job opportunities in other communities which may offer greater long-term career advancement as well as more opportunities for changing jobs and careers in the future.

Don't ever take to the road until you have done your homework by researching communities, organizations, and individuals.

In recent years economic development has shifted toward the West, Southwest, and Southeast as well as to selected metropolitan areas in the East and South. Even the Midwest has experienced an economic turnaround. Indeed, in 1993 the fastest growing states in terms of population were Nevada, Idaho, Colorado, Utah, and Arizona; the slowest growing and declining places were the District of Columbia, Rhode Island, Connecticut, North Dakota, Maine, and Massachusetts. Millions of job seekers will continue to migrate to the growth areas throughout the 1990s in response to growing job opportunities. Perhaps you, too, will look toward these areas as you change jobs and careers in the future.

In this chapter we examine how to conduct both a long-distance and a community-based job search campaign. We use the example of Washington, DC to illustrate the importance of conducting community research as well as for identifying alternative job networks. Nowhere do we recommend that you pull up stakes and take to the road in search of new opportunities. Many people did so in the 1980s as they headed for the reputed promised lands of Houston and Denver. As the booming economies in these communities went bust by the mid-1980s, many of these people experienced a new round of unemployment. The situation is likely to happen in the new reputed promised lands of the early 1990's—Cincinnati, Seattle, and Las Vegas.

Don't ever take to the road until you have done your homework by researching communities, organizations, and individuals as well as created the necessary bridges for contacting employers in a new community. Most important, be sure you have the appropriate work-content and networking skills for finding employment in specific communities.

TARGET COMMUNITIES

Many people are attached to their communities. Friends, relatives, churches, schools, businesses, and neighborhoods provide an important sense of identity which is difficult to leave for a community of strangers. As a member of the military, you are one of the few truly mobile occupational groups accustomed to moving to new communities every few years.

The increased mobility of society is partly due to the nature of the job market. Many people voluntarily move to where job opportunities are most plentiful. Thus, Atlanta becomes a boom city with hundreds of additional cars entering the already congested freeways each week. The corporate structure of large businesses, with branches geographically spread throughout the national production and distribution system, requires the movement of key personnel from one location to another—much like military and diplomatic personnel.

When you begin your job search, you face two alternative community approaches. You can concentrate on a particular job, regardless of its geographic setting, or you can focus on one or two communities. The first approach, which we term follow-the-job, is widely used by migrant farm workers, cowboys, bank robbers, mercenaries, oil riggers, construction workers, newspaper reporters, college and university professors, and city managers. These people move to where the jobs are in their particular profession. Not surprising, many of these job seekers end up in boring communities which may limit their lifestyle options.

If you follow-the-job, you will need to link into a geographically mobile communication system for identifying job opportunities. This often means subscribing to specialized trade publications, maintaining contacts with fellow professionals in other communities, joining a nationwide electronic resume and networking bank, or creatively advertising yourself to prospective employers through newspaper ads or letter blitzes.

On the other hand, you may want to target a community. This may mean remaining in your present community or locating a community you find especially attractive because of job opportunities, climate, recreation, or social and cultural environments. Regardless of rumored job opportunities, many people, for instance, would not move to South Dakota—the state with the lowest unemployment rate in the country (2.4%)—or to the "deep South" where the weather is relatively hot and humid and where the local economies, cultures, and public services are less supportive of desired lifestyles best found in other regions of the country. The same is true for Southerners who are not particularly interested in moving to what are reputed to be cold, dreary, and crime ridden northern cities. At the same time, Raleigh-Durham, Minneapolis, Austin, Boston, Indianapolis, Cincinnati, Orlando, Atlanta, San Jose, Seattle, Las Vegas, Phoenix, and Washington, DC are reputed to be the new promised lands for many people. Seeming oases of prosperity and centers for attractive urban lifestyles, these cities are on the community target list of many job seekers.

We recommend using this second approach of targeting specific communities. The follow-the-job approach is okay if you are young, adventuresome, or desperate; you find yourself in a geographically mobile profession; your career takes precedence over all other aspects of your life; or you have a bad case of wanderlust and thus let others arrange your travel plans. By targeting a community, your job search will be more manageable. Furthermore, moving to another community can be a liberating experience which will have a positive effect on both your professional and personal lives.

Why not find a great job in a community you really love? Fortunately you live in a very large country consisting of numerous communities that offer a terrific range of career and lifestyle opportunities. Let's identify some communities that might be a good "fit" for you as well as eliminate many which you may wish to avoid.

KNOW THE GROWING
STATES AND COMMUNITIES

Frictional unemployment—the geographic separation of underemployed and unemployed individuals from high labor demand regions and communities—should present new options for you. Numerous job opportunities may be available if you are willing to relocate.

As noted in the following statistics, unemployment during the later half of the 1980s was unevenly distributed among the states.

UNEMPLOYMENT IN THE STATES

	1000's OF PERSONS	PERCENTAGE
West Virginia	116	15.0
Michigan	488	11.2
Alabama	200	11.1
Mississippi	116	10.8
Louisiana	194	10.0
Alaska	25	10.0
Washington	194	9.5
Ohio	481	9.4
Oregon	125	9.4
Kentucky	160	9.3
Illinois	511	9.1
Washington, DC	290	9.1
Pennsylvania	499	9.1
Arkansas	93	8.9
Indiana	226	8.6
Tennessee	190	8.6
North Dakota	17	8.1
Nevada	39	7.8
California	972	7.8
New Mexico	47	7.5
Montana	30	7.4
Wisconsin	176	7.3
Missouri	172	7.2
Idaho	33	7.2
New York	584	7.2
South Carolina	105	7.1
Oklahoma	109	7.0
Iowa	100	7.0
North Carolina	205	6.7
Utah	47	6.5
Minnesota	141	6.3
Florida	322	6.3
Wyoming	16	6.3
New Jersey	236	6.2
Delaware	19	6.2
New Hampshire	34	6.1
Maine	34	6.1
Georgia	166	6.0
Texas	466	5.9
Colorado	96	5.6
Hawaii	27	5.6
Maryland	121	5.4
Rhode Island	26	5.3
Vermont	14	5.2
Kansas	63	5.2
Virginia	143	5.0
Arizona	71	5.0
Massachusetts	145	4.8

Connecticut	77	4.6
Nebraska	35	4.4
South Dakota	15	4.3

Unemployment was most pronounced in the states of West Virginia, Michigan, Alabama, Mississippi, and Louisiana. South Dakota, Nebraska, Connecticut, Massachusetts, and Arizona had the lowest unemployment rates.

These patterns of unemployment will shift in the 1990s depending on the state of the economy. In 1993, for example, unemployment nationwide stood at 6.8 percent. It was differentially distributed by state and metropolitan areas as follows:

UNEMPLOYMENT BY STATE AND METROPOLITAN AREAS, July 1993

	1000's OF UNEMPLOYED	PERCENTAGE
Alabama	**159.0**	**8.1**
Birmingham	27.6	6.1
Huntsville	9.5	6.8
Mobile	19.5	8.5
Montgomery	9.5	6.6
Tuscaloosa	4.6	6.2
Alaska	**18.0**	**6.4**
Anchorage	6.8	5.5
Arizona	**100.0**	**5.8**
Phoenix	48.3	4.6
Tucson	12.5	3.0
Arkansas	**67.4**	**5.7**
Fayetteville-Springdale	1.9	2.7
Fort Smith	5.4	5.7
Little Rock-North Little Rock	13.0	4.6
Pine Bluff	3.2	8.7
California	**1,543.9**	**9.9**
Anaheim-Santa Ana	103.6	7.4
Bakersfield	42.4	14.7
Fresno	53.3	13.9
Los Angeles-Long Beach	431.0	9.5
Modesto	31.9	16.4
Oakland	88.2	7.7
Oxnard-Ventura	41.2	10.4
Riverside-San Bernardino	159.4	13.6
Sacramento	70.6	8.7
Salinas-Seaside-Monterey	19.4	10.7

San Diego	112.4	9.2
San Francisco	65.7	7.3
San Jose	66.3	7.9
Santa Barbara-Santa Maria-Lompoc	16.0	8.6
Santa Rose-Petaluma	16.4	7.4
Stockton	33.1	14.6
Vallejo-Fairfield-Napa	21.5	9.7
Colorado	**94.8**	**5.2**
Boulder-Longmont	6.0	4.0
Denver	48.1	5.2
Connecticut	**122.6**	**6.7**
Bridgeport-Milford	17.7	7.5
Hartford	29.6	6.9
New Britain	6.7	6.6
New Haven-Meriden	19.6	6.8
Stamford	5.1	4.2
Waterbury	9.8	8.8
Delaware	**19.3**	**5.0**
Wilmington	17.8	5.6
District of Columbia	**22.4**	**8.0**
Washington	107.5	4.7
Florida	**516.3**	**7.6**
Daytona Beach	12.4	7.6
Fort Lauderdale-Hollywood-Pompano Beach	51.4	7.1
Fort Myers-Cape Coral	10.6	6.6
Gainesville	5.4	4.5
Jacksonville	31.1	6.4
Lakeland-Winter Haven	22.1	11.9
Melbourne-Titusville-Palm Bay	17.1	8.2
Miami-Hialeah	82.1	8.1
Orlando	42.9	6.1
Pensacola	9.2	5.6
Sarasota	7.3	5.5
Tallahassee	6.3	4.2
Tampa-St. Petersburg-Clearwater	75.0	7.0
West Palm Beach-Boca Raton-Delray Beach	43.8	9.8
Georgia	**176.6**	**5.3**
Albany	3.6	6.6
Athens	2.8	3.7
Atlanta	78.6	4.9
Augusta	12.2	6.1
Columbus	6.8	6.7

Macon-Warner Robins	6.7	5.1
Savannah	6.5	5.3
Hawaii	**28.6**	**4.9**
Honolulu	14.9	3.6
Idaho	**29.1**	**5.4**
Boise City	4.4	3.4
Illinois	**433.0**	**6.9**
Aurora-Elgin	13.7	6.7
Bloomington-Normal	3.4	4.2
Champaign-Urbana-Rantoul	5.5	5.9
Chicago	225.9	6.8
Davenport-Rock Island-		
Moline	10.7	5.6
Decatur	5.4	8.4
Joliet	16.6	7.0
Kankakee	3.9	7.5
Lake County	14.6	4.3
Peoria	11.4	6.5
Rockford	15.6	9.4
Springfield	6.0	4.9
Indiana	**123.3**	**4.1**
Anderson	3.7	6.1
Bloomington	1.8	2.8
Elkhart-Goshen	3.2	3.2
Evansville	6.2	4.0
Fort Wayne	8.0	3.8
Gary-Hammond	13.7	5.1
Indianapolis	22.6	3.1
Kokomo	3.9	7.5
Lafayette-West Lafayette	1.8	2.5
Muncie	2.9	4.5
South Bend-Mishawaka	4.9	3.7
Terre Haute	3.0	4.6
Iowa	**59.7**	**3.7**
Cedar Rapids	3.1	3.1
Des Moines	11.9	4.6
Dubuque	1.6	3.5
Iowa City	1.2	1.7
Sioux City	1.7	2.6
Waterloo-Cedar Falls	3.3	4.3
Kansas	**63.2**	**4.6**
Lawrence	1.7	3.7
Topeka	4.8	4.9
Wichita	15.0	5.6
Kentucky	**113.9**	**6.3**
Lexington-Fayette	8.6	4.2

Louisville	26.2	4.8
Owensboro	3.2	6.9
Louisiana	**141.1**	**7.4**
Alexandria	4.2	7.2
Baton Rouge	19.4	6.9
Houma-Thibodaux	4.8	7.0
Lafayette	5.9	5.6
Lake Charles	6.1	7.4
Monroe	4.5	6.5
New Orleans	40.2	7.1
Shreveport	10.2	6.5
Maine	**43.6**	**6.5**
Lewiston-Auburn	4.0	9.1
Portland	6.2	4.5
Maryland	**175.0**	**6.6**
Baltimore	96.8	7.8
Massachusetts	**208.2**	**6.6**
Boston	89.3	5.8
Brockton	7.7	8.1
Fall River	8.3	10.9
Fitchburg-Leominster	3.8	8.1
Lawrence-Haverhill	15.9	8.2
Lowell	11.2	7.8
New Bedford	8.8	10.2
Pittsfield	2.8	6.8
Springfield	19.4	7.7
Worcester	14.4	6.5
Michigan	**373.2**	**7.8**
Ann Arbor	7.4	4.5
Battle Creek	4.9	7.3
Benton Harbor	6.4	7.9
Detroit	184.1	8.3
Flint	20.8	11.1
Grand Rapids	23.9	5.9
Jackson	5.9	8.6
Kalamazoo	5.8	4.7
Lansing-East Lansing	12.9	5.3
Muskegon	7.0	10.2
Saginaw-Bay City-Midland	14.6	7.4
Minnesota	**108.6**	**4.3**
Duluth	6.9	5.9
Minneapolis-St. Paul	58.9	4.0
Rochester	1.9	2.8
St. Cloud	4.8	4.4
Mississippi	**77.0**	**6.3**
Jackson	10.6	5.1

Missouri	**166.5**	**6.2**
Kansas City	45.9	5.2
St. Louis LMA	80.1	6.3
Springfield	6.6	4.8
Montana	**22.8**	**5.4**
Nebraska	**24.0**	**2.7**
Lincoln	3.1	2.2
Omaha	11.2	3.1
Nevada	**48.7**	**6.7**
Las Vegas	32.0	6.7
Reno	8.7	5.8
New Hampshire	**38.4**	**6.0**
Manchester	4.6	5.4
Nashua	6.8	6.8
Portsmouth-Dover-Rochester	6.1	4.3
New Jersey	**290.0**	**10.3**
Atlanta City	14.9	7.5
Bergen-Passaic	49.0	7.4
Jersey City	26.8	10.3
Middlesex-Somerset-Hunterdon	36.8	6.2
Monmouth-Ocean	32.2	6.4
Newark	71.7	7.8
Trenton	9.6	5.7
Vineland-Millville-Bridgeton	6.8	11.2
New Mexico	**55.3**	**7.4**
Albuquerque	14.3	5.1
Las Cruces	6.5	10.6
Santa Fe	3.1	4.0
New York	**643.7**	**7.4**
Albany-Schenectady-Troy	20.5	4.6
Binghamton	7.5	6.2
Buffalo	32.7	7.0
Elmira	2.2	5.2
Glens Falls	3.5	5.9
Nassau-Suffolk	82.8	6.1
New York	355.6	8.9
New York City	320.0	9.5
Orange County	9.3	6.5
Poughkeepsie	10.8	9.4
Rochester	29.4	5.6
Syracuse	18.8	5.8
Utica-Rome	8.1	5.8
North Carolina	**173.5**	**4.9**
Asheville	3.9	3.9

Charlotte-Gastonia-Rock Hill	31.5	4.7
Greensboro-Winston-Salem-		
High Point	22.5	4.1
Raleigh-Durham	16.8	3.6
North Dakota	**12.9**	**4.0**
Bismarck	1.7	3.4
Fargo-Moorhead	2.7	3.0
Grand Forks	1.4	3.8
Ohio	**366.3**	**6.6**
Akron	20.5	5.9
Canton	13.5	6.7
Cincinnati	44.1	5.4
Cleveland	60.1	6.2
Columbus	41.0	5.3
Dayton-Springfield	26.0	5.4
Toledo	22.1	7.1
Youngstown-Warren	18.6	8.1
Oklahoma	**93.5**	**6.1**
Enid	1.3	4.4
Lawton	3.0	5.8
Oklahoma City	26.8	5.3
Tulsa	23.4	6.7
Oregon	**123.9**	**7.8**
Eugene-Springfield	12.5	8.1
Medford	7.8	9.8
Portland	47.4	6.5
Salem	11.9	7.7
Pennsylvania	**447.0**	**7.3**
Allentown-Bethlehem-Easton	25.3	7.2
Altoona	4.7	7.1
Beaver County	7.1	10.9
Erie	10.7	7.3
Harrisburg-Lebanon-Carlisle	17.1	4.9
Johnstown	11.4	10.7
Lancaster	11.9	4.9
Philadelphia	177.8	7.3
Pittsburgh	72.7	6.9
Reading	11.6	6.3
Scranton-Wilkes-Barre	34.4	8.9
Sharon	5.2	9.8
State College	4.3	6.0
Williamsport	5.1	8.2
York	13.8	5.7
Rhode Island	**36.6**	**6.9**
Pawtucket-Woonsocket-		
Attleboro	11.9	7.1
Providence	24.3	7.0

South Carolina	**135.2**	**7.3**
Charleston	17.0	6.6
Columbia	14.1	5.4
Greenville-Spartanburg	20.8	5.7
South Dakota	**9.2**	**2.4**
Rapid City	1.0	2.3
Sioux Falls	1.3	1.6
Tennessee	**144.4**	**5.7**
Chattanooga		
Johnson City-Kingsport-		
Bristol	12.8	5.7
Knoxville	14.9	4.7
Memphis	24.2	5.0
Nashville	22.8	4.1
Texas	**643.6**	**7.2**
Abilene	3.6	6.8
Amarillo	5.3	5.2
Austin	22.6	4.7
Beaumont-Port Arthur	19.7	10.7
Brazoria	8.3	9.0
Brownsville-Harlingen	13.1	11.4
Bryan-College Station	2.6	3.8
Corpus Christi	14.8	8.6
Dallas	93.6	6.2
El Paso	27.2	10.1
Fort Worth-Arlington	51.3	6.7
Galveston-Texas City	10.3	8.2
Houston	136.2	7.5
Killeen-Temple	7.8	7.1
Laredo	6.0	9.7
Longview-Marshall	7.4	8.9
Lubbock	7.0	5.9
McAllen-Edinburg-Mission	26.9	16.3
Midland	3.5	7.1
Odessa	5.1	9.5
San Angelo	2.7	5.9
San Antonio	39.3	6.0
Sherman-Denison	3.8	8.0
Texarkana	4.5	7.6
Tyler	5.7	7.2
Victoria	2.3	5.5
Waco	6.0	6.3
Wichita Falls	3.6	6.6
Utah	**32.7**	**3.8**
Provo-Orem	4.6	3.7
Salt Lake City-Odgen	20.0	3.6
Vermont	**17.0**	**5.2**
Burlington	3.4	4.1

Virginia	**185.1**	**5.4**
Charlottesville	2.9	4.0
Danville	4.5	8.4
Lynchburg	3.7	4.7
Norfolk-Virginia Beach- Newport News	42.3	6.2
Richmond-Petersburg	24.3	5.0
Roanoke	6.6	5.0
Washington	**185.1**	**5.4**
Seattle	82.0	7.1
West Virginia	**76.7**	**9.8**
Charleston	9.2	7.6
Huntington-Ashland	11.4	8.8
Parkersburg-Marietta	5.8	7.8
Wheeling	5.7	7.8
Wisconsin	**119.7**	**4.4**
Appleton-Oshkosh-Neenah	7.1	3.7
Eau Claire	3.5	4.7
Green Bay	4.6	3.8
Janesville-Beloit	5.2	6.7
Kenosha	4.0	6.7
La Crosse	2.5	4.3
Madison	5.0	2.0
Milwaukee	34.3	4.3
Racine	5.7	7.2
Sheboygan	2.3	3.7
Wausau	2.9	4.2
Wyoming	**13.5**	**5.5**
Casper	2.4	7.9

Throughout the 1990s we expect Colorado, the District of Columbia, Georgia, Hawaii, Idaho, Indiana, Iowa, Kansas, Minnesota, Montana, Nebraska, North Carolina, North Dakota, South Dakota, Tennessee, Utah, Vermont, Virginia, and Wisconsin to have above average employment rates. Numerous communities within these states will offer some of the best job opportunities.

Growing regions and communities are relatively predictable for the 1990s. Several metropolitan areas that experienced high population growth rates in the 1970s continued with similar growth rates in the 1980s:

- Los Angeles-Long Beach, San Francisco-Oakland, CA
- Washington, DC
- Baltimore, MD
- Dallas-Fort Worth, TX

- Houston, TX
- Minneapolis-St. Paul, MN
- Atlanta, GA
- Anaheim-Santa Ana-Garden Grove, CA
- San Diego, CA
- Denver-Boulder, CO
- Seattle-Everett, WA
- Miami, FL
- Tampa-St. Petersburg, FL
- Riverside-San Bernardino-Ontario, CA
- Phoenix, AZ
- Portland, OR
- San Antonio, TX
- Fort Lauderdale-Hollywood, FL
- Salt Lake City-Ogden, UT

Many of these same metropolitan areas will continue to be growth areas throughout the 1990s. The major exception will be California. This state has been hard hit by defense cutbacks, a large influx of unskilled immigrant labor, several natural disasters (fires, earthquakes, floods), and a recession in Asia that affects the state's growing export economy. While most states in 1993 showed signs of climbing out of the recession, California's economy remained mired in recession; its recovery could be slow. For the first time in decades, California was no longer a promised land for job seekers. Indeed, hundreds of individuals were leaving California each week in search of employment in other states.

According to U.S. Census Bureau, the fastest growing cities between 1980 and 1990 were the following:

FASTEST GROWING CITIES, 1980-1990

City	1980	1990	% Gain
Mesa, AZ	152,404	288,091	89%
Rancho Cucamonga, CA	55,250	101,409	84%
Plano, TX	72,331	128,713	78%
Irvine, CA	62,134	110,330	78%
Escondido, CA	64,355	108,635	69%
Oceanside, CA	76,698	128,398	67%
Bakersfield, CA	105,611	174,820	66%
Arlington, TX	160,113	261,721	64%
Fresno, CA	217,491	354,202	63%
Chula Vista, CA	83,927	135,163	61%

The fastest growing metropolitan area between 1986 and 1993 were the following:

FASTEST GROWING METRO AREAS,
1986-1993

City	1986	1993	% Gain
Punta Gorda, FL	84,100	132,055	57.0
Las Vegas, NV-AZ	661,800	983,313	48.6
Riverside-San			
Bernardino, CA	2,001,100	2,892,733	44.6
Yuma, AZ	86,800	124,026	42.9
Naples, FL	121,400	172,909	42.4
Fort Pierce-			
Port St. Lucie, FL	205,700	282,012	37.1
Fort Myers-			
Cape Coral, FL	279,100	381,263	36.6
Orlando, FL	1,030,900	1,388.941	34.7
Modesto, CA	316,600	416,794	31.6
West Palm Beach-			
Boca Raton, FL	755,600	973,630	28.9
Daytona Beach, FL	339,100	435,637	28.5
Sarasota-			
Bradenton, FL	424,700	542,530	27.7
Myrtle Beach, SC	130,600	164,912	26.3
Santa Rosa, CA	343,600	432,055	25.7
Ocala, FL	171,000	214,601	25.5

Disproportionately found in the West, Southwest and Southeast—especially Florida and California—many of these communities, along with a few in the Northeast and Midwest, should continue with medium to high growth rates throughout the remainder of the 1990s. Depending on the extent of another energy crisis in the 1990s, several communities in the energy rich Rocky Mountain states may once again become boom towns. Communities with large concentrations of high-tech and service industries, supported by a strong higher education infrastructure—will continue to expand both demographically and economically. Cities with large college and university complexes, such as Boston, Minneapolis-St. Paul, Omaha, Raleigh-Durham-Chapel Hill, Oklahoma City, Salt Lake City, Madison (WI), Columbia (SC), Knoxville, Atlanta, Austin (TX), Columbus (OH), San Francisco, Seattle, Honolulu, Iowa City, Ann Arbor, and Washington DC should experience steady employment growth throughout the 1990s. These cities will also generate some of the best paying, high quality jobs.

We foresee major population and economic growth in and around several large cities: Seattle, Portland, Las Vegas, Salt Lake City-Ogden,

Denver, Minneapolis-St. Paul, Rochester (MN), Milwaukee, Dallas-Ft. Worth, Houston, Austin, San Antonio, Albuquerque, Phoenix, Atlanta, Tampa-St. Petersburg, Raleigh-Durham, Pittsburgh, Philadelphia, Washington-Baltimore, Boston, Indianapolis, Louisville, and Cleveland. Contrary to some recent projections, we no longer expect Southern California—especially the Los Angeles-San Diego corridor—to be a major growth region for population and jobs. California is likely to experience at least three years of little or no economic growth as it comes to terms with its own recession. We would expect the California economy to begin turning around after 1995, largely driven by its exports to newly revitalized Pacific Rim economies, which experienced a mild recession in 1993 and 1994, and Mexico. The California economy and job market should rebound in the second half of the 1990s. However, we do not expect California to transform itself into a new job mecca. Its recovery and future growth will be slow.

Even though the overall growth predictions point to the Southeast and West, these trends should not deter you from considering older cities in the Northeast and North Central regions. After all, 1-2 million new jobs are created nationwide each year. New jobs will continue to develop in cities such as Chicago, Philadelphia, and New York; these are still the best places to pursue careers in the fields of banking, publishing, and advertising. Boston will again become an attractive employment center. Several communities in the Midwest—especially those with strong educational infrastructures—will rebound as they transform their local economies in the direction of new high-tech and service industries. Minneapolis-St. Paul, Madison, Chicago, Detroit, St. Louis, Kansas City, Indianapolis, Columbus, Cleveland, and Cincinnati in the Midwest and Baltimore, Washington DC, Raleigh-Durham-Chapel Hill, and Atlanta in the central to southern Atlantic coast area will remain some of the best cities for jobs and lifestyles throughout the 1990s.

CONSIDER THE BEST
PLACES WITH JOB GROWTH

If you contemplate relocating to a new community, you should consider communities that are experiencing the greatest job growth as well as avoid those that are losing jobs. Between 1993 and 1998, the following metropolitan areas are expected to gain and lose the largest number of jobs:

PROJECTED JOB WINNERS, 1993-1998

Metro Area	Total New Jobs
Washington, DC-MD-VA-WV	206,767
Orange County, CA	177,898
Atlanta, GA	168,300
Phoenix-Mesa, AZ	148,703
Los Angeles-Long Beach, CA	139,108
San Diego, CA	134,863
Tampa-St. Petersburg-Clearwater, FL	123,672
Orlando, FL	119.336
Philadelphia, PA-NJ	116,815
Riverside-San Bernardino, CA	110,695
Dallas, TX	110,363
Houston, TX	95,324
Chicago, IL	95,324
Seattle-Bellevue-Everett, WA	90,313
Detroit, MI	86,601
Minneapolis-St. Paul, MN-WI	80,045
Baltimore, MD	73,730
Charlotte-Gastonia-Rock Hill, NC-SC	72,598

PROJECTED JOB LOSERS, 1993-1998

Metro Area	Employment Decline
Lawton, OK	-2.67%
Great Falls, MT	-2.14
Houma, LA	-1.59
New York, NY	-0.91
Flint, MI	-0.68
Beaumont-Port Arthur, TX	-0.63
Enid, OK	-0.52
Jacksonville, NC	-0.44
Abilene, TX	-0.38
Grand Forks, ND-MN	-0.10
Amarillo, TX	-0.05

Source: Woods & Poole Economics, Inc., employment forecasts, 1993, as reported in *Places Rated Almanac,* p. 57.

A recent *Fortune Magazine* survey (November 15, 1993) identified ten cities as the best places for businesses in need of knowledgeable workforces. These cities have highly educated and skilled populations capable of providing businesses with the skills necessary for operating in the 21st century:

1. Raleigh-Durham
2. New York

3. Boston
4. Seattle
5. Austin
6. Chicago
7. Houston
8. San Jose
9. Philadelphia
10. Minneapolis

Located outside the Sunbelt, most of these cities are likely to experience solid growth throughout the 1990s. The cities of Raleigh-Durham and Minneapolis are already star performers because of their extensive medical facilities and high-tech infrastructure as well as their attractive lifestyles. These two cities will probably continue to be great growth communities during the coming decade. They will generate a disproportionate number of high paying jobs due to the high quality nature of their jobs and workforces. They may well provide models of a new economy and workforce for the 21st century.

SEEK OUT THE BEST EMPLOYERS

You might also want to consider some of America's best employers when identifying your ideal community. According to Robert Levering and Milton Moskowitz in their new edition of *The 100 Best Companies to Work for in America,* the companies listed on pages 274 and 275 are the best ones to work for in America. While the headquarters will be the main employment centers for most of these companies, please keep in mind that many of these companies—such as Federal Express, Delta Air Lines, Avis, IBM, Lowe's, J.C. Penney, Wal-Mart, and Nordstrom—have offices, plants, and stores in other locations throughout the United States as well as abroad. If you are interested in working for one of these companies, contact the headquarters for information on their other locations as well as refer to *The 100 Best Companies to Work for in America* for more detailed information on each company.

LOOK FOR SOLID METRO AREAS

Metropolitan areas exhibiting strong performance in several sectors—cost of living, jobs, housing, transportation, education, health care, crime, the arts, recreation, and climate—should prove to be very attractive areas in the long-term. The most recent edition of *Places Rated Almanac* found

100 BEST COMPANIES IN AMERICA, 1993

Company	Headquarters
Acipco	Birmingham, AL
Advanced Micro Devices	Sunnyvale, CA
Alagasco	Birmingham, AL
Anheuser-Busch	St. Louis, MO
Apogee Enterprise	Minneapolis, MN
Armstrong	Lancaster, PA
Avis	Garden City, NY
Baptist Hospital of Miami	Miami, FL
BE&K	Birmingham, AL
Ben & Jerry's Homemade	Waterbury, VT
Beth Israel Hospital Boston	Boston, MA
Leo Burnett	Chicago, IL
Chaparral Steel	Midlothian, TX
Compaq Computer	Houston, TX
Cooper Tire	Findlay, OH
Corning	Corning, NY
Cray Research	Eagan, MN
Cummins Engine	Columbus, TN
Dayton Hudson	Minneapolis, MN
John Deere	Moline, IL
Delta Air Lines	Atlanta, GA
Donnelly	Holland, MI
Du Pont	Wilmington, DE
A. G. Edwards	St. Louis, MO
Erie Insurance	Erie, PA
Federal Express	Memphis, TN
Fel-Pro	Skokie, IL
First Federal Bank of California	Santa Monica, CA
H. B. Fuller	St. Paul, MN
General Mills	Minneapolis, MN
Goldman Sachs	New York, NY
W. L. Gore & Associates	Newark, DE
Great Plains Software	Fargo, ND
Hallmark Cards	Kansas City, MO
Haworth	Holland, MI
Hersey Foods	Hersey, PA
Hewitt Associates	Lincolnshire, IL
Hewlett-Packard	Palo Alto, CA
Honda of America Manufacturing	Marysville, OH
IBM	Armonk, NY
Inland Steel	Chicago, IL
Intel	Santa Clara, CA
Johnson & Johnson	New Brunswick, NJ
SC Johnson Wax	Racine, WI
Kellogg	Battle Creek, MI
Knight-Ridder	Miami, FL
Lands' End	Dodgeville, WI
Lincoln Electric	Cleveland, OH
Los Angeles Dodgers	Los Angeles, CA

Lotus Development	Cambridge, MA
Lowe's	North Wilkesboro, NC
Lyondell Petrochemical	Houston, TX
Marquette Electronics	Milwaukee, WI
Mary Kay Cosmetics	Dallas, TX
McCormick	Hunt Valley, MD
Merck	Whitehouse Station, NJ
Methodist Hospital	Houston, TX
Microsoft	Redmond, CA WA
Herman Miller	Zeeland, MI
3M	St. Paul, MN
Moog	East Aurora, NY
J. P. Morgan	New York, NY
Morrison & Foerster	San Francisco, CA
Motorola	Schaumburg, IL
Nissan Motor Manufacturing	Smyrna, TN
Nordstrom	Seattle, WA
Northwestern Mutual Life	Milwaukee, WI
Odetics	Anaheim, CA
Patagonia	Ventura, CA
J. C. Penney	Plano, TX
Physio-Control	Redmond, WA
Pitney Bowes	Stamford, CT
Polaroid	Cambridge, MA
Preston Trucking	Preston, MD
Procter & Gamble	Cincinnati, OH
Publix Super Markets	Lakeland, FL
Quad/Graphics	Pewaukee, WI
Reader's Digest	Pleasantville, NY
Recreational Equipment, Inc.	Seattle, WA
Rosenbluth International	Philadelphia, PA
SAS Institute	Cary, NC
J. M. Smucker	Orrville, OH
Southwest Airlines	Dallas, TX
Springfield ReManufacturing	Springfield, MO
Springs	Fort Mill, SC
Steelcase	Grand Rapids, MI
Syntex	Palo Alto, CA
Tandem	Cupertino, CA
TDIndustries	Dallas, TX
Tennant	Minneapolis, MN
UNUM	Portland, ME
USAA	San Antonio, TX
U S WEST	Eaglewood, CO
Valassis Communications	Livonia, MI
Viking Freight System	San Jose, CA
Wal-Mart	Bentonville, AR
Wegmans	Rochester, NY
Weyerhaeuser	Tacoma, WA
Worthington Industries	Columbus, OH
Xerox	Stamford, CT

five metropolitan areas it considers to be super-solid metropolitan areas:

SUPER-SOLID METRO AREAS

Metro Area (Overall Rank)	Highest Rank	Lowest Rank
Boise City, ID	Crime	Health Care
Indianapolis	Jobs	Crime
Lexington, KY	Health Care	Crime
Louisville, KY-IN	Climate	Recreation
Salt Lake City-Ogden, UT	Transportation	Housing

These places should be excellent locations for jobs and lifestyles.

However, keep in mind that while many of these communities are *statistically* good places to live, they may or may not be the best places for *you* to find a job and start a new career. Be sure to thoroughly investigate communities before deciding to target your job search on one.

FIND THE BEST PLACE TO LIVE

Community growth and decline trends should be considered as part of your job and career options. If you live in a declining community with few opportunities for your skills and interests, seriously consider relocating to a growth community. Depressed communities simply do not generate enough jobs. Many communities with populations of 100,000 to 500,000 offer a nice variety of job and lifestyle options.

Except for a few people, one's work should not become one's life. After all, there are more important things in life than one's work. Different communities offer many life choices in addition to jobs. Economic development and job generation are only two of many important community choice concerns. Using ten indicators of "living," the 1993 edition of *Places Rated Almanac* identifies what it considers to be the 50 best communities in North America (USA and Canada) in terms of their mix of cost of living, jobs, housing, transportation, education, health care, crime, the arts, recreation, and climate:

NORTH AMERICA'S TOP 50 METRO AREAS

1. Cincinnati, OH-KY-IN
2. Seattle-Bellevue-Everett, WA
3. Philadelphia, PA-NJ
4. Toronto, ON
5. Pittsburgh, PA
6. Raleigh-Durham-Chapel Hill, NC

  7. Washington, DC-MD-VA-WV
  8. Indianapolis, IN
  8. Salt Lake City-Ogden, UT
10. Louisville, KY-IN
11. Vancouver, BC
12. Atlanta, GA
13. Portland, OR
14. Cleveland-Lorain-Elyria, OH
14. Knoxville, TN
16. San Diego, CA
17. Boston, MA
18. San Francisco, CA
18. Greensboro-Winston-Salem-High Point, NC
20. Syracuse, NY
21. Baltimore, MD
22. St. Louis, MO
23. Orange County, CA
24. Detroit, MI
25. Eugene-Springfield, OR
26. Oklahoma City, OH
27. Johnson City-Kingsport-Bristol, TN-VA
27. Los Angeles-Long Beach, CA
29. Tucson, AZ
30. Quebec City, PQ
31. Nashville, TN
32. Denver, CO
33. Miami, FL
34. Milwaukee-Waukesha, WI
35. Kansas City, MO-KS
36. Lexington, KY
37. Albuquerque, NM
38. Phoenix-Mesa, AZ
39. Buffalo-Niagara Falls, NY
40. Minneapolis-St. Paul, MN-WI
41. Long Island, NY
42. Rochester, NY
43. Akron, OH
44. Chicago, IL
45. Houston, TX
46. Columbus, OH
47. Spokane, WA
48. Montreal, PQ
49. San Jose, CA
50. Dayton-Springfield, OH

These rankings will undoubtedly change for the second half of the 1990s. It is best to consult the latest edition of *Places Rated Almanac* to see how particular communities rank according to each and every indicator. This book is available in libraries, bookstores, and from Impact Publications.

SELECT A LOCATION PROPERLY

You and your family must take into consideration several factors and
questions when deciding on which communities to target your job search:

- Where would you like to live for the next 5, 10, or 20 years?

- If you are about to retire or retain certain military privileges
  through participation in the VSI or SSB exit programs, how
  important is continued access to military facilities, such as the
  commissary, post exchange, recreational facilities, and the
  Army hospital or clinic?

- If you're leaving active duty without retiring but want to
  continue serving your country through Army reserve duty,
  which locations have military reserve units with openings for
  your Military Occupational Specialty?

- What is the relative cost of living?

- How attractive are the educational, social, and cultural activities?

- What are the economic and psychological costs of making a
  move?

- What job and career opportunities are there for me/us?

- How can I/we best conduct a job search in another community?

Many people answer these questions by remaining in their community
or by targeting growth communities. The exodus from the declining
industrial cities in the Northeast and North Central regions to the Sunbelt
began in the 1960s, expanded in the 1970s, and continued into the 1980s
with the inclusion of the energy-rich Rocky Mountain states. Several
metropolitan areas in all regions will have abundant job opportunities for
skilled workers during the 1990s. Targeting a job search in metropolitan
Seattle, Phoenix, Minneapolis, Atlanta, Raleigh-Durham, and Washington
DC may be a wise move. While these areas will experience numerous
urban problems over the next decade, their problems are ones of
growth—traffic congestion, pollution, city planning, crime, and housing

shortages—not ones of decline. We believe it is better to experience the problems of growth than of decline. In a situation of decline, your livelihood becomes threatened. In a situation of growth, your major problem may be fighting the traffic congestion in order to get to a job which offers a promising career.

New frontiers for renewed job and career prosperity abound throughout America if you are willing to pack your bags and move. But most such frontiers require highly skilled individuals. If you lack the necessary skills for industries in other communities, consider getting retrained before making a move. Unfortunately, many people making moves today do not have the necessary skills to succeed in new communities.

Making a community move on your own involves taking risks. Many people, for example, are locked into financial obligations, such as a mortgaged house which doesn't sell well in what may be a depressed housing market. If you find yourself locked in financially, you may want to consider taking an immediate financial loss in anticipation of renewed prosperity in a community which is experiencing promising growth and prosperity. You may recoup your immediate losses within a year or two. However, you will have to pass through a transition period which can be difficult if you don't approach it in a positive, up-beat manner. The old saying, "There is no gain without pain" is appropriate in many situations involving community moves.

CONSIDER YOUR FINANCIAL COSTS

The financial costs of relocating will vary depending on your situation. They can be major, especially if you move to a community with high housing costs. In addition, your cost of living will be less in areas where you have access to military facilities. Free medical care and access to the commissary, PX, and recreational facilities can save you thousands of dollars each year in cost of living expenses.

Studies conducted by Runzheimer International, for example, found the average costs of relocating in 1992 to be $48,426 for homeowners and $9,329 for non-homeowners. The major costs include:

1. Search for housing—travel, child care, and associated expenses.

2. Closing costs on both the old and new homes.

3. Increases in mortgage payments or apartment rent.

4. Temporary living expenses.

5. Cost of a bridge, equity, or swing loan.

6. Costs of maintaining two residences during the relocation period—very high if the old home does not sell immediately.

7. Shipment of household goods.

8. Final moving expenses.

9. Possible increase in cost of living—property and sales taxes, food, utilities.

10. Travel and job search costs for working spouse.

11. Expenses for marketing a home or subletting an apartment.

12. Miscellaneous costs—deposits, decorating costs, fees, dues.

Housing can be a major cost if you move to a community with expensive housing. The National Association of Realtors reported the median home price for the top 25 metropolitan areas in 1992 to be as follows:

MEDIAN HOME PRICES FOR THE
TOP 25 METROPOLITAN AREAS

1.	Honolulu, HI	$349,000
2.	San Francisco Bay Area, CA	$254,600
3.	Orange County, CA	$234,900
4.	Los Angeles, CA	$213,200
5.	Bergen/Passaic, NJ	$187,600
6.	Newark, NJ	$184,400
7.	San Diego, CA	$183,600
8.	New York/Northern New Jersey-Long Island, NY-NJ-CT	$172,700
9.	Boston, MA	$171,100
10.	Middlesex/Somerset/Hunterdon, NJ	$168,900
11.	Washington, DC/MD/VA	$167,800
12.	Nassau/Suffolk, NY	$158,600
13.	New Haven/Meriden, CT	$145,800
14.	Seattle, WA	$145,700
15.	Hartford, CT	$141,100
16.	Monmouth/Ocean, NJ	$139,200
17.	Trenton, NJ	$138,100

18.	Chicago, IL	$136,800
19.	Riverside/San Bernardino, CA	$136,200
20.	Sacramento, CA	$132,000
21.	Worcester, MA	$128,000
22.	Lake County, IL	$119,600
23.	Aurora/Elgin, IL	$118,800
24.	Providence, RI	$118,500
25.	Wilmington, DE/NJ/MD	$117,200

On the other hand, once you buy into these communities, your housing investment should appreciate. In the long-term, you will probably realize a return on your investment. The basic problem is initially buying into the higher priced housing, and especially if comparable housing was much less expensive in your last community.

When considering a community move, you should be aware of the relative cost of living in various communities. According to *Places Rated Almanac,* the following metropolitan areas exhibited the highest and lowest cost of living in 1993:

HIGHEST COST OF LIVING, 1993

1. San Francisco, CA
2. New York, NY
3. San Jose, CA
4. Honolulu, HI
5. Orange County, CA
6. Santa Cruz-Watsonville, CA
7. Santa Barbara-Santa Maria-Lompoc, CA
8. Long Island, NY
9. Los Angeles-Long Beach, CA
10. Northern New Jersey, NJ

LOWEST COST OF LIVING, 1993

1. Joplin, MO
2. Enid, OK
3. Gadsden, AL
4. St. Joseph, MO
5. McAllen-Edinburg-Mission, TX
6. Anniston, AL
7. Texarkana, TX-Terarkana, AR
8. Pine Bluff, AR
9. Florence, AL
10 Terre Haute, IN

Unfortunately, communities with the lowest cost of living also tend to offer limited opportunities. Offering few job opportunities, many of these communities generate a disproportionate number of low paying jobs—the reason they have a low cost of living. Not surprising, communities with the highest cost of living tend to offer more job opportunities which also pay the highest wages. Our advice to people with marketable skills: consider heading for communities with a high cost of living. You'll find better job opportunities and face quality lifestyle options in these places.

You should also consider the costs and time of commuting to and from work in different communities. Metropolitan areas with the longest and shortest average commutes include the following:

LONGEST COMMUTE

1.	New York, NY	75.8 minutes
2.	Long Island, NY	64.6
3.	Washington, DC-MD-VA-WV	63.0
4.	Chicago, IL	61.5
5.	Riverside-San Bernardino, CA	59.3
6.	Orange County, NY	58.5
7.	Monmouth-Ocean, NJ	58.3
8.	Oakland, CA	57.5
9.	Houston, TX	56.9
10.	Vallejo-Fairfield-Napa, CA	56.8

SHORTEST COMMUTE

1.	Bismarck, ND	27.1
2.	Grand Forks, ND-MN	27.4
3.	Cheyenne, WY	29.5
4.	Dubuque, IA	30.1
5.	Fargo-Moorhead, ND-MN	30.7
6.	Enid, OK	30.8
7.	Great Falls, MT	30.9
8.	Sheboygan, WI	31.5
9.	Rochester, MN	31.6
10.	Waterloo-Cedar Falls, IA	31.9

Source: *Places Rated Almanac,* 1993, p. 100

CONDUCT A LONG-DISTANCE JOB SEARCH

How do you target your job search on a particular community? If you decide to remain in your present community, your job search is relatively manageable on a day-to-day basis. If you target another community, you will need to conduct a long-distance job search which requires more extensive use of the mail and telephone as well as carefully planned visits to the community. In fact, you will probably use your job search time more efficiently with a long-distance campaign. In both situations, you need to conduct community research prior to initiating the major communication steps in your job search.

Most of your community research can be conducted in the library. You need names, addresses, and phone numbers of potential employers. Use the major directories we identified in Chapter 10, such as the *Dun & Bradstreet's Middle Market Directory* and *Who's Who in Commerce and Industry*. The *National Directory of Addresses and Telephone Numbers* is an especially useful directory for anyone contemplating a long-distance job search.

We particularly recommend starting with *The Sourcebook of ZIP Code Demographics: 1990 Census Edition* (CACI Marketing Systems). Found in the reference section of many libraries, this two-volume directory gives detailed information on population, housing, employment, education, income, and transportation in all communities throughout the United States. Organized by zip code, this directory yields a wealth of information on zip coded communities. For example, if you turn to the section on your current zip code, you will discover how your community is structured according to population, housing, employment, language, education, income, and transportation. You can compare your current community to thousands of other zip code communities throughout the country. In some cities with five or more zip codes, you will learn average median family incomes can fluctuate from $13,000 to $65,000, depending on the particular community zip code. We recommend consulting this directory *before* committing yourself to relocating to another community.

As noted in Chapter 10, four publishers—Bob Adams, Inc., Surrey Books, NET Research, and Gale Research—publish job bank books which identify hundreds of employers and job search services in the following cities and states: Atlanta, Boston, the Carolinas, Chicago, Dallas/Fort Worth, Denver, Detroit, Florida, Houston, Los Angeles, Minneapolis, New York City, Ohio, Philadelphia, Phoenix, Portland, San Diego, San Francisco, Seattle, St. Louis, Tennessee, and Washington, DC. Each book includes annotated descriptions of employers along with addresses and telephone numbers. While these books are available in some bookstores and public libraries, all of the books can be ordered directly from Impact Publications by completing the order information at the end of this book.

The Yellow Pages of telephone directories are especially useful sources for identifying the business and commercial structure of communities as well as for addresses and telephone numbers. The larger the community, the more specialized the businesses. For example, New York City has several businesses specializing in manufacturing manhole covers! At the same time, write to chambers of commerce for information on the community and to companies for annual reports and other organizational literature.

Homequity Company provides relocation counseling services. If you call their toll-free number (800/243-1033), you can receive free information on housing and schools in any community as well as spouse career counseling. You can also write to them for information: Homequity Destination Services, 107 Newtown Road, Danbury, CT 06813.

United Van Lines' Betty Malone Relocation Services (800/325-3870) will send you free information on 7,000 cities, and many banks will supply you with relocation information.

You should also examine the *Moving and Relocation Sourcebook* (Omnigraphics) which profiles the 100 largest metropolitan areas in the United States. This comprehensive volume includes information on everything from population, education, health care, arts, recreation, media, and shopping centers to government, religion, racial and ethnic groups, death rates, and per capita income. The book may be available in some major libraries. It can be purchased through Impact Publications by completing the order form at the end of this book. If you are planning to relocate abroad, we recommend consulting *Craighead's International Business, Travel, and Relocation Guide to 71 Countries* (Gale Research)

Another good source for conducting a job search is Fran Bastress' comprehensive job search guide for spouses: *The New Relocating Spouse's Guide to Employment* (Impact Publications). Based on research conducted with the Department of Defense, this book is especially relevant to Army families.

Part of your research may involve narrowing the number of communities you are considering. If you identify ten alternative communities, outline the criteria by which to evaluate them. For example, you may be particularly interested in moving to a community which has a good climate, excellent cultural facilities, unique recreational opportunities, military facilities, and a sound educational infrastructure in addition to numerous job and career opportunities in your area of interest and skill. Select three communities and initiate a writing campaign for more information. If at all possible, schedule a trip to the cities to get an on-site view or feel for the relative environments. Further try to narrow your choices by rank-ordering your preferences among the three communities. Concentrate your job search efforts on your top priority community.

Your next step is to develop a strategy for penetrating both the advertised and hidden job markets. If you are conducting a job search outside your present community, the advertised job market will be most accessible to you. However, you need to link into the hidden job market, where most of the good jobs are located. While doing this from a distance is somewhat difficult, nonetheless it can be managed.

PENETRATE THE LOCAL JOB MARKET

The advertised job market is always the easiest to access. Buy a newspaper and read the classified ads. Contact an employment firm and they will eagerly assist you. Walk into a personnel office and they may permit you to fill out an application form.

If you target a community from a distance, begin by subscribing to a local newspaper; the Sunday edition will most likely meet your needs. This newspaper also will give you other important information on the community—housing market, economics, politics, society, culture, entertainment, and recreation. Survey the help wanted ads to get a feel for the structure of the advertised job market. Remember, these are not necessarily indicative of the true employment picture in a community—only 20 to 30 percent of the job market. Write letters to various companies and ask about job opportunities. You also may want to contact one or more reputable employment agencies or job search firms for job leads. But remember our previous warnings about possible frauds and hucksters!

Efforts to penetrate the advertised job market should be geared toward uncovering the hidden job market. For example, in reading the Sunday newspaper, watch for names of important people in the society or *"Living"* section. You may want to contact some of these people by using an approach letter as outlined in Chapters 10 and 11. The employment agencies may give some indication of the general employment situation in the community—both advertised and hidden job markets. The chamber of commerce might be able to give you some job leads other than those advertised. Perhaps you can develop local contacts through membership in an alumni network, professional association, or church. Be sure to use your military contacts, especially individuals associated with the groups in Chapter 4—NCOA, TROA, AUSA, ACAP, JAC.

If you are conducting a long-distance job search, we recommend following the same procedures we outlined in Chapter 11 on networking. Preparation is the key to success. Do your research on potential employers, write letters, make phone calls, and schedule informational and referral interviews. The major difference in this situation is your timing. In addition, you need to give more information to your contacts. In your letter mention that you are planning to move to their community and would appreciate their advice on job opportunities for someone with your qualifications. Mention that you plan to visit the community on such and such a date and would appreciate an opportunity to discuss your job search plan at that time. In this case, enclose your resume with the letter and request a reply to your inquiry. Most people will reply and schedule an interview or refer you to someone else.

You should set aside one or two weeks—preferably more—to literally blitz the community with informational and referral interviews. This requires doing a considerable amount of advance work. For example, use your present community to practice informational and referral interviewing. Contact employers in your area who are in similar positions. Many of them may give you referrals to friends and colleagues in your targeted community.

If you have limited contacts when conducting a long-distance job search, you will probably need to use the "cold turkey" approach more frequently. You should make most of your key contacts at least four weeks before you plan to visit your targeted community. Within two weeks of your visit, you should have scheduled most of your interviews.

Try to schedule at least three interviews each day. You will probably do more because each interview will yield one or two referrals to others. Five interviews a day are manageable if you don't need to spend a lot of time traveling from one site to another. Plan to keep the sites near each other for each day. Within a two week period, you should be able to conduct 40 to 60 interviews. Use the weekends to research the community further. Contact a realtor who will be happy to show you around the community and inform you of different housing alternatives, neighborhoods, schools, taxes, public services, shopping centers, and a wealth of other community information. You should reserve the last two days for following up on referrals. Scheduling interviews with referrals will have to be made by telephone because of the time factor.

After concluding your one to two week visit, follow up your interviews with thank you letters, telephone calls, and letters indicating continuing interest and requesting referrals.

If you receive an invitation to a formal job interview in another city, be sure to clarify the financial question of who pays for the interview. Normally if the employer has requested the interview, the company pays the expense to and from the out of town interview. However, if you have invited yourself to an interview by stating that you will be "in town," expect to pay your own expenses. If you are unclear about who initiated the interview, simply ask the employer "How should we handle the travel expenses?" This question should clarify the matter so there will be no misunderstanding.

BUT I'M OVERSEAS

If you are currently stationed abroad, you face unique problems in conducting your long-distance job search. Again, we strongly recommend contacting personnel with the ACAP program who can get you started in planning your career transition from abroad. Be sure you have your mini-resume in the DORS electronic resume database. Become a member of NCOA or TROA and use their placement services. Get a listing of NCOA's upcoming job fairs which you may be able to attend if you are on permissive TDY. You also may want to join one of the commercial electronic resume banks, such as Job Bank USA, Connexion, or kiNexus. If you have on-line computer access to Internet, explore their bulletin board and e-mail options; you may be able to do some important electronic networking with employers both in the United States and abroad. Make sure you use the career resources in your base library and Army Community Services center for identifying potential employers. Many of the resources we identify in Chapters 10 and 18 will be found in these places. Network with people on your base as well as get out that Christmas list and start writing to family, friends, and colleagues who may be helpful in giving you job information and referrals.

Whatever you do, don't postpone the rest of your life by waiting until you return to the United States to start your job search. You can do a great deal while you are overseas to get your job search and relocation plans on the right track. Once you return to the United States, you can literally hit the ground running with your job search. You will have established important job contacts with whom you can now conduct informational interviews according to our advice in Chapter 11.

IDENTIFY OPPORTUNITY STRUCTURES

Each community has its own set of social, economic, political, and job market structures. Your job is to understand and use the particular job market structure in your targeted community. Therefore, we outline the case of Washington, DC for illustrative purposes. The principles for identifying and using the institutional and personal networks will remain the same for most communities even though the individuals, groups, and institutions differ for different communities.

The degree of structure differs for every community. However, one thing is relatively predictable: most communities lack a coherent structure for processing job information efficiently and effectively. But communities are made up of networks which enable individuals to network for job information, advice, and referrals. Each community consists of numerous individuals, groups, organizations, and institutions—many of which constitute mutually dependent networks—that are involved in pursuing their own interests in cooperation and competition with one another. The Yellow Pages of your telephone book best outline the major actors. Banks, mortgage companies, advertising firms, car dealers, schools, churches, small businesses, industries, hospitals, law firms, governments, and civic and voluntary groups do their "own thing" and have their own internal power structure. No one dominates except in small communities which also are company towns—paper mills, mining companies, universities, or steel mills. At the same time, the groups overlap with each other because of economic, political, and social needs. The bank, for example, needs to loan money to the businesses and churches. The businesses, in turn, need the educational institutions. And the educational institutions need the businesses to absorb their graduates. Therefore, individuals tend to cooperate in seeing that people playing the other games also succeed. Members of school boards, medical boards, and the boardrooms of banks and corporations will overlap and give the appearance of a "power structure" even though power is structured in the loosest sense of the term. The game players compete and cooperate with each other as well as co-op one another. The structures they create are your opportunity structures for penetrating the hidden job market. They are networks for locating job opportunities.

Examine the case of Washington, DC. The opportunity structures for your job search networks are relatively well defined in this city. While government is the major institution, other institutions are well defined in relation to the government. Within government, both the political and administrative institutions function as alternative opportunity structures in the Washington networks: congressional staffs, congressional committees, congressional subcommittees, congressional bureaucracy, executive staff, departments, independent executive agencies, and independent regulatory agencies. Outside, but clinging to, government are a variety of other groups and networks: interest groups, the media, professional associations, contractors, consultants, law firms, banks, and universities and colleges. As illustrated on page 290, these groups are linked to one another for survival and advancement. Charles Peters (*How Washington Really Works*) calls them "survival networks" which function in the "make believe world" of Washington, DC. Ripley and Franklin (*Congress, Bureaucracy, and Public Policy*) identify the key political dynamics as "subgovernments"—the interaction of interest groups, agencies, and congressional committees.

Washington is the ultimate networking community. For years Washington insiders have learned how to use these "survival networks" and "subgovernments" to advance their careers. A frequent career pattern would be to work in an agency for three to four years. During that time, you would make important contacts on Capitol Hill with congressional staffs and committees as well as with private consultants, contractors, and interest groups. Your specialized knowledge on the inner workings of government is marketable to these other people. Therefore, you make a relatively easy job change from a federal agency to a congressional committee or to an interest group. After a few years here, you move to another group in the network. Perhaps you work on your law degree at the same time so that in another five years you can go into the truly growth industry in the city—law firms. The key to making these moves is the personal contact—whom you know. Particular attention is given to keeping a current SF 171 or resume, just in case an opportunity happens to come by for you. Congressional staff members usually last no more than two years; they set their sights on consulting and contracting firms, agencies, or interest groups for their next job move.

Whatever community you decide to focus your job search on, expect it to have its particular networks. Do as much research as possible to identify the structure of the networks as well as the key people who can provide access to various elements in the opportunity structures. Washington is not unique in this respect; it is just better known, and Washingtonians talk about it more because of their frequent job moves.

WASHINGTON NETWORKS

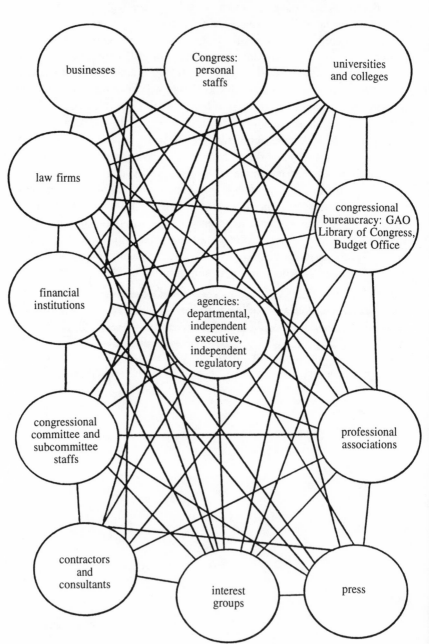

15

START YOUR OWN BUSINESS

While the previous chapters examined strategies for finding employment in other peoples' organizations, you may also be interested in working for yourself. Your self-assessment activities in Chapters 5, 6, and 7 may indicate your motivated abilities and skills (MAS) are entrepreneurial in nature and thus you may be best suited for self-employment.

We expect the 1990s to be another strong decade for entrepreneurship in America. Millions of small businesses will develop in response to new opportunities in high-tech and service industries. Self-employment and start-up businesses will remain great frontiers for career changes in the 1990s. They offer important career alternatives for military personnel.

ALTERNATIVE FOR ARMY RETIREES

Going into business can be an especially attractive career alternative for retired members of the Army who have a monthly pension and medical coverage provided by the U.S. Government. These Army benefits help minimize many of the risks associated with starting a business.

But starting your own business is risky. After all, few retiring Army members have considerable business experience. On the other hand, many have been in positions where they were responsible for a large number of personnel and a sizeable budget, often in the millions of dollars. Much of this experience may transfer well into the world of self-employment.

CONSIDER YOUR ALTERNATIVES

The largest number of job and career opportunities in America are found among small businesses—not large Fortune 500 corporations. Indeed, between 1980 and 1990, Fortune 500 companies eliminated 3.4 million jobs; companies employing fewer than 500 people generated more than 13 million new jobs.

We expect large corporations in the 1990s to continue emphasizing productivity by introducing new cost-cutting technologies and management systems to improve the efficiency and effectiveness of the work place. In other words, they will continue to cut back on the fastest growing corporate expense—personnel. The advancement hierarchies of large companies will shorten and career opportunities narrow as these companies further automate as well as reduce the number of middle management personnel. Many of these displaced personnel will become entrepreneurs, starting both small and medium-sized businesses—often in competition with their former employers.

Since nearly 90 percent of all new jobs will be created by small businesses employing fewer than 500 individuals, you may wish to target your job search toward opportunities with such businesses. Finding a job with a small business will require a great deal of research because most of these businesses are not well known among job seekers.

One other alternative is to start your own business. Indeed, nearly 700,000 new businesses are started each year. During the 1990s millions of individuals will be "pushed" or "pulled" from what were once seen as promising jobs and careers with companies to form their own businesses. As work becomes more centralized, advancement opportunities become more limited, and starting a business becomes easier, millions of individuals will opt for starting their own businesses in the 1990s.

While nearly 700,000 new businesses are started each year, grim business statistics also sober as well as discourage many would-be entrepreneurs; another 500,000 to 600,000 businesses fail each year; 50 percent fail within the first 38 months; and nearly 90 percent fail within 10 years. Unfortunately, starting a business is a risky business; the statistical odds are against anyone becoming a successful entrepreneur.

Nonetheless, owning your business is a viable career alternative to working for someone else—if you approach business intelligently. Many people fail because they lack the necessary ingredients for success. In this chapter we outline the basics for getting started in owning your business and employing yourself.

EXAMINE RISKS AND MOTIVATIONS

You will find few challenges riskier than starting your own business. At the same time, you may experience your greatest professional satisfaction in running your own business.

Starting a business means taking risks. First, while you had grandiose visions of becoming an overnight success, you will probably go into debt and realize little income during the first two years of building your business. You may be under-capitalized or have overhead costs higher than anticipated. It takes time to develop a regular clientele. What profits you do realize are normally plowed back into the business in order to expand operations and guarantee larger future profits. Second, business is often a trial and error process in which it is difficult to predict or ensure outcomes. Due to unforeseen circumstances beyond your control, you may fail even though you work hard and make intelligent decisions. Third, you could go bankrupt and lose more than just your investments of time and money.

At the same time, owning your own business can be tremendously satisfying. It is the ultimate exercise of independence. Being your own boss means you are in control, and no one can fire you. You are rewarded in direct proportion to your productivity. Your salary is not limited by a boss, nor are your accomplishments credited to others. Unless you decide otherwise, you are not wedded to a 9 to 5 work routine or a two-week vacation each year. Depending on how successful your business becomes, you may be able to retire young and pursue other interests. You can turn what you truly enjoy doing, such as hobbies, into a profitable, rewarding, and fun career.

But such self-indulgence and gratification have costs which you may or may not be willing to ensure. You will probably need at least $30,000 to $50,000 of start-up capital, or perhaps as much as $350,000, depending on the type of business you enter. No one will send you a paycheck every two weeks so you can regularly pay your bills. You may work 12 and 14 hour days, seven days a week, and have no vacation during the first few years. And you may become heavily indebted, experience frequent cash flow problems, and eventually have creditors descend on you. If you are an Army retiree, your military benefits will help ease some of these financial strains.

Why, then, start your own business? If you talk to people who have worked for others and then started their own businesses, they will tell you similar stories. They got tired of drawing a salary while making someone else rich. They got bored with their work and hated coming to an office everyday to engage in a 9 to 5 work routine. They wanted control over what they did. Some worked for jerks; others were victims of organizational politics; and others had difficulty working in an environment structured by others whom they considered less competent than themselves. Many simply couldn't work for others—they had to be in charge of their work. On a more positive note, many started businesses because they had a great idea they wanted to pursue, or they wanted the challenge of independently accomplishing their own goals.

This is the old fashioned way of making money—hard work and long hours.

If you decide to go into business for yourself, be sure you know what you want to do and be willing to take risks and work hard. Don't expect to get rich overnight or sit back and watch your business grow on its own. Starting a business is usually a very sobering experience that tests your motivations, abilities, and skills. Success in a bureaucratic or corporate career may not transfer well to starting your own business which initially requires entrepreneurial skills. Be prepared to work long and hard hours, experience disappointments, and challenge yourself to the limits. You will quickly discover this is the old fashioned way of making money—hard work and long hours. But at least you can choose which 12 to 14 hours of each day you want to work!

There are few things that are more self-actualizing than running your own business. But you must have realistic expectations as well as a motivational pattern which is conducive to taking risks and being an entrepreneur. In Chapters 5, 6, and 7 you identified your motivational patterns and skills. If you like security, predictability, and stability, you probably are a candidate for a position where someone hands you a paycheck each week. If you read and believe in a get-rich-quick book, video, or seminar which tries to minimize your risks and uncertainty, you probably have been ripped-off by an enterprising individual who is getting rich producing books, videos, and seminars for naive people!

POSSESS THE RIGHT STRENGTHS FOR SUCCESS

How can you become self-employed and successful at the same time? No one has a magical success formula for the budding entrepreneur—only advice based on experience. We do know why many businesses fail, and we can identify some basic characteristics for success. Poor management and decision-making lie at the heart of business failures. Many people go into business without doing sufficient market research; they under-capitalize; they select a poor location; they incur extremely high and debilitating overhead costs; they lack commitment; they are unwilling to sacrifice; they can't read or count; and they lack interpersonal and salesmanship skills.

On the positive side, studies continue to identify something called "drive," or the need to achieve, as a key characteristic of successful entrepreneurs. As Kellogg (*Fast Track,* McGraw-Hill) and others have found, young achievers and successful entrepreneurs possess similar characteristics: "A high energy level, restless, a willingness to work hard and take risks, a desire to escape from insecurity."

Successful business people combine certain motivations, skills, and circumstances. Contrary to popular myths, you don't need to be rich or have an MBA or business experience to get started. If you are willing to gamble and are a self-starter, self-confident, an organizer, and you like people, you should consider this entrepreneurial alternative in changing careers. These characteristics along with drive, thinking ability, human relations, communication, technical knowledge, hard work, persistence, and good luck are essential ingredients for business success.

If these are among your strengths (Chapter 7), you may be a good candidate for starting your own business with a high probability of success. If you feel you have recurring weaknesses in certain areas, you may want to find a business partner who has particular complementary strengths for running a business. As someone just coming out of the Army, be careful whom you trust with your money. You may encounter some unscrupulous people who will take advantage of you.

KNOW YOURSELF

There are many different ways to get started in business. You can buy into a franchise which can initially cost you $20,000 to $500,000. Advertisements in the *Wall Street Journal* are a good source for hundreds of franchise opportunities from flipping hamburgers to selling animals. You can join someone else's business on a full-time or part-time basis as a partner or employee in order to get some direct business experience. You can try your hand at a direct-sales business such as Amway, Shaklee, or Avon. Hundreds of new direct-sales businesses modeled after Amway's multi-level business methods are now marketing every conceivable product—soap, computers, canoes, motor oil, and milk. You can buy someone else's business or you can start your own business from scratch.

Your decision on how to get started in business should be based upon the data you generated on your skills and goals in Chapters 5, 6, and 7. Do not go into business for negative reasons—get fired, hate your job, can't find work. Unfortunately, many people go into business with totally unrealistic expectations as well as with little understanding of their own goals, skills, and motivations. For example, while it is nice to work around food and beverages, owning a restaurant requires handling inventory and personnel as well as paying taxes and rent, doing bookkeeping, and advertising. Getting all those wonderful dishes served to demanding customers is hard work! Many people don't understand how the business world works. It requires a great deal of interpersonal skill to develop and expand personal networks of creditors, clients, and colleagues.

Therefore, you should do two things before you decide to go into business. First, thoroughly explore your goals and motivations. The questions are familiar:

- What do you want to do?
- What do you do well?
- What do you enjoy doing?

Second, research different types of businesses in order to better understand advantages, disadvantages, procedures, processes, and possible problems. Talk to business persons about their work. Try to learn as much as possible about the reality before you invest your time and money. Surprisingly, few people do this. Many people leap into a business that they think will be great and then later learn it was neither right for them nor did they have realistic expectations of what was involved. This is precisely why so many businesses fail each year.

You should approach business opportunities the same way you approach the job market: do research, develop networks, and conduct informational and referral interviews. Most business people, including your competition, will share their experiences with you and assist you with advice and referrals. Such research is absolutely invaluable. If you fail to do it initially, you will pay later on by making the same mistakes that millions of others have made in starting their own businesses in isolation of others. Don't be high on motivation but low on knowledge and skills, for "thinking big" is no substitute for doing the work!

LOOK FOR NEW OPPORTUNITIES

Most business people will tell you similar stories of the reality of running your own business. Do your market research, spend long hours, plan, and be persistent. They also will give you advice on what businesses to avoid and what business routines you should be prepared to handle.

Many service and high-tech businesses will be growing in the 1990s. Given the changing demographic structure—fewer young people, more elderly, the two career family—numerous opportunities are arising for small personal service businesses to meet the needs of the elderly and career-oriented families. Businesses relating to restaurants, home maintenance, health care, housing for the elderly, and mortuaries and cemeteries should expand considerably during the next two decades.

Opportunities are also available for inventive business persons who can make more productive use of busy peoples' time—fast foods, financial planning, and mail-order shopping. The information and high-tech revolutions are taking place at the same time two career families do not have time to waste standing in lines at banks, grocery stores, and department stores. Mail-order or computer assisted home and office-based shopping should increase dramatically during the next decade.

A service business is particularly attractive. It is easy to establish, many require a small initial investment, and the bookkeeping is relatively simple. You may be able to operate from your home and thus keep your overhead down.

Knowing these trends and opportunities is important, but they should not be the only determining factors in choosing a business. You should start with yourself by again trying to identify a business that is fit for you rather than one you think you might fit into.

PREPARE THE BASICS

You also need to consider several other factors before starting a business. Since a business requires financing, locating, planning, developing customer relationships, and meeting legal requirements, be prepared to address these questions:

1. **How can I best finance the business?** Take out a personal or business loan with a bank? Go into a partnership in order to share the risks and costs? Get a loan from the Small Business Administration?

2. **How much financing do I need?** Many businesses fail because they are under-capitalized. Others fail because of over-spending on rent, furnishings, inventory, personnel, and advertising.

3. **Where is my market?** Just in this community, region, nationwide, or international? Mail-order businesses enable you to expand your market nationwide whereas retail and service businesses tend to be confined to particular neighborhoods or communities.

4. **Who are my suppliers?** How many must I work with? What about credit arrangements?

5. **Where is the best location for the business?** Do you need to open a store or operate out of your home? If you need a store or office, is it conveniently located for your clientele? "Location is everything" still best summarizes the success of many businesses, especially McDonald's and Wal-Mart.

6. **How should the business be legally structured?** Sole proprietorship, partnership, or corporation? Each has certain advantages and disadvantages. A corporation has several tax advantages.

7. **What licenses and permits do I need?** These consist of local business licenses and permits, federal employee identification numbers, state sales tax number, state occupational licenses, federal licenses and permits, and special state and

local regulations which vary from state to state and from community to community. What type of insurance do I need? Fire, theft, liability, workers' compensation, and auto?

8. **How many employees do I need?** Can I do without personnel initially until the business expands? Should I use part-time and temporary help?

9. **What business name should I use?** If incorporated, is anyone else using the name? If a trade name, is it registered?

10. **What accounting system should I use?** Cash or accrual? Can I handle the books or do I need a part-time or full-time accountant? Who will handle the timely calculation and payment of payroll, sales, and corporate taxes as well as insurance, retirement plans, and workers compensation?

11. **Do I need a lawyer?** What type of lawyer? What legal work can I do myself?

12. **How do I develop a business plan?** A business plan should include a definition of the business, a marketing strategy, operational policies, purchasing plans, financial statements, and capital raising plans.

GET USEFUL ADVICE

If you decide to go into business, make sure you choose the right business for your particular skills, abilities, motivation, and interests. A good starting point is Douglas Gray's *Have You Got What It Takes? The Entrepreneur's Complete Self-Assessment Guide* (Self-Counseling Press). This book provides you with useful exercises for assessing your suitability for becoming an entrepreneur. One book includes information on franchises for veterans: *The Veteran's Survival Guide to Good Jobs in Bad Times* (Grant's Guides). For a good overview of the many decisions you must make in establishing a small business, see Bernard Kamaroff's *Small-Time Operators* (Bell Springs Publishing). This book provides you with all the basic information you need for starting your own business, including ledger sheets for setting up your books. Albert Lowry's *How to Become Financially Successful by Owning Your Own Business* (Simon and Schuster) also outlines the basics for both small-time and big-time operators. Several other books provide similar how-to advice for the neophyte entrepreneur:

James W. Holloran, *The Entrepreneur's Guide to Starting a Successful Business* (TAB Books)

Lyle Maul and Dianne Mayfield, *The Entrepreneur's Road Map to Business Success* (Saxton River Publications)

Gregory and Patricia Kishel, *How to Start, Run, and Stay in Business* (Wiley and Sons)

Arnold S. Goldstein, *Starting on a Shoestring: Building a Business Without a Bankroll* (Wiley and Sons)

Patricia A. Way, *Small Businesses That Grow and Grow and Grow* (Betterway Publications)

The J. K. Lasser Tax Institute, *How to Run a Small Business* (St. Martin's Press)

C. D. Peterson, *How to Leave Your Job and Buy a Business of Your Own* (St. Martin's Press)

Joseph Anthony, *Kiplinger's Working for Yourself* (Kiplinger)

Ina Lee Selden, *Going Into Business for Yourself: New Beginnings After 50* (American Association of Retired Persons)

Paul and Sarah Edwards, *The Best Home-Based Businesses for the 90s* (Putnam).

Sharon Kahn and Philip Lief Group, *101 Best Businesses to Start* (Bantam Books)

C. Revel, *184 Businesses Anyone Can Start* (Bantam Books)

The federal government will help you with several publications available through the U.S. Small Business Administration: 1441 L Street, NW, Washington, DC 20416, Tel. 800/368-5855. SBA field offices are located in 85 cities. The Consumer Information Center publishes a free booklet entitled *More Than a Dream: Running Your Own Business:* Dept. 616J, Pueblo, CO 81009. The Internal Revenue Service sponsors several one-day tax workshops for small businesses. Your local Chamber of Commerce also can give you useful information.

The U.S. Small Business Administration also sponsors a non-profit association which offers excellent assistance in starting and improving small businesses. SCORE, the Service Corps of Retired Executives Association, provides counseling, workshops, and educational programs on small business throughout the United States. Each year the various local chapters of SCORE conduct nearly 4,000 workshops to assist entrepreneurs with their small businesses. For more information on SCORE and the chapter nearest to you, contact SCORE, 409 3rd Street, SW, Suite 5900, Washington, DC 20024-3212, Tel. 800/634-0245.

Buying into a franchise may be a good business decision since the franchise often provides business training to help ensure success. For information on franchises for veterans, contact VETFRAM (The Veterans' Transition Franchise Initiative), a non-profit program whose member franchisors give discounts and provide financing for veterans wishing to acquire a franchise. You can contact them by calling 817/753-4555. You should also consult *The Franchise Opportunities Guide* which lists over 2,500 franchise opportunities. This guide is available through The International Franchise Association, 1350 New York Avenue, NW, Suite 900, Washington, DC. You can order by credit card by calling 1-800-543-1038 ($15 + $6 shipping/handling). The U.S. Department of Commerce also publishes *The Franchise Opportunities Handbook* (U.S. Government Printing Office).

If you are interested in how to get started in a particular small business, write for information from the American Entrepreneurs Association, 2392 Morse Avenue, Irving, CA 92714-6234 or use their toll-free numbers: 800/421-2300 or 800/421-2345. This organization offers a comprehensive set of services for starting small businesses. These include a free catalog of products and services, the magazine *Entrepreneur,* and the Entrepreneur Institute. To help you get off in the right direction, this organization also publishes over 300 helpful small business start-up and operation manuals which include businesses such as energy stores, video stores, seminars, pet cemeteries, health clubs, pizza parlors, travel agencies, dating services, rent-a-hot tub, furniture stripping, pipe shop, discos, and maid services. For a six-month free subscription to *Money Making Opportunities* magazine, which lists hundreds of mail order ads, write to Money Making Opportunities, 11071 Ventura Blvd., Studio City, CA 91604. These publications will give you a sampling of alternative businesses you can establish. However, beware of hucksters who may advertise in business magazines. Many want your money for "proven success" and "get-rich-quick" formulas that don't even work for the advertisers!

CONTINUE YOUR SUCCESS

The factors for operating a successful business are similar to the 21 principles we outlined in Chapter 3 for conducting a successful job search. Once your initial start-up problems are solved, you must organize, plan, implement, and manage in relation to your goals. Many people lack these abilities. Some people are good at initially starting a business, but they are unable to follow-through in managing day-to-day routines once the business is established. And others have the ability to start, manage, and expand businesses successfully.

Be careful about business success. Many business people become obsessed with their work, put in 12 and 14 hour days continuously, and spend seven day weeks to make the business successful. Unwilling to delegate, they try to do too much and thus become a prisoner to the business. The proverbial "tail wagging the dog" is a common phenomenon in small businesses. For some people, this lifestyle feeds their ego and makes them happy. For others, the 9 to 5 routine of working for someone else on salary may look very attractive only after a few months of self-employment. Therefore, you must be prepared to change your lifestyle when embarking on your own business. Your major limitation will be yourself.

So think it over carefully, do your research, and plan, organize, implement, and manage for success. Even though running your own business is risky and involves hard work, the thrill of independence and success is hard to beat!

16

IMPLEMENT YOUR GOALS

*U*nderstanding without action is a waste of time. And buying a how-to book without implementing it is a waste of money. Many people read how-to books, attend how-to seminars, and do nothing other than read more books, attend more seminars, and engage in more wishful thinking. While these activities become forms of therapy for some individuals, they should lead to positive actions for you. After all, as an Army member you are used to putting plans in place and achieving assigned objectives.

From the very beginning of this book we stressed the importance of understanding the job market and developing appropriate job search strategies for getting the job you want. We make no assumptions nor claim any magic is contained in this book. Rather, we have attempted to assemble useful information to help you organize an effective job search

303

which will best communicate your qualifications to potential employers. Individual chapters examined the present and future job markets as well as outlined in how-to terms specific skills for shaping your own future. We have done our part in getting you to the implementation stage. What happens next is your responsibility.

The methods we outlined in previous chapters have worked for thousands of individuals who have paid $2,000 to $12,000 to get similar information from the highly-paid professionals. While you may want to see a professional for assistance at certain steps in your job search, if you are self-motivated you can do everything on your own with a minimum expenditure of money. The major cost will be your time and effort.

But you must make the effort and take the *risk of implementing* this book. Changing careers takes work and is a risky business. You try something new and place your ego on the line. You subject yourself to the possibility of being rejected several times. And this is precisely the major barrier you will encounter to effective implementation. For many people are unwilling to take more than a few rejections.

Understanding without action is a waste of time. And buying a how-to book without implementing it is a waste of money.

WELCOME REJECTIONS
AS LEARNING OPPORTUNITIES

Planning is the easiest part of any task. Turning plans into reality is the most difficult challenge. It's relatively simple to set goals and outline a course of action divorced from the reality of actually doing it. But if you don't take action, you will not get your expected results. You must implement if you want desired results.

Once you take action, be prepared for rejections. Employers will tell you "Thank you—we'll call you," but they never do. Other employers will tell you "We have no positions available at this time for someone with your qualifications" or "You don't have the qualifications necessary for this position." Whatever the story, you will face many disappointments on the road to success.

Rejections are a normal part of the process of finding employment as well as getting ahead in life. Rejections offer an important learning experience which should help you better understand yourself, employers, and the job finding process. Expect ten rejections or "nos" for every acceptance or "yes" you receive. If you quit after five or eight rejections, you prematurely end your job search. If you persist in collecting two to five more "nos," you will likely receive a "yes." Most people quit prematurely because their ego is not prepared for more rejections. Therefore, you should welcome rejections as you seek more and more acceptances.

GET MOTIVATED AND WORK HARD

Assuming you have a firm understanding of each job search step and how to relate them to your goals, what do you do next? The next steps involve *motivation and hard work.* Just how motivated are you to seek a new job or career and thus your life? Our experience is that individuals need to be sufficiently *motivated* to make the first move and do it properly. If you go about your job search half-heartedly—you just want to "test the waters" to see what's out there—don't expect to be successful. You must be committed to achieving specific goals. Make the decision to properly develop and implement your job search and be prepared to work hard in achieving your goals.

FIND TIME

Once you've convinced yourself to take the necessary steps to find a job or change and advance your career, you need to find the *time* to properly implement your job search. This requires setting aside specific blocks of time for identifying your motivated abilities and skills, developing your resume, writing letters, making telephone calls, and conducting the necessary research and networking required for success. This whole process takes time. If you are a busy person, like most people, you simply must make the time. As noted in our examination of your time management practices in Chapter 3 (pages 57-59), you should practice your own versions of time management or cutback management. Get better organized, give some things up, or cut back on all your activities. If, for example, you can set aside one hour each day to devote to your job search, you will spend seven hours a week or 28 hours a month on your search. However, you should and can find more time than this.

Time and again we find successful job hunters are the ones who routinize a job search schedule and keep at it. They make contact after contact, conduct numerous informational interviews, submit many applications and resumes, and keep repeating these activities in spite of encountering rejections. They learn that success is just a few more "nos" and informational interviews away. They face each day with a positive attitude fit for someone desiring to change their life—I must collect my ten "nos" today because each "no" brings me closer to another "yes"!

Success is just a few more "nos" and informational interviews away.

COMMIT YOURSELF IN WRITING

You may find it useful to commit yourself in writing to achieving job search success. This is a very useful way to get both motivated and directed for action. Start by completing the job search contract on page 307 and keep it near you—in your briefcase or on your desk.

In addition, you should complete weekly performance reports. These reports identify what you actually accomplished rather than what your good intentions tell you to do. Make copies of the performance and planning report form on page 308 and use one each week to track your actual progress and to plan your activities for the next week.

If you fail to meet these written commitments, issue yourself a revised and updated contract. But if you do this three or more times, we strongly suggest that you question your motivation and commitment to find a job. Start over again, but this time consult a professional career counselor who can provide you with the necessary structure to make progress in finding a job.

A professional may not be cheap, but if paying for help gets you on the right track and results in the job you want, it's money well spent. Do not be "penny wise but pound foolish" with your future. If you must seek professional advice, be sure you are an informed consumer according to our "shopping" advice in Chapter 3.

JOB SEARCH CONTRACT

1. I'm committed to changing my life by changing my job. Today's date is _____ .

2. I will manage my time so that I can successfully complete my job search and find a high quality job. I will complete my time management inventory (pages 57-59) and begin changing my time management behavior on _____ .

3. I will begin my job search on _____ .

4. I will involve _____ with my job search.
                    (individual/group)

5. I will spend at least one week conducting library research on different jobs, employers, and organizations. I will begin this research during the week of _____ .

6. I will complete my skills identification step by _____ .

7. I will complete my objective statement by _____ .

8. I will complete my resume by _____ .

9. Each week I will:

   - make ____ new job contacts.
   - conduct ____ informational interviews.
   - follow-up on ____ referrals.

10. My first job interview will take place during the week of _____ .

11. I will begin my new job by _____ .

12. I will make a habit of learning one new skill each year.

Signature: _____

Date: _____

WEEKLY JOB SEARCH PERFORMANCE AND PLANNING REPORT

1. The week of: _____.

2. This week I:
   - wrote ___ job search letters.
   - sent ___ resumes and ___ letters to potential employers.
   - completed ___ applications.
   - made ___ job search telephone calls.
   - completed ___ hours of job research.
   - set up ___ appointments for informational interviews.
   - conducted ___ informational interviews.
   - received ___ invitations to a job interview.
   - followed up on ___ contacts and ___ referrals.

3. Next week I will:
   - write ___ job search letters.
   - send ___ resumes and ___ letters to potential employers.
   - complete ___ applications.
   - make ___ job search telephone calls.
   - complete ___ hours of job research.
   - set up ___ appointments for informational interviews.
   - conduct ___ informational interviews.
   - follow up on ___ contacts and ___ referrals.

4. Summary of progress this week in reference to my Job Search Contract commitments:

   _____

   _____

   _____

   _____

   _____

   _____

CHANGE CAREERS FOR
SECURING YOUR FUTURE

The continuing transformation of American society will require millions of individuals to change careers in the years ahead. The nature of jobs and careers are changing as the work place becomes transformed due to the impact of new technology and unique events. Many career fields in demand today may well be glutted tomorrow.

Throughout this book we have emphasized the importance of *being prepared* for turbulent times. The age of the generalist armed with job search skills alone is passing. The emerging society requires a new type of *generalist-specialist* who is trained for today's technology, *flexible* enough to be retrained in tomorrow's technology, and *adaptive* to new jobs and careers that will arise today and tomorrow. In other words, the society needs more and more generalist-specialists who welcome change by being willing and able to change careers. Knowing and practicing the job search skills outlined in this book, these people also are continuously learning new work-content skills in order to better position themselves in tomorrow's job market.

> *Make an effort to learn one new skill each year.*

If you want to change your life, you should be prepared to develop and practice careering competencies for the decades ahead. We recommend two final career actions on your part. First, make an effort to learn one new skill each year; the skill can be related to work, family, community, or a hobby such as building bookcases, operating different computer software packages, repairing appliances, or remodeling your home. If you do this, you will be better prepared for making the career transitions necessary for functioning effectively in turbulent times.

Second, develop your own five-year plan which incorporates yearly career check-ups. At the end of each year, ask yourself: To what degree have I achieved my goals? Which goals do I need to revise? What actions do I need to take to better achieve my goals?

Careers and jobs should not be viewed as life sentences. You should feel free to change jobs and careers when you want to or need to. In fact, thousands of people make successful career transitions each year. Some are more successful than others in finding the right job. If you plan your career transition according to the methods outlined in previous chapters, you should be able to successfully land the job you want.

Treat yourself right. Take the time and effort to sail into today's job market with a plan of action that links your qualifications to the needs of employers. You are first and foremost an individual with knowledge, abilities, and skills that many employers need and want. If you follow the advice of this book, you will put your best foot forward in communicating your qualifications to employers. You will find a job fit for you and a career that is both satisfying and rewarding. You'll discover your best years still lie ahead as you pursue your new post-Army career and lifestyle.

17

COMPUTER PATHWAYS TO CAREER FITNESS

*Y*ou can link your job search to today's information highway via your computer. Indeed, there's an electronic revolution taking place in the employment field. It is changing the way people find jobs and how employers conduct the hiring process. You would be wise to understand this revolution. For you may want to join it today as well as participate in it for many years to come. It will increase your power to change jobs throughout your life. Central to this revolution is the emerging concept of "career fitness"—a process for constantly keeping your career healthy.

WELCOME TO THE REVOLUTION

The way people go about finding jobs—responding to classified ads, networking, using employment firms, executive search firms or headhunt-

ers, and career counselors—has not changed greatly during the past fifty
years. The same is true for how employers go about locating candidates
and hiring—networking, placing classified ads, and using employment
firms and headhunters. In such a system, job hunters and employers come
together in a highly decentralized and fragmented job market characterized by poor communication, intrigue, uncertainty, numerous rejections,
high levels of anxiety, and random luck. While no one really likes this
system—especially job seekers who must learn to communicate their
qualifications to strangers and absorb numerous rejections—no one has
developed a better system to link talented individuals to vacant positions—at least not until now. In the meantime, individuals learn entrepreneurial strategies for operating within this less than perfect system.

---

*The electronic communication revolution
promises to dramatically improve
communication between employers
and job seekers.*

The electronic communication revolution has the potential to
significantly change job search and hiring approaches. It may eliminate
much of the decentralization, fragmentation, uncertainty, chaos, and
anxiety in the hiring process. Most important of all, it promises to
dramatically improve communication between employers and job seekers
and, in the process, redefine the structure and coherence of the job
market.

OLD DREAMS, NEW UTOPIAS

Employment specialists have long dreamed of creating a nationwide
computerized information highway for employment. Ideally, a computerized job bank would list all available job vacancies throughout the nation.
Job seekers and employers could use such a system to quickly develop
linkages to each other through an efficient and effective electronic
network system. No longer would employers need to engage in a costly
and time consuming process of placing classified ads or hiring employ-

ment firms to find needed personnel. Job seekers would be able to quickly identify vacancies for which they are most qualified. They could eliminate the time consuming and frustrating process of responding to classified ads, broadcasting resumes and letters, networking, and literally knocking on doors. So goes the dream.

The job search revolution taking place today is not exactly what employment specialists have long envisioned. While many state employment offices, libraries, and educational institutions have computerized job banks on-line, such as America's Job Bank, most of these systems are limited in scope, include only certain types of jobs, and focus on a few geographic areas. They are by no means at the forefront of the much touted "national information highway" of the future. No comprehensive, nationwide computerized job bank has yet been created to centralize job vacancy information and thereby create a truly national job market. In the meantime, the job market remains decentralized, fragmented, and chaotic. Success in this market primarily requires formal application and interpersonal strategies for linking individual qualifications to employer needs.

Nonetheless, signs of a job search/hiring revolution are readily apparent for the 1990s and into the 21st century. It's taking on a new and unexpected form. Using computer technology to link job seekers to employers, this revolution is organized and directed by a few innovative computerized job bank firms that use sophisticated search and retrieval software that quickly links employers to job seekers. Employers and individuals become members, paying yearly or per search fees to participate in the database. The key to making the system work efficiently and effectively is for a large number of both employers and job seekers to belong to the database. The larger the number of members and the broader the mix of skills and opportunities, the better the choices for all members involved.

In its simplest form, this revolution is an efficient way of linking employers to candidates. For you the job seeker, it's a high-tech way of broadcasting your resume to hundreds of employers. Within the next ten years electronic networks will transform the way job seekers market themselves to potential employers. Working from their personal computers, or through computerized job search services with extensive electronic resume and employer banks, job seekers will be able to quickly broadcast their qualifications to thousands of employers. No longer will they need to spend three, six, or nine months pounding the pavement, responding to classified job ads, attending meetings, making cold telephone calls, contacting strangers, or scheduling informational interviews. Indeed, many of the traditional job search methods outlined in this book may well become obsolete in this new electronic employment era. At least these appear to be the promises of the electronic revolution for the job markets of today and tomorrow.

> ## *This revolution is an efficient way of linking employers to candidates.*

Since electronic job search methods are likely to cut job search time by 50 to 70 percent, they should prove to be a cost effective way of linking candidates to employers. Employers will find they cost less and may generate better quality candidates than their more traditional recruitment methods of placing classified ads, hiring employment firms, or broadcasting vacancy announcements. Job seekers will discover that electronic networking enables them to reach a very broad sample of employers that would not be available through other job search methods.

Offering new job search and hiring options for individuals and employers alike, electronic job search services have quickly become one of the most efficient and effective ways of matching qualified candidates to employers. It will displace many current inefficient and ineffective employment services. It drastically improves communication as well as creates a certain degree of centralization in what is inherently a decentralized job market.

But that is just part of the story, the most visible part most people understand. So far computer technology has been used to make a traditional process more efficient—improve communication between job seekers and employers. The next stage is now evolving as the technology is literally redefining the process. The really revolutionary dimension of these electronic job banks is their potential to significantly alter the way people view their careers, conduct a job search, and hire.

The concept of "career fitness" explains what may well become a normal way of managing your career in the future. It's a concept worth understanding and exploring.

CAREER FITNESS IN
THE ELECTRONIC AGE

"Career fitness" is an obvious health analogy adapted to the career field. Emphasizing development and growth, this concept implies keeping your career healthy not just today or tomorrow but throughout your worklife. As enunciated by Peter Weddle, CEO of Job Bank USA, it's a lifelong concept of how you go about managing your career. Rather than initiate a job search only when you lose your job or become dissatisfied with your work—the career crisis approach—you should constantly manage your career by keeping yourself marketable and available for alternative opportunities. You can easily do this by becoming a member of one or more electronic job banks where you can literally be in the job market 24 hours a day, 7 days a weeks, and 365 days a year. Your membership does not mean you are actively seeking employment; rather, you are constantly keeping yourself marketable or "fit" for new and exciting opportunities that may come your way because you keep an updated resume in the database. While you work, your resume is always working for you. Your electronic resume is the key element for defining and directing your career fitness. As envisioned by "career fitness" advocates, individuals should seriously consider becoming lifelong members of such groups, regardless of whether or not they are actively seeking new employment.

You can literally be in the job market 24 hours a day, 7 days a week, and 365 days a year.

THE NEW ELECTRONIC RESUME

Computerized job banks use electronic resumes for linking candidates to employers. While similar in many ways to traditional resumes, the electronic resume is different. It requires close attention to the choice of resume *language* because your resume must be "read" by search and retrieval software. The software literally takes key words identified in employers' vacancy announcements and matches them with similar key words found on resumes. If, for example, an employer is looking for a human resources manager with ten years of progressive experience in developing training programs for mining engineers, a search for candidates meeting these qualifications may result in making matches with 15 resumes in the database. The employer receives hard copies of the electronic resumes and further sorts the batch of candidates through more traditional means such as telephone screening interviews.

These new electronic job search and hiring systems have important implications for resume writing. When you write an electronic resume, you must focus on using *proper resume language* that would be most responsive for the search and retrieval software. This means knowing what key words, such as the functional skills language in Chapter 5, are best to include on an electronic resume. You need not be as concerned with such cosmetic elements as resume layout, type faces, and paper texture and color. While important to a traditional paper job search, these "dressed for success" elements are not important to the search and retrieval software of electronic job banks. Therefore, you will need to write a different type of resume for your "career fitness". The degree to which your resume is "software sensitive" will determine how many employers will contact you.

MEET THE NEW
GENERATION OF PLAYERS

During the past few years numerous firms have gotten into the electronic resume business. Many of them use electronic e-mail communications, on-line bulletin boards, and existing nationwide on-line computer networks such as America OnLine, CompuServe, and Prodigy. Primarily funded by large Fortune 1,000 corporations, membership in these electronic employment data-based companies includes individuals, professional associations, and alumni, retirement, military, and other groups who are interested in linking electronic resumes to member companies. These electronic resume services become new employer-employee networks which are redefining the job marketplace. The marketplace is no longer confined to the classified ads, employment firms, or executive search firms. These firms may bring together over 100,000 members into an electronic network which is constantly seeking to find "good fits" between the needs of employers and the key words appearing on members' electronic resumes.

Several electronic job search networks designed specifically for military personnel should prove useful for your job search:

DORS (Defense Outplacement Referral System)
ATTN: Operation Transition
99 Pacific St.
Suite 155A
Monterey, CA 93940-2453
Tel. 800-727-3677

TOPS: TROA's Officer Placement Service
The Retired Officers Association
201 N. Washington St.
Alexandria, VA 22314-2539
Tel. 800-245-8762 or 703-549-2311

Veterans Employment Assistance (VEA) Program
Non Commissioned Officers Association
10635 IH 35 North
San Antonio, TX 78233
Tel. 210-653-6161

Each of these organizations operates resume databases for matching candidates with employers. Most of these programs are open to active duty personnel and their spouses. Some also are open to veterans, reservists, and national guard members. You should contact each of the organizations for information on their specific services.

The DORS system, for example, includes a Transition Bulletin Board (TBB) and calendar of events as well as incorporates America's Job Bank for on-line employment services. Active duty members and those separated for up to six months, and their spouses, can use DORS free of charge at 300 different sites. Call their 800 telephone number for further information. You can use DORS by participating in the ACAP program.

The placement programs offered by TROA and NCOA also include electronic resume databases. Both organizations use a specific form of mini-resume for using the system. NCOA, for example, operates a Mini Resume People Bank. See Chapter 4 for further information on these organizations.

Several commercial electronic job banks offer unique resume and job search services. The major firms include the following:

JOB BANK USA: 1420 Spring Hill Road, Suite 480, McLean, VA 22102, Tel. 800-296-1USA or Fax 703-847-1494. Advertised as "the nation's premier database company," Job Bank USA is an all purpose employment resource for both employers and job seekers. More than 35 educational institutions participate, including the University of Notre Dame, Fairleigh Dickinson University, The American University, University of California (Irvine), the University of Texas (Arlington), the University of Arkansas, the University of Maryland, the United States Military Academy, and the University of Louisville. Graduating seniors and alumni associated with these institutions give employers access to a growing pool of degreed professionals, from entry-level to senior executive. Individuals can enroll in the Job Bank USA database for a basic annual fee of $48.50. Other levels of enrollment cost $78.00 and $129.00. The basic enrollment gives you the following services:

- Conversion of your work experience and employment credentials into a unique electronic resume.

- Storage of your electronic resume in Job Bank USA's computer for one year.

- Access to a toll free telephone number to make a reasonable number of updates and corrections to your electronic resume.

- Exclusive discounts on a wide range of career management and job search services, books, and other resources.

- Unlimited referral to Job Bank USA clients who have open positions for which you qualify.

- A quarterly newsletter—*CAREERPLUS*—published exclusively for database enrollees. Includes important job market observations as well as useful ideas and tips for job seekers.

Guaranteeing privacy, Job Bank USA only releases your resume to prospective employers with your prior approval. Job Bank USA also offers testing/assessment and resume writing services. Its executive search service is aimed at linking high quality candidates to employers. This service normally deals with positions offering a base salary of $100,000 or more.

KINEXUS: Information Kinetics, Inc., 640 N. LaSalle St., Suite 560, Chicago, IL 60610, Tel. 800-229-6499, Fax 312-642-0616. Advertises itself as "the nation's first and largest computerized database of experienced executives, college and university students and alumni seeking part-time and full-time employment." Its current database includes over 150,000 active job seekers. Designed primarily for graduating college students and companies interested in communicating directly with career and placement centers in advertising job vacancies and identifying and interviewing candidates, this on-campus electronic job listing and advertising system operates "Career Network" on 100 colleges and universities such as Indiana University, University of Tennessee (Knoxville), Harvard, University of Houston, Brigham Young University, University of California (Davis), Syracuse University, and the University of North Carolina. The network is sponsored by companies such as Aetna, ALCOA, Burlington Industries, Monsanto Chemical, MITRE, Motorola, The Prudential, Procter & Gamble, Sears Roebuck & Company, and Watkins-Johnson as well as includes in its membership companies such as ADP, AT&T, Blue Cross, EDS, M&M Mars, IDS, Johnson & Johnson, Merrill Lynch, TRW, and UPS. Its members also include government agencies, such as the Department of Energy, SBA, TVA, and the Department of Navy. The kiNexus system uses search (kiNexus keyWord[SM]) and retrieval software for aligning resume information with the hiring needs identified by its member employers. It uses the nationwide on-line computer network provided and supported by PRODIGY as well as electronic E-Mail communications and on-line Bulletin Board, electronic Billboard, and 3 screen Profile. Organizational users can access job information from their personal computers in offices and at home. The PC-based system is stored and accessible from a CD-ROM drive and works with existing Lotus, Dbase, MicroSoft World, WordPerfect, and WordStar programs. Students and alumni at nearly 800 colleges and universities can register with kiNexus through their Career Center at no charge. They register with the database for one year and also can update their electronic resume at any time. If your college or university is not a member of kiNexus, you can still register with this organization for an annual fee of $30 ($50 if you want confidentiality) by calling their toll-free number—800-229-6499. kiNexus is also available through numerous professional organizations, associations, outplacement firms, and public libraries. If you have any questions on your free eligibility or wish to enroll directly, contact kiNexus for information on their services.

CONNEXION®: Peterson's Connexion® Services, 202 Carnegie Center, P.O. Box 2123, Princeton, NJ 08543-2123, Tel. 800-338-3282, Ext. 561 or Fax 609-243-9150. Advertised as "the innovative recruitment network that links you with thousands of employers and graduate schools who may be seeking candidates with your specific experience or training." Unlike other electronic networks, Connexion® includes graduate schools in its recruitment base. Membership is free for currently enrolled full-time students. Other individuals can enroll for an annual fee of $40. Individuals who do not want their resumes sent to employers, but who want access to other Connexion® privileges and communiques, can join as Associate Members for an annual fee of $24.95. This network can be accessed on CompuServe.

CAREER PLACEMENT REGISTRY: Career Placement Registry, Inc., 302 Swann Ave., Alexandria, VA 22301, Tel. 800-368-3093 or 703-683-1085. Includes over 110,000 employers in its database. Individuals can register for a six month period for a variety of fees, depending on desired salary level. For example, students can register for $15; individuals seeking a job up to $20,000 register for $25; those with salary expectations in the $20,001-$40,000 range register for $35; those expecting a salary of $40,000+ register for $45. Recruiters can access the Career Placement Registry on DIALOG.

INTERNET: Online Career Center, Online Resume Service, 1713 Hemlock Lane, Plainfield, IN 46168. This nonprofit organization, sponsored by 40 major corporations, allows job seekers to review hundreds of vacancy announcements posted in its computer database. It also accepts resumes so that companies can search for talented employees. For a fee of only $6.00, job seekers can have their resume entered into the computer database for a 90 day period. Computer users can browse through hundreds of vacancy announcements and resumes by accessing Internet, a worldwide group of 11,000 public and private computer networks used by nearly 10 million people. Approximately 3,000 companies use Internet for recruiting purposes. The key to accessing the Online Career Center database to using this system is having access to Internet. Those with such access should send an electronic mail message to: occmsen.com and type "info" on the subject line. You will receive instructions on what to do next. If you do not yet have access to Internet—but you do have a computer and modem—you can gain access to Internet by contacting the following companies: America OnLine (800-827-6364); CompuServe (800-848-8199); Delphi (800-491-3393); IDS (401-884-7856); or Worldline (800-NET-2-YOU). Finally, if you do not have a computer and modem, send a copy of your resume along with $6.00 to: Online Resume Service, 1713 Hemlock Lane, Plainfield, IN 46168. If your resume runs more than three pages, add $1.50 for each additional page. Your resume will be entered in the database for 90 days. Our advice: now may be the time to acquire that computer and modem you have been putting off for so long! For less than $1,000 you can be fully equipped to use such an electronic job network 24 hours a day, 7 days a week, and 365 days a year. Finding a good job with the assistance of a computer will more than pay for the cost of equipment. But make this purchase only if you can afford it. You should justify its use for other job search activities, such as producing resumes, writing letters, and organizing job search activities. It also should improve your overall computer literacy for today's job market.

Individuals interested in environmental jobs should contact the following electronic database system:

JOBSource
ATTN: Robert Ackerman
Colorado State University
Tel. 303-491-5511 (for current information)

For a broad offering of nationwide job vacancies, contact the following organization:

ADNET ONLINE
ADNET Employment Advertising Network
5987 E. 71 St., Suite 206
Indianapolis, IN 46220
Tel. 800-543-9974 or 317-579-6922

Adnet Online claims to have nearly 1.5 million resumes in their system. This network can be accessed on Prodigy.

For individuals interested in human resources positions, contact the following organization:

HUMAN RESOURCE INFORMATION NETWORK
Executive Telecom System, Inc.
9585 Valparaiso Ct.
Indianapolis, IN 46268
Tel. 800-421-8884 or 317-872-2045

If you are interested in manufacturing, engineering, or computer positions, contact the following job-matching resume database ($19.95 for 3 months):

CAREERS ONLINE
710 Fehr Road
Louisville, KY 40206
Tel. 502-894-9887

You might also consider the employment networking potential of the three major telecommunications services which operate as electronic bulletin boards. Each includes a "career corner" of job vacancies and career services:

AMERICA ONLINE
8619 Westwood Center Dr.
Vienna, VA 22182
Tel. 800-827-6364

COMPUSERVE
CompuService Information Service
5000 Arlington Centre Boulevard
P.O. Box 20212
Columbus, OH 43220
Tel. 800-848-8199

PRODIGY
Prodigy Services Company
445 Hamilton Avenue
White Plains, NY 10601
Tel. 800-776-3449 or 914-993-8000

You will need a computer, modem, and communications software to interact with these services. Chances are you will electronically meet new people and organizations that can provide job leads for someone with your interests and qualifications.

KEY ELECTRONIC NETWORKING RESOURCES

A few new books provide useful information on the new electronic job search and hiring era. The most useful such resources include:

> Kennedy, Joyce Lain and Thomas J. Morrow, *Electronic Job Search Revolution* (New York: Wiley, 1994).

> Kennedy, Joyce Lain and Thomas J. Morrow, *Electronic Resume Revolution* (New York: Wiley, 1994).

> Lauber, Daniel, *The Professional's Private Sector Job Finder* (River Forest, IL: Planning/Communications, 1994).

> Weddle, Peter D., *Electronic Resumes for the New Job Market: Resumes That Work for You 24 Hours a Day* (Manassas Park, VA: Impact Publications, 1994).

During the next ten years we expect an explosion of new electronic job search and hiring services—from electronic resume banks and on-line job vacancy bulletin boards to CD-ROM programs for developing new forms of job search communication. While you may encounter a chaotic and bewildering array of such services, each competing for more and more database enrollees, one thing is certain: electronic job search and hiring services are here to stay. Employers will use these services more and more because they offer efficient and effective ways of tapping into nationwide talent pools. Job seekers will increasingly use the services because they can reach many more employers electronically than they could through more traditional direct-mail and networking methods.

BEWARE OF THE LAZY WAY TO SUCCESS

While electronic job search services may well be the wave of the future, they will by no means displace the more traditional job search methods outlined in previous chapters of this book. Indeed, there is a danger in thinking that the electronic revolution will offer *the* solution to the inefficiencies and ineffectiveness associated with traditional job search methods. As presently practiced, electronic networking is primarily a method for disseminating resumes to potential employers. As such, it is a high-tech resume broadcasting method. This revolution will most likely move to other levels, especially multi-media communication forms, which integrate resumes with audio and video presentations of candidate's qualifications.

The problems with present forms of electronic networking are fourfold. First, these networks are primarily designed for and controlled by employers. Job seekers are only included in the networks for the benefit of employers. Indeed, these electronic networks are mostly funded by employers who have on-line access to participants' resume data. Job seekers' involvement in the network is that of passive participant who submits an electronic resume and then waits to hear from employers who may or may not access their resume. Not surprising, many job seekers may never hear from employers. From the perspective of the job seeker, such a network is merely a high-tech version of the broadcast resume that is mass mailed to numerous employers—one of the most ineffective resume distribution approaches.

Second, electronic resume services give employers limited, albeit important, information on candidates. These services are primarily efficient resume screening techniques that communicate little information about the individual beyond traditional resume categories. Employers still need to screen candidates on other criteria, especially in face-to-face settings, which enable them to access a candidate's personal chemistry. Such information is best communicated through the networking process we identified in Chapter 11.

Third, the major sponsors and participants—large Fortune 1000 companies—in the electronic resume banks are not the ones that do most of the hiring. These are the same companies that have been shedding jobs—more than 3 million in the past five years—rather than adding them to the job market. What hiring these companies do is largely for highly skilled and hard-to-find individuals. Most small companies—those that generate the most jobs—do not participate in these electronic job search and hiring networks. Therefore, you are well advised to target your job search toward the companies that generate the most jobs. You do so by using the major networking techniques outlined earlier in this book. If you decide to participate in an electronic job bank, do so only as a supplement to your other job search activities.

Fourth, like many predictions of futurists, the electronic job search revolution is often overstated and highly overrated. It tends to disproportionately appeal to people who prefer quick and easy approaches to the job search. They often look for the "magic pill" for job search success—one that involves the least amount of time and effort and few interpersonal contacts with potential employers. Research, networking, informational interviews, and cold calling techniques involve a great deal of interpersonal skill and have unpredictable outcomes. On the other hand, computers, modems, and electronics give many people a false sense of making progress in what is inherently a difficult and highly ego-involved process—communicating your qualifications to strangers who are likely to reject you.

We recommend that you include electronic job search services in your overall repertoire of job search methods. But put this electronic networking alternative in its proper perspective—an efficient way to broadcast your qualifications to employers through an electronic resume. Don't approach electronic networking as the easy way to job search success; there's nothing magical about this resume dissemination method. Sending a $6, $20, $30, $50, or $100 membership fee and a resume to one of these firms ensures you nothing other than a presence in an electronic resume bank. What happens next—whether or not you are contacted by employers—depends on an unpredictable mix of factors, such as the number and quality of employer members in the system, employer hiring needs at any specific time, and the quality of your electronic resume, especially your choice of resume language.

DO WHAT WORKS BEST

Finding a job still remains hard work. It requires a great deal of initiative on your part. Above all, you must take action aimed at specific organizations and employers on a daily basis. And that's what our high impact job search strategies and techniques in previous chapters are all about. If you use them in conjunction with electronic job search services, you will be in the best position to find great jobs in the 1990s as well as into the 21st century.

18

RESOURCES FOR STARTING OUT RIGHT

A successful career change also involves knowing which resources are the most useful for conducting a job search. While you chose this book as one of your resources, you should also discover many other resources that complement as well as extend this book into other critical job search steps. As we noted earlier, many of these resources can be found throught your ACAP program, Job Assistance Center, base library, and Army Community Service center.

In this chapter we include some of the best resources available for further expanding your job search beyond this book. Since many of these books, videos, audiocassettes, and computer software and CD-ROM programs cannot be found in local bookstores or libraries, you may need

326

to order them directly from the publishers. For your convenience, you can order most of the books, videos, audiocassettes, and computer software and CD-ROM programs through Impact Publications by completing the order form at the end of this book. For a more complete listing of career planning and job search resources, contact our publisher to receive a free copy of their annotated catalog of over 1,000 resources.

We primarily include books here, because they are the least expensive and most easily accessible resources in bookstores and libraries. However, more and more computer software and CD-ROM programs are available to assist you with two stages in your job search: self-assessment and resume writing. As mentioned in previous chapters, many career planning centers and some libraries and computer stores offer these resources.

BOOKS

Key Directories and Reference Works

Bob Adams, Inc. (eds.), *The JobBank Guide to Employment Services* (Holbrook, MA: Bob Adams, Inc., 1994)

Career Associates (eds.), *Encyclopedia of Career Choices for the 1990s* (New York: Putnam, 1991).

Columbia Books, Inc. (eds.), *National Trade and Professional Associations* (Washington, DC: Columbia Books, Inc., 1994).

Craighead Publications, Inc. (eds.), *Craighead's International Business, Travel, and Relocation Guide to 71 Countries* (Detroit, MI: Gale Research, 1993).

Darnay, Arsen (ed.), *American Salaries and Wages Survey* (Detroit, MI: Gale Research, 1993).

Dorgan, Charity Anne and Jennifer Mast (ed.), *Job Seeker's Guide to Private and Public Companies* (Detroit, MI: Gale Research, 1993).

Ferguson (eds.), *Encyclopedia of Careers and Vocational Guidance* (4 vols.) (Chicago, IL: Ferguson and Co., 1993).

Hoover, Gary, Alta Campbell, Patrick J. Spain, and Alan Chai (eds.), *The Hoover Handbooks: American Business; Emerging Companies;* and

World Business (Austin, TX: Ready Reference Press, 1994).

JIST Works (eds.), *The Enhanced Guide for Occupational Exploration* (Indianapolis, IN: JIST Works, Inc., 1992).

Kennedy Publications (eds.), *Directory of Executive Recruiters* (Fitzsimmons, NH: Kennedy Publications, 1994).

Le Compte, Michelle (ed.), *Job Hunter's Sourcebook* (Detroit, MI: Gale Research, 1991).

McLean, Janice (ed.), *Consultants and Consulting Organizations Directory* (Detroit, MI: Gale Research, 1994).

McLean, Janice (ed.), *Training and Development Organizations Directory* (Detroit, MI: Gale Research, 1991).

O'Meara, Meghan A. and Kimberley A. Peterson (eds.), *World Business Directory* (Detroit, MI: Gale Research, 1994).

Omnigraphics, Inc. (eds.) *Government Directory of Addresses and Telephone Numbers* (Detroit, MI: Omnigraphics, Inc., 1994).

Savage, Kathleen M. and Charity Anne Dorgan (eds.), *Professional Careers Sourcebook* (Detroit, MI: Gale Research, 1993).

Schwartz, Carol A. (ed.), *Encyclopedia of Associations* (Detroit, MI: Gale Research, 1994).

Smith, Darren L. (ed.), *National Directory of Addresses and Telephone Numbers* (Detroit, MI: Omnigraphics, 1994).

Spomer, Cindy (ed.), *Personnel Executives Contactbook* (Detroit, MI: Gale Research, 1993).

U.S. Department of Labor, *Dictionary of Occupational Titles* (Washington, DC: Government Printing Office, 1991).

U.S. Department of Labor, *Occupational Outlook Handbook* (Washington, DC: Government Printing Office, 1992). Biannual publication.

Job Search Strategies and Tactics

Elderkin, Kenton W., *How to Get Interviews From Classified Job Ads* (Manassas Park, VA: Impact Publications, 1993).

Figler, Howard E., *The Complete Job Search Handbook* (New York: Holt, Rinehart, and Winston, 1988).

Irish, Richard K., *Go Hire Yourself an Employer* (New York: Doubleday, 1987).

Jackson, Tom, *Guerrilla Tactics in the New Job Market* (New York: Bantam, 1991).

Kennedy, Joyce Lain and Darryl Laramore, *The Joyce Lain Kennedy's Career Book* (Lincolnwood, IL: National Textbook, 1992).

Kennedy, Joyce Lain and Thomas J. Morrow, *Electronic Job Search Revolution* (New York: Wiley, 1994).

Krannich, Ronald L., *Change Your Job, Change Your Life* (Manassas Park, VA: Impact Publications, 1994).

Lathrop, Richard, *Who's Hiring Who* (Berkeley, CA: Ten Speed Press, 1989).

Lucht, John, *Rites of Passage at $100,000+* (New York: Holt, Rinehart, and Winston, 1993).

McDonald, Scott A., *The Complete Job Finder's Guide for the 90's* (Manassas Park, VA: Impact Publications, 1993).

Rogers, Edward J., *Getting Hired* (Englewood, NJ: Prentice Hall, 1982).

Siegal, Barbara and Robert, *The Five Secrets to Finding a Job* (Manassas Park, VA: Impact Publications, 1994).

Studner, Peter K., *Super Job Search* (Los Angeles, CA: Jamenair Ltd., 1987).

Wegmann, Robert and Robert Chapman, *The Right Place at the Right*

Time (Berkeley, CA: Ten Speed Press, 1990).

Wegmann, Robert, Robert Chapman, and Miriam Johnson, *Work in the New Economy* (Indianapolis, IN: JIST Works, 1989).

Wendleton, Kate, *Through the Brick Wall* (New York: Villard Books, 1992).

Skills Identification, Testing, and Self-Assessment

Bolles, Richard N., *The New Quick Job Hunting Map* (Berkeley, CA: Ten Speed Press, 1990).

Bolles, Richard N., *The Three Boxes of Life* (Berkeley, CA: Ten Speed Press, 1981).

Bolles, Richard N., *What Color Is Your Parachute?* (Berkeley, CA: Ten Speed Press, 1994).

Crystal, John C. and Richard N. Bolles, *Where Do I Go From Here With My Life?* (Berkeley, CA: Ten Speed Press, 1979).

Gale, Barry and Linda Gale, *Discover What You're Best At* (New York: Simon and Schuster, 1990).

Holland, John L., *Making Vocational Choices* (Englewood Cliffs, NJ: Prentice-Hall, 1985).

Krannich, Ronald L. and Caryl Rae Krannich, *Discover the Best Jobs for You!* (Manassas Park, VA: Impact Publications, 1993).

Miller, Arthur F. and Ralph T. Mattson, *The Truth About You: Discover What You Should Be Doing With Your Life* (Berkeley, CA: Ten Speed Press, 1989).

Pilkington, Maya, *The Real-Life Aptitude Test* (New York: St. Martin's Press, 1989).

Sher, Barbara, *Wishcraft: How to Get What You Really Want* (New York: Ballantine, 1983).

Sturman, Gerald M., *Career Discovery Project* (New York: Bantam, 1993).

Research On Cities, Fields, and Organizations

Adams Inc., Bob (ed.), *The JobBank Series: Atlanta, Boston, Carolinas, Chicago, Dallas, Denver, Detroit, Florida, Houston, Los Angeles, Minneapolis, New York, Ohio, Philadelphia, Phoenix, San Francisco, Seattle, St. Louis, Tennessee, Washington, DC* (Holbrook, MA: Bob Adams, Inc., 1994).

Adams Inc., Bob (ed.), *Bob Adams Jobs Almanac 1994* (Holbrook, MA: Bob Adams, 1993).

Adams Inc., Bob (ed.), *The National JobBank* (Holbrook, MA: Bob Adams, 1994).

Basta, Nicholas, *Top Professions* (Princeton, NJ: Peterson's Guides, 1989).

Camden, Bishop, Schwartz, Greene, Fleming-Holland, *"How to Get a Job in..." Insider's City Guides: Atlanta, Boston, Chicago, Houston, Dallas/Ft. Worth, Los Angeles/San Diego, New York, San Francisco, Seattle/Portland, Washington, DC* (Chicago, IL: Surrey Books, 1993-1994).

Diefenbach, Greg and Phil Giordano, *Jobs in Washington, DC* (Manassas Park, VA: Impact Publications, 1992).

Harkavy, Michael, *101 Careers* (New York: Wiley, 1990).

Harrington, Thomas F. and Arthur J. O'Shea (eds.), *Guide for Occupational Exploration* (Circle Pines, MN: American Guidance Service, 1989).

Kleiman, Carol, *The 100 Best Jobs for the 1990s and Beyond* (Chicago, IL: Dearborn Financial Publishing, Inc., 1992).

Krannich, Ronald L. and Caryl Rae Krannich, *Best Jobs for the 1990s & Into the 21st Century* (Manassas Park, VA: Impact Publications, 1993).

Krantz, Les, *The Jobs Rated Almanac* (New York: Pharos Books, 1992).

Levering, Robert and Milton Moskowitz, *The 100 Best Companies to Work for in America* (New York: Doubleday, 1993).

Morgan, Bradley J. (ed.), *The Career Directory Series: Advertising, Book Publishing, Business and Finance, Computing and Software Design, Environmental, Magazines, Marketing and Sales, Mental Health and Social Work, Newspapers, Public Relations, Radio and Television, Technologists and Technicians, Therapists and Allied Health Professionals, Travel and Hospitality* (Detroit, MI: Visible Ink Press, 1993-1994).

Norback, Craig T., *Careers Encyclopedia* (Lincolnwood, IL: National Textbook, 1992).

Petras, Ross and Kathryn, *Jobs 1994* (New York: Simon and Schuster, 1994).

Savageau, David and Richard Boyer, *Places Rated Almanac* (New York: Simon and Schuster, 1993).

Schwartz, Lester and Irv Brechner, *The Career Finder* (New York: Ballantine, 1990).

Wright, John W., *The American Almanac of Jobs and Salaries* (New York: Avon, 1993).

Resumes and Letters

Beatty, Richard H., *The Perfect Cover Letter* (New York: Wiley, 1989).

Bostwick, Burdette E., *Resume Writing* (New York: Wiley, 1984).

Frank, William S., *200 Letters for Job Hunters* (Berkeley, CA: Ten Speed Press, 1993).

Fry, Ronald W., *Your First Resume* (Hawthorne, NJ: Career Press, 1992).

Good, C. Edward, *Resumes for Re-Entry* (Manassas Park, VA: Impact Publications, 1993).

Jackson, Tom, *The Perfect Resume* (New York: Doubleday, 1990).

Kaplan, Robbie Miller, *Sure-Hire Resumes* (New York: Amacom, 1990).

Kennedy, Joyce Lain and Thomas J. Morrow, *Electronic Resume Revolution* (New York: Wiley, 1994).

Krannich, Ronald L. and Caryl Rae Krannich, *Dynamite Cover Letters* (Manassas Park, VA: Impact Publications, 1992).

Krannich, Ronald L. and Caryl Rae Krannich, *Dynamite Resumes* (Manassas Park, VA: Impact Publications, 1992).

Krannich, Ronald L. and William J. Banis, *High Impact Resumes and Letters* (Manassas Park, VA: Impact Publications, 1992).

Krannich, Ronald L. and Caryl Rae Krannich, *Job Search Letters That Get Results* (Manassas Park, VA: Impact Publications, 1992).

Parker, Yana, *The Damn Good Resume Guide* (Berkeley, NY: Ten Speed Press, 1986).

Parker, Yana, *The Resume Catalog* (Berkeley, NY: Ten Speed Press, 1988).

Schuman, Nancy and William Lewis, *Revising Your Resume* (New York: Wiley, 1987).

Swanson, David, *The Resume Solution* (Indianapolis, IN: JIST Works, 1990).

Yate, Martin John, *Resumes That Knock 'Em Dead* (Holbrook, MA: Bob Adams, 1992).

Weddle, Peter D., *Electronic Resumes for the New Job Market: Resumes That Work for You 24 Hours a Day* (Manassas Park, VA: Impact Publications, 1994).

Networking

Baber, Anne and Lynne Waymon, *Great Connections: Small Talk and Networking for Businesspeople* (Manassas Park, VA: Impact Publications, 1992).

Boe, Anne and Bettie B. Youngs, *Is Your "Net" Working?* (New York: Wiley, 1989).

Krannich, Ronald L. and Caryl Rae Krannich, *The New Network Your Way to Job and Career Success* (Manassas Park, VA: Impact Publications, 1993).

Raye-Johnson, Venda, *Effective Networking* (Palo Alto, CA: Crisp Publications, 1990).

Roane, Susan, *How to Work a Room* (New York: Warner Books, 1989).

Roane, Susan, *The Secrets of Savvy Networking* (New York: Warner Books, 1993).

Vilas, Donna and Sandy, *Power Networking* (Austin, TX: MountainHarbour Publications, 1992).

Dress, Appearance, and Image

Karpinski, Kenneth J., *Red Socks Don't Work! Messages From the Real World About Men's Clothing* (Manassas Park, VA: Impact Publications, 1994).

Martin, Judith, *Miss Manners' Guide to the Turn-of-the Millennium* (New York: St. Martin's Press, 1989).

Molloy, John T., *John Molloy's New Dress for Success* (New York: Warner, 1989).

Molloy, John T., *The Woman's Dress for Success Book* (New York: Warner, 1977).

Nicholson, JoAnne and Judy Lewis-Crum, *Color Wonderful* (New York: Bantam, 1986).

Stran, Pamela Redmond, *Dressing Smart* (New York: Doubleday, 1990).

Interviews and Salary Negotiations

Beatty, R. H., *The Five Minute Interview* (New York: Wiley, 1986).

Chapman, Jack, *How to Make $1000 A Minute: Negotiating Salaries and Raises* (Berkeley, CA: Ten Speed Press, 1987).

Krannich, Caryl Rae and Ronald L. Krannich, *Dynamite Answers to Interview Questions: No More Sweaty Palms!* (Manassas Park, VA: Impact Publications, 1992).

Krannich, Caryl Rae and Ronald L. Krannich, *Interview for Success* (Manassas Park, VA: Impact Publications, 1993).

Krannich, Ronald L. and Caryl Rae Krannich, *Dynamite Salary Negotiations* (Manassas Park, VA: Impact Publications, 1990).

Medley, H. Anthony, *Sweaty Palms* (Berkeley, CA: Ten Speed Press, 1991).

Meyer, Mary Coeli and Inge M. Berchtold, *Getting the Job: How To Interview Successfully* (Princeton, NJ: Petrocelli, 1982).

Ryan, Robin, *60 Seconds and You're Hired!* (Manassas Park, VA: Impact Publications, 1994).

Vlk, Suzee, *Interviews That Get Results* (New York: Simon and Schuster, 1984).

Yate, Martin, *Knock 'Em Dead* (Holbrook, MA: Bob Adams, 1994).

Educators

Krannich, Ronald L., *The Educator's Guide to Alternative Jobs and Careers* (Manassas Park, VA: Impact Publications, 1991).

Pollack, Sandy, *Alternative Careers for Teachers* (Boston, MA: Harvard Common Press, 1986).

Public-Oriented Careers

Krannich, Ronald L. and Caryl Rae Krannich, *The Almanac of American Government Jobs and Careers* (Manassas Park, VA: Impact Publications 1991).

Krannich, Ronald L. and Caryl Rae Krannich, *The Complete Guide to Public Employment* (Manassas Park, VA: Impact Publications, 1994).

Krannich, Ronald L. and Caryl Rae Krannich, *Find a Federal Job Fast* (Manassas Park, VA: Impact Publications, 1992).

Krannich, Ronald L. and Caryl Rae Krannich, *Jobs and Careers With Nonprofit Organizations* (Manassas Park, VA: Impact Publications 1994).

Lauber, Daniel, *The Government Job Finder* (River Forest, IL: Planning Communications, 1994).

Lauber, Daniel, *The Nonprofit's Job Finder* (River Forest, IL: Planning Communications, 1994).

Lewis, William and Carol Milano, *Profitable Careers in Nonprofit* (New York: Wiley, 1987).

Smith, Devon Cottrell (ed.), *Great Careers: The Fourth of July Guide to Careers, Internships, and Volunteer Opportunities in the Nonprofit Sector* (Garrett Park, MD: Garrett Park Press, 1990).

Smith, Russ, *The Right SF 171 Writer* (Manassas Park, VA: Impact Publications, 1994).

Waelde, David E., *How to Get a Federal Job* (Washington, DC: FED HELP, 1989).

International and Overseas Jobs

Foreign Policy Association (ed.), *Guide to Careers in World Affairs* (Manassas Park, VA: Impact Publications, 1993).

Kocher, Eric, *International Jobs* (Reading, MA: Addison-Wesley, 1993

Krannich, Ronald L. and Caryl Rae Krannich, *The Almanac of International Jobs and Careers* (Manassas Park, VA: Impact Publications, 1994).

Krannich, Ronald L. and Caryl Rae Krannich, *The Complete Guide to International Jobs and Careers* (Manassas Park, VA: Impact Publications, 1992).

Krannich, Ronald L. and Caryl Rae Krannich, *Jobs for People Who Love Travel* (Manassas Park, VA: Impact Publications, 1993).

Sanborn, Robert, *How to Get a Job in Europe* (Chicago, IL: Surrey Books, 1992).

Sanborn, Robert, *How to Get a Job in the Pacific Rim* (Chicago, IL: Surrey Books, 1992).

Win, David, *International Careers: An Insider's Guide* (Charlotte, VT: Williamson Publishing, 1987).

Military

Fitzpatrick, William G. and C. Edward Good, *Does Your Resume Wear Combat Boots?* (Charlottesville, VA: Blue Jeans Press, 1990).

Henderson, David G., *Job Search: Marketing Your Military Experience in the 1990s* (Harrisburg, PA: Stackpole Books, 1991).

Jacobsen, Kennth C., *Retiring From the Military* (Annapolis, MD: Naval Institute Press, 1990).

Nyman, Keith O., *Re-Entry: Turning Military Experience Into Civilian Success* (Harrisburg, PA: Stackpole Books, 1990).

Savino, Carl S. and Ronald L. Krannich, *From Army Green to Corporate Gray* (Manassas Park, VA: Impact Publications, 1994).

Women and Spouses

Bastress, Fran, *The New Relocating Spouse's Guide to Employment* (Manassas Park, VA: Impact Publications, 1993).

Bloomberg, Gerri and Margaret Holden, **Women's Job Search Handbook** (Charlotte, VT: Williamson Publishing, 1991).

King, Julie Adair and Betsy Sheldon, **Smart Woman's Guide to Resumes and Job Hunting** (Hawthorne, NJ: Career Press, 1993).

College Students and Graduates

Bouchard, Jerry, **Graduating to the 9-5 World** (Manassas Park, VA: Impact Publications, 1991).

LaFevre, John L., **How You Really Get Hired** (New York: Simon and Schuster, 1992).

Munschauer, John L., **Jobs for English Majors and Other Smart People** (Princeton, NJ: Peterson's, 1990).

Nadler, Burton Jay, **Liberal Arts Jobs** (Princeton, NJ: Peterson's, 1985).

Phifer, Paul, **College Majors and Careers** (Garrett Park, MD: Garrett Park Press, 1987).

Minorities and Physically Challenged

Graham, Lawrence Otis, **Best Companies for Minorities** (New York: Penguin Books, 1993)

Hoffa, Helynn and Gary Morgan, **Yes You Can** (New York, St. Martin's, 1990).

Johnson, Willis L. (ed.), **Directory of Special Programs for Minority Group Members** (Garrett Park, MD: Garrett Park Press, 1991).

Kastre, Michael, Alfred Edwards, and Nydia Rodriguez Kastre, **The Minority Career Guide** (Princeton, NJ: Peterson's, 1993).

Rivera, Miquela, **The Minority Career Book** (Holbrook, MA: Bob Adams, 1991).

Shields, Cydney and Leslie Shields, **Work, Sister, Work** (New York: Simon and Schuster, 1993).

Witt, Melanie Astaire, *Job Strategies for People With Disabilities* (Princeton, NJ: Peterson's, 1992).

Experienced and Retired

Birsner, E. Patricia, *The 40+ Job Hunting Guide* (New York: Facts on File, 1991).

Falvey, Jack, *What's Next? Career Strategies After 35* (Charlotte, VT: Williamson Publishing, 1986).

Marsh, DeLoss L., *Retirement Careers* (Charlotte, VT: Williamson Publishing, 1992).

Petras, Kathryne and Ross, *The Over 40 Job Hunting Guide* (New York: Simon and Schuster, 1993).

Ray, Samuel N., *Job Hunting After 50* (New York: Wiley, 1990).

Alternative Career Fields

Basta, Nicholas, *Environmental Career Guide* (New York: Wiley and Sons, 1991).

Basta, Nicholas, *Careers in High Tech* (Lincolnwood, IL: National Textbook, 1992).

Carter, David, *You Can't Play the Game If You Don't Know the Rules: Career Opportunities in the Sports Industry* (Manassas Park, VA: Impact Publications, 1994).

Edward, Kenneth W., *Your Successful Real Estate Career* (New York: AMACOM, 1992).

Field, Shelly, *Career Opportunities In the Music Industry* (New York: Facts on File, 1986).

Munneke, Gary, *Careers in Law* (Lincolnwood, IL: National Textbook, 1992).

"Opportunities in..." Career Series (145 titles), (Lincolnwood, IL: National Textbook, 1984-1993).

Peterson's, *Job Opportunities in Business* (Princeton, NJ: Peterson's, 1993).

Peterson's, *Job Opportunities in Engineering and Technology* (Princeton, NJ: Peterson's, 1993).

Peterson's, *Job Opportunities in Environment* (Princeton, NJ: Peterson's, 1993).

Peterson's, *Job Opportunities in Health Care* (Princeton, NJ: Peterson's, 1993).

Rosenberg, Howard G., *How to Succeed Without a Career Path: Jobs for People With No Corporate Ladder* (Manassas Park, VA: Impact Publications, 1993).

Rubin, K., *Flying High In Travel: A Complete Guide to Careers In the Travel Industry* (New York: Wiley, 1992).

Rucker, T. Donald and Martin D. Keller, *Careers in Medicine* (Garrett Park, MD: Garrett Park Press, 1987).

Shenk, Ellen, *Outdoor Careers* (Harrisburg, PA: Stackpole Books, 1992).

VIDEOS

Dialing for Jobs (Indianapolis, IN: JIST Works, Inc., 1992).

Find the Job You Want...and Get It (Aurora, CO: Pat Sladey & Associates, 1991).

Insider's Guide to Competitive Interviewing (Carmel, CA: RNC Productions, 1991).

Negotiating Your Job Offer (New York: Drake Beam Morin, 1992).

Networking Process (New York: Drake Beam Morin, 1992).

Networking Your Way to Success (New York: American Management Association, 1992).

Researching the Job Market (New York: Drake Beam Morin, 1992).

Winning at Job Hunting in the 90s (Highland Park, IL: Successful Job Hunting, Inc., 1991).

AUDIO PROGRAMS

The Edge Rx For Success (Conshohocken, PA: Career Care, Inc., 1993).

Find the Job You Want...and Get It (Aurora, CO: Pat Sladey and Associates, 1993).

Five Secrets to Getting a Job (St. Louis, MO: Career Center, 1994).

Job Search: The Total System (Houston, TX: Dawson and Associates, 1989).

COMPUTER SOFTWARE PROGRAMS

Career Navigator (New York: Drake Beam Morin, 1989).

Computerized Career Assessment and Planning Program (S. Charleston, WV: Cambridge Career Products, 1993).

FOCIS: Federal Occupational and Career Information System (Washington, DC: U.S. Office of Personnel Management, 1993).

INSTANT Job Hunting Letters (Englewood, CO: CareerLab, 1993).

JOBHUNT (Charlotte, NC: Scope International, 1993).

Quick and Easy 171s (Harrisburg, PA: DataTech, 1993).

ResumeMaker (Pleasanton, CA: Individual Software, Inc., 1993).

The Ultimate Job Finder (Orem, UT: InfoBusiness, 1993).

CD-ROM

America's Top Jobs (Indianapolis, IN: JIST Works, Inc., 1994).

Companies International (Detroit, MI: Gale Research, 1994).

Encyclopedia of Associations (Detroit, MI: Gale Research, 1994).

Job Power Source: Job Finding Skills for the 90s (Orem, UT: InfoBusiness, 1994).

Appendix

KEY NETWORKS FOR MILITARY PERSONNEL

*T*he following membership associations provide excellent opportunities to network for job information, advice, and referrals amongst fellow members of the military. Some of these associations provide placement services, sponsor job fairs, and publish membership directories. Contact them directly for information on their membership and services.

Army Associations

**Association of the
United States Army**
2425 Wilson Blvd.
Arlington, VA 22201
703/841-4300

**U.S. Army Warrant
Officers Association**
462 Herndon Parkway
Herndon, VA 22070-5235
703/742-7727

Joint Service Associations

**Non Commissioned
Officers Associations**
255 North Washington St.
Alexandria, VA 22314-2537
703/549-0311

**Association of Military
Surgeons of the United
States**
9320 Old Georgetown Road
Bethesda, MD 20814-1653
301/897-8800

**Commissioned Officers
Association of the
United States Public
Health Service, Inc.**
1400 Eye St., Suite 725
Washington, D.C. 20005-9990
202/289-6400

**Enlisted Association of
the National Guard**
1219 Prince St.
Alexandria, VA 22314
703/519-3846

**Jewish War Veterans of
the United States of
America**
1811 R St., N.W.
Washington, D.C. 20009
202/265-6280

**Military Chaplain
Association of the
United States of
America**
P.O. Box 42660
Washington, D.C. 20015-0660
202/574-2423

**National Association
for Uniformed
Services/Society of
Military Widows**
5525 Hempstead Way
Springfield, VA 22151-4094
703/519-3846

**National Guard
Association**
1 Massachusetts Ave., N.W.
Washington, D.C. 20001
202/789-0031

**National Military
Family Association**
6000 Stevenson Ave., Suite 304
Alexandria, VA 22304-3526

Reserve Officers Association
1 Constitution Ave., N.E.
Washington, D.C. 20002-5624
202/479-2200

**The Retired Enlisted
Association**
909 North Washington St.
Suite 300
Alexandria, VA 22314
703/684-1981

**The Retired Officers
Association**
201 North Washington St.
Alexandria, VA 22314-2529
703/549-2311

**United Armed Forces
Association**
15 Falcon Court
Stafford, VA 22554-5316
703/659-3760

THE
AUTHORS

CARL S. SAVINO, a former active duty Major, successfully transitioned to the corporate world after participating in an Army-sponsored career transition program. A graduate of the U.S. Military Academy at West Point and the University of Pennsylvania, he is currently serving as a technical consultant with Booz, Allen & Hamilton, Inc. He can be contacted at Competitive Edge, P.O. Box 342, Fairfax Station, VA 22039.

RONALD L. KRANNICH, Ph.D., is one of America's leading career specialists. He is author of over 25 career books, including such bestsellers as *Change Your Job Change Your Life, High Impact Resumes and Letters, Dynamite Resumes, Dynamite Cover Letters, Dynamite Salary Negotiations, Complete Guide to International Jobs and Careers, Find a Federal Job Fast,* and *The Best Jobs for the 1990s and Into the 21st Century.* He is president of Development Concepts Incorporated, a training, consulting, and publishing firm. He can be contacted through the publisher.

INDEX

CAREER
RESOURCES

Contact Impact Publications to receive a free copy of their latest comprehensive and annotated catalog of over 1,000 career resources (books, subscriptions, training programs, videos, audiocassettes, computer software, and CD-ROM).

The following career resources, many of which are mentioned in previous chapters, are available directly from Impact Publications. Complete the following form or list the titles, include postage (see formula at the end), enclose payment, and send your order to:

IMPACT PUBLICATIONS
9104-N Manassas Drive
Manassas Park, VA 22111
Tel. 703/361-7300 or FAX 703/335-9486

Orders from individuals must be prepaid by check, moneyorder, Visa or MasterCard number. We accept telephone and FAX orders with a Visa or MasterCard number.

Qty.	TITLES	Price	TOTAL
MILITARY TO CIVILIAN TRANSITION			
___	Beyond the Uniform	$12.95	_____
___	Civilian Career Guide	$12.95	_____
___	Does Your Resume Wear Combat Boots?	$9.95	_____

___ Drawdown Survival Guide	$11.95	_____
___ From Army Green to Corporate Gray	$15.95	_____
___ How to Locate Anyone Who is or Has Been in		
the Military: Armed Forces Locator Directory	$14.95	_____
___ Job Search: Marketing Your Military Experience	$14.95	_____
___ Re-Entry	$13.95	_____
___ Retiring From the Military	$22.95	_____
___ Veteran's Survival Guide to Good Jobs in Bad Times	$12.95	_____

RELOCATION AND RETIREMENT

___ 50 Fabulous Places to Retire in America	$17.95	_____
___ 100 Best Small Towns in America	$12.00	_____
___ Complete Guide to Life in Florida	$14.95	_____
___ Complete Relocation Kit	$17.95	_____
___ Country Careers	$14.95	_____
___ Craighead's International Business, Travel,		
and Relocation Guide to 71 Countries	$425.00	_____
___ Guide to Military Installations	$17.95	_____
___ Moving and Relocation Directory	$149.00	_____
___ Places Rated Almanac	$21.95	_____

CITY AND STATE JOB FINDERS

___ Finding a Job in Florida	$14.95	_____
___ Jobs in Washington, DC	$11.95	_____

How to Get a Job in . . .

___ Atlanta	$15.95	_____
___ Boston	$15.95	_____
___ Chicago	$15.95	_____
___ Dallas/Fort Worth	$15.95	_____
___ Houston	$15.95	_____
___ New York	$15.95	_____
___ San Francisco	$15.95	_____
___ Seattle/Portland	$15.95	_____
___ Southern California	$15.95	_____
___ Washington, DC	$15.95	_____

Bob Adams' JobBanks to:

___ Atlanta	$15.95	_____
___ Boston	$15.95	_____
___ Chicago	$15.95	_____
___ Dallas/Fort Worth	$15.95	_____
___ Denver	$15.95	_____
___ Florida	$15.95	_____
___ Houston	$15.95	_____
___ Los Angeles	$15.95	_____
___ Minneapolis	$15.95	_____
___ New York	$15.95	_____

___ Phoenix	$15.95	_____
___ San Francisco	$15.95	_____
___ Seattle	$15.95	_____
___ Washington, DC	$15.95	_____

Job Seekers Sourcebooks to:

___ Boston and New England	$14.95	_____
___ Los Angeles and Southern California	$14.95	_____
___ Mid-Atlantic	$14.95	_____
___ Mountain States	$14.95	_____
___ New York and New Jersey	$14.95	_____
___ Northern Great Lakes	$14.95	_____
___ Pacific Northwest	$14.95	_____
___ Southern States	$14.95	_____
___ Southwest	$14.95	_____

KEY DIRECTORIES AND REFERENCE WORKS

___ American Salaries and Wages Survey	$94.95	_____
___ Career Training Sourcebook	$24.95	_____
___ Careers Encyclopedia	$39.95	_____
___ Complete Guide for Occupational Exploration	$29.95	_____
___ Consultants and Consulting Organizations Directory	$835.00	_____
___ Dictionary of Occupational Titles	$39.95	_____
___ Directory of Executive Recruiters (annual)	$44.95	_____
___ Directory of Special Programs for Minority Group Members	$31.95	
___ Encyclopedia of Careers and Vocational Guidance	$129.95	_____
___ Enhanced Guide for Occupational Exploration	$29.95	_____
___ Government Directory of Addresses and Telephone Numbers	$129.95	_____
___ Hoover's Business Directories: American Business, Emerging Companies, World Business	$99.95	_____
___ Job Bank Guide to Employment Services (annual)	$149.95	_____
___ Job Hunter's Sourcebook	$59.95	_____
___ Job Seeker's Guide to Private and Public Companies	$359.95	_____
___ National Directory of Addresses & Telephone Numbers	$99.95	_____
___ National Job Bank (annual)	$249.95	_____
___ National Trade and Professional Associations	$79.95	_____
___ Occupational Outlook Handbook	$22.95	_____
___ Personnel Executives Contactbook	$149.00	_____
___ Professional Careers Sourcebook	$79.95	_____

JOB SEARCH STRATEGIES AND TACTICS

___ 40+ Job Hunting Guide	$23.95	_____
___ 110 Biggest Mistakes Job Hunters Make	$12.95	_____
___ Change Your Job, Change Your Life	$14.95	_____
___ Complete Job Finder's Guide to the 90s	$13.95	_____
___ Complete Job Search Handbook	$12.95	_____
___ Cracking the Over-50 Job Market	$11.95	_____

___ Dynamite Tele-Search	$10.95	_____
___ Electronic Job Search Revolution	$12.95	_____
___ Five Secrets to Finding a Job	$12.95	_____
___ Go Hire Yourself an Employer	$9.95	_____
___ Guerrilla Tactics in the New Job Market	$5.99	_____
___ How to Get Interviews From Classified Job Ads	$14.95	_____
___ Job Hunting After 50	$12.95	_____
___ Joyce Lain Kennedy's Career Book	$29.95	_____
___ Knock 'Em Dead	$19.95	_____
___ Professional's Job Finder	$18.95	_____
___ Right Place At the Right Time	$11.95	_____
___ Rites of Passage At $100,000+	$29.95	_____
___ Super Job Search	$22.95	_____
___ Through the Brick Wall	$13.00	_____
___ Who's Hiring Who	$9.95	_____
___ Work in the New Economy	$14.95	_____

BEST JOBS AND EMPLOYERS FOR THE 90s

___ 100 Best Companies to Work for in America	$27.95	_____
___ 100 Best Jobs for the 1990s and Beyond	$19.95	_____
___ 101 Careers	$12.95	_____
___ American Almanac of Jobs and Salaries	$17.00	_____
___ America's 50 Fastest Growing Jobs	$9.95	_____
___ America's Fastest Growing Employers	$14.95	_____
___ Best Jobs for the 1990s and Into the 21st Century	$12.95	_____
___ Job Seeker's Guide to 1000 Top Employers	$22.95	_____
___ Jobs! What They Are, Where They Are, What They Pay	$13.95	_____
___ Jobs 1994	$15.95	_____
___ Jobs Rated Almanac	$15.95	_____
___ New Emerging Careers	$14.95	_____
___ Top Professions	$10.95	_____
___ Where the Jobs Are	$15.95	_____

ALTERNATIVE JOBS AND CAREERS

___ Adventure Careers	$9.95	_____
___ Advertising Career Directory	$17.95	_____
___ Business and Finance Career Directory	$17.95	_____
___ Career Opportunities in the Sports Industry	$27.95	_____
___ Career Opportunities in TV, Cable, and Video	$27.95	_____
___ Careers for Animal Lovers	$12.95	_____
___ Careers for Foreign Language Speakers	$12.95	_____
___ Careers for Sports Nuts	$12.95	_____
___ Careers for Travel Buffs	$12.95	_____
___ Careers in Computers	$16.95	_____
___ Careers in Education	$16.95	_____
___ Careers in Health Care	$16.95	_____
___ Careers in High Tech	$16.95	_____
___ Careers in Medicine	$16.95	_____
___ Careers in the Outdoors	$12.95	_____
___ Encyclopedia of Career Choices for the 1990s	$19.95	_____

___ Environmental Career Guide $14.95   _____
___ Environmental Jobs for Scientists and Engineers $14.95   _____
___ Health Care Job Explosion $14.95   _____
___ Marketing and Sales Career Directory $17.95   _____
___ Nurses and Physicians Career Directory $17.95   _____
___ Opportunities in Accounting $13.95   _____
___ Opportunities in Civil Engineering $13.95   _____
___ Opportunities in Computer Science $13.95   _____
___ Opportunities in Environmental Careers $13.95   _____
___ Opportunities in Financial Career $13.95   _____
___ Opportunities in Fitness $13.95   _____
___ Opportunities in Health & Medical Careers $13.95   _____
___ Opportunities in Law $13.95   _____
___ Opportunities in Medical Technology $13.95   _____
___ Opportunities in Microelectronics $13.95   _____
___ Opportunities in Paralegal Careers $13.95   _____
___ Opportunities in Teaching $13.95   _____
___ Opportunities in Telecommunications $13.95   _____
___ Opportunities in Television & Video $13.95   _____
___ Outdoor Careers $14.95   _____
___ Radio and Television Career Directory $17.95   _____
___ Travel and Hospitality Career Directory $17.95   _____

INTERNATIONAL, OVERSEAS, AND TRAVEL JOBS

___ Almanac of International Jobs and Careers $14.95   _____
___ Complete Guide to International Jobs & Careers $13.95   _____
___ Flying High in Travel $16.95   _____
___ Getting Your Job in the Middle East $19.95   _____
___ Guide to Careers in World Affairs $14.95   _____
___ How to Get a Job in Europe $17.95   _____
___ How to Get a Job in the Pacific Rim $17.95   _____
___ Jobs for People Who Love Travel $12.95   _____
___ Jobs in Russia and the Newly Independent States $15.95   _____

PUBLIC-ORIENTED CAREERS

___ Almanac of American Government Jobs and Careers $14.95   _____
___ Complete Guide to Public Employment $19.95   _____
___ Federal Jobs in Law Enforcement $15.95   _____
___ Find a Federal Job Fast! $9.95   _____
___ Government Job Finder $14.95   _____
___ Jobs and Careers With Nonprofit Organizations $15.95   _____
___ Non-Profit's Job Finder $16.95   _____
___ The Right SF 171 Writer $19.95   _____

JOB LISTINGS & VACANCY ANNOUNCEMENTS

___ Community (Nonprofit) Jobs (1 year) $69.00   _____
___ Federal Career Opportunities (6 biweekly issues) $38.00   _____
___ International Employment Gazette (6 biweekly issues) $35.00   _____
___ The Search Bulletin (6 issues) $97.00   _____

SKILLS, TESTING, SELF-ASSESSMENT, EMPOWERMENT

___ 7 Habits of Highly Effective People	$11.00 ___
___ Discover the Best Jobs for You	$11.95 ___
___ Do What You Are	$14.95 ___
___ Do What You Love, the Money Will Follow	$10.95 ___
___ Finding the Hat That Fits	$10.00 ___
___ What Color Is Your Parachute?	$14.95 ___
___ Where Do I Go From Here With My Life?	$10.95 ___
___ Wishcraft	$10.95 ___

RESUMES, LETTERS, & NETWORKING

___ 200 Letters for Job Hunters	$17.95 ___
___ Best Resumes for $70,000+ Executive Jobs	$14.95 ___
___ Dynamite Cover Letters	$9.95 ___
___ Dynamite Resumes	$9.95 ___
___ Electronic Resume Revolution	$12.95 ___
___ Electronic Resumes for the New Job Market	$11.95 ___
___ Great Connections	$11.95 ___
___ High Impact Resumes and Letters	$12.95 ___
___ How to Work a Room	$9.95 ___
___ Job Search Letters That Get Results	$12.95 ___
___ New Network Your Way to Job and Career Success	$12.95 ___
___ The Resume Catalog	$15.95 ___
___ Resumes for Re-Entry: A Woman's Handbook	$10.95 ___
___ The Secrets of Savvy Networking	$11.99 ___

DRESS, APPEARANCE, IMAGE

___ John Molloy's New Dress for Success	$10.95 ___
___ Red Socks Don't Work!	$14.95 ___
___ The Winning Image	$17.95 ___
___ Women's Dress for Success	$9.95 ___

INTERVIEWS & SALARY NEGOTIATIONS

___ 60 Seconds and You're Hired!	$9.95 ___
___ Dynamite Answers to Interview Questions	$9.95 ___
___ Dynamite Salary Negotiation	$12.95 ___
___ Interview for Success	$11.95 ___
___ Sweaty Palms	$9.95 ___

WOMEN AND SPOUSES

___ Balancing Career and Family	$7.95 ___
___ Doing It All Isn't Everything	$19.95 ___
___ New Relocating Spouse's Guide to Employment	$14.95 ___
___ Resumes for Re-Entry: A Woman's Handbook	$10.95 ___
___ Smart Woman's Guide to Resumes and Job Hunting	$9.95 ___
___ Survival Guide for Women	$16.95 ___
___ Women's Job Search Handbook	$12.95 ___

MINORITIES AND PHYSICALLY CHALLENGED

___ Best Companies for Minorities $12.00 _____
___ Directory of Special Programs for
Minority Group Members $31.95
___ Job Strategies for People With Disabilities $14.95 _____
___ Minority Organizations $49.95 _____
___ Work, Sister, Work $19.95 _____

COLLEGE STUDENTS AND GRADUATES

___ 150 Best Companies for Liberal Arts Grads $12.95
___ Graduating to the 9-5 World $11.95 _____
___ How You Really Get Hired $11.00 _____
___ Kiplinger's Career Starter $10.95 _____

ENTREPRENEURSHIP AND SELF-EMPLOYMENT

___ 101 Best Businesses to Start $15.00
___ 184 Businesses Anyone Can Start $12.95 _____
___ Best Home-Based Businesses for the 90s $10.95 _____
___ Entrepreneur's Guide to Starting a Successful Business $16.95 _____
___ Have You Got What It Takes? $12.95 _____
___ How to Start, Run, and Stay in Business $12.95 _____
___ Mid-Career Entrepreneur $17.95 _____
___ When Friday Isn't Payday $12.99 _____

COMPUTER SOFTWARE

___ Career Navigator $59.95 _____
___ FOCIS: Federal Occupational and
Career Information System $59.95
___ JOBHUNT™ Quick and Easy Employer Contacts $49.95 _____
___ INSTANT™ Job Hunting Letters $39.95 _____
___ ResumeMaker $49.95 _____
___ Ultimate Job Finder $59.95 _____

CD-ROM

___ America's Top Jobs $395.00 _____
___ Companies International $1995.00 _____
___ Encyclopedia of Associations $995.00 _____
___ Job Power Source $49.95 _____

VIDEOS

___ Dialing for Jobs $129.00 _____
___ Find the Job You Want...and Get It! (4 videos) $229.95 _____
___ How to Present a Professional Image (2 videos) $149.95 _____
___ Inside Secrets of Interviewing $39.95 _____
___ Insider's Guide to Competitive Interviewing $59.95 _____

___ Networking Your Way to Success $89.95   _____
___ Very Quick Job Search $129.00   _____
___ Winning at Job Hunting in the 90s $89.95   _____

AUDIO PROGRAMS

___ Edge Rx For Success $159.95   _____
___ Find the Job You Want...And Get It! $49.95   _____
___ Five Secrets to Finding a Job $29.95   _____
___ Job Search: The Total System $199.95   _____

SUBTOTAL   _____

Virginia residents add 4½% sales tax   _____

POSTAGE/HANDLING ($4.00 for first
title and $1.00 for each additional book) $4.00

Number of additional titles x $1.00 ----------- _____

TOTAL ENCLOSED ---------------- _____

SHIP TO:

NAME _____

ADDRESS _____

_____

_____

[ ] I enclose check/moneyorder for $ _____ made
     payable to IMPACT PUBLICATIONS.

[ ] Please charge $ _____ to my credit card:

Card # _____

Expiration date: _____/_____

Signature _____

SEND YOUR ORDER TO:

IMPACT PUBLICATIONS
9104-N Manassas Drive
Manassas Park, VA 22111
Fax 703/335-9486 (Visa/MasterCard)

ARMY GREEN TO CORPORATE GRAY CAREER TRANSITION KIT

The following books constitute a basic career transition kit for Army personnel. It includes the best job search books designed for experienced individuals interested in pursuing jobs and careers in the private sector.

- **FROM ARMY GREEN TO CORPORATE GRAY**. *Carl S. Savino and Ronald L. Krannich*. Provides essential information and guidance on making a career transition. Dispels myths and shows Army personnel how to best assess skills, conduct market research, write resumes, dress properly, interview for the job, negotiate salary, and much more. Includes unique chapters on transition services, relocation, and starting a business. 1994. $15.95

- **THE PROFESSIONAL'S PRIVATE SECTOR JOB FINDER**. *Daniel Lauber*. Packed with useful and hard-to-find information on *"where the jobs are"* for professionals in the private sector. Includes sources for job listings, from trade publications to job hotlines. 1994. $18.95

- **JOB SEARCH LETTERS THAT GET RESULTS: 201 Great Examples!** *Drs. Ron & Caryl Krannich*. Includes 201 examples of powerful letters that open the doors to job search success: letters to start your job search; letters that lay the ground work; letters for approaching employers; letters that respond to vacancy announcements; cover letters; resume letters, follow-up letters; thank you letters; letters to start your job in the right direction; and special and unusual letters. 1993. $12.95

- **HIGH IMPACT RESUMES AND LETTERS** (5th Edition). *Ron Krannich & William Banis*. Four times excerpted in the *National Business Employment Weekly* of *The Wall Street Journal,* here's the book that shows how to understand today's job market, develop job search skills, select appropriate resume formats, write each resume section, and distribute resumes and letters into the most responsive channels. Debunks resume myths and includes the forms for producing and evaluating each resume section. 1992. $12.95

- **THE *NEW* NETWORK YOUR WAY TO JOB AND CAREER SUCCESS** (2nd Edition). *Drs. Ron & Caryl Krannich*. Here's the first book to provide practical guidance on how to organize and mobilize effective job networks, prospect for new job leads, write effective networking letters, and conduct informational interviews. 1993. $12.95

- **INTERVIEW FOR SUCCESS** (4th Edition). *Drs. Caryl & Ron Krannich.* Featured in the *National Business Employment Weekly* of *The Wall Street Journal,* here's one of today's most comprehensive interview books. Shows how to best prepare for different types of interviews, handle stress, observe etiquette, gather information, formulate key questions, rehearse tough questions, dress appropriately, communicate class, listen effectively, negotiate salary figure, and handle the critical post-interview period. 1993. $11.95

- **HOW TO GET INTERVIEWS FROM CLASSIFIED JOB ADS** (2nd Edition). *Kenneth W. Elderkin.* The only book devoted exclusively to showing how to get interview offers from newspaper and magazine advertisements and articles. Shows how to analyze them, whom to write, what to say, when to follow-up, where to find the best ads, why to pursue news articles, how to crack blind ads, and much more. 1993. $14.95

- **DYNAMITE SALARY NEGOTIATIONS** (2nd Edition). *Drs. Ron & Caryl Krannich.* Outlines the major issues involved in determining salaries; secrecy, salary history, salary requirements, salary ranges, and negotiating tactics. Dispelling numerous myths and outlining many mistakes, this book reveals how to value positions; acquire salary information; calculate your worth; respond to ads and applications requesting salary history; handle tough interview questions; negotiate your salary and terms of employment; and finalize the job offer. 1994. $13.95

- **DIRECTORY OF EXECUTIVE RECRUITERS**. *Kennedy Publications.* Latest edition of this indispensable guide to executive recruiters. Includes 3,200 offices of 1965 firms in the U.S., Canada, and Mexico. Complete with names, addresses, and telephone numbers for contacting key firms with employment contacts. 1994. $39.95

- **THE 100 BEST COMPANIES TO WORK FOR IN AMERICA**. *Robert Levering & Milton Moskowitz.* Identifies 100 companies that have been able to maintain the people values that are the hallmarks of a good workplace. Rates companies on pay and benefits, job security, chances to move up, openness and fairness, and workplace pride. 1993. Cloth: $27.95

SPECIAL OFFER ON COMPLETE SET: Purchase the complete set of 10 books for $169.95. Please add $8.00 shipping for complete package. If ordering individual titles, add $4.00 for first item and $1.00 for each additional item. Send your order to: IMPACT PUBLICATIONS, 9104-N Manassas Drive, Manassas Park, VA 22111 or Fax 703/335-9486 (Visa/MasterCard).

FIND A FEDERAL JOB FAST KIT

The federal government is the single largest employer in the United States. With a workforce of nearly three million, it hires close to 1,000 employees each day. Many jobs are well paid and secure. They come with attractive benefits and generous retirement plans. Unknown to many, over 85 percent of all federal employees work outside Washington. California has as many federal employees as the Nation's capital!

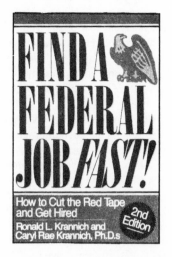

A federal job is an ideal career alternative for many non commissioned officers. However, getting a federal job can be difficult. Few individuals understand how the hiring process operates, where to locate job vacancies, and how to apply for and land a job. A seeming maze of agencies, regulations, and red tape discourage many would-be job seekers.

Impact Publications is pleased to offer a complete package for understanding the federal hiring process, targeting specific agencies, and producing job-winning applications. This package consists of three books and two computer software programs:

- **FIND A FEDERAL JOB FAST! How to Cut the Red Tape and Get Hired.** (2nd Edition). *Drs. Ron & Caryl Krannich.* The first book all federal job hunters need to read *prior to* targeting agencies and completing applications. Provides a sound overview of the federal hiring process. Reveals the inside story on locating job vacancies, completing a winning SF 171, marketing oneself among agencies, and getting quickly hired for many jobs. 197 pages. 1992. $9.95

- **THE ALMANAC OF AMERICAN GOVERNMENT JOBS AND CAREERS.** *Drs. Ron & Caryl Krannich.* This directory provides the critical contact information on thousands of federal government agencies. Identifies job opportunities with executive, legislative, and judicial branches of government. Includes names, addresses, and phone numbers of personnel offices and job hotlines. Describes the work of specific agencies. 289 pages. 1991. $14.95

- **THE RIGHT SF 171 WRITER.** *Dr. Russ Smith.* Finally, a comprehensive guide to completing the critical federal application form—The Standard form

171 (SF 171). Outlines what federal employers look for on the SF 171, major writing principles, the best language to use (KASO's), how to customize the form, and much more. Includes examples of completed SF 171's; special chapters on distribution and resources; and treatment of the SF 172 and veterans preferences. Useful appendices include sample forms, critical sections from the all-important *X-118 Handbook*, and addresses of the Federal Job Information Centers. A critical book every federal job seeker needs in order to produce the right application package. 180 pages. 1994. $19.95.

- **QUICK AND EASY 171s.** *DataTech.* Here's the most advanced computerized SF 171 production program available today. If you plan to apply for a federal job, it's best to produce your SF 171 with this powerful software program. Turns blank paper into a completed SF 171 using most printers on the market. Direct support provides for over 50 dot matrix printers, the DeskJet 500, and laser printers that are compatible with the Hewlett Packard LaserJet II. Prints the form. Approved by the U.S. Office of Personnel Management. Available in 4 versions: **Personal** (single user only): $49.95; **Family** (2 users only): $59.95; **Office** (8 users only): $129.95; **Organization** (unlimited users): $399.95. For IBM or compatible systems only. Also available for Windows (please specify).

- **FOCIS: FEDERAL OCCUPATIONAL & CAREER INFORMATION SYSTEM.** *U.S. Office of Personnel Management.* This interactive program helps federal employees and job seekers obtain information about federal careers, occupations, agencies, current job openings, and training. Contains database on nearly 600 federal occupations and 300 federal organizations. Users with modems can dial into an OPM bulletin board, electronically transfer current job vacancy listings to their computer, and search for job openings using FOCIS. Federal employees can access in formation on more than 1,000 nationwide training courses. Software: three 3½" diskettes, 1.44 M high density. Documentation included. System: IBM-PC or compatible, PC-DOS 3.0 or higher operating system, 400K. Hard disk requires 2.5 to 12.7 Mb depending on the combination of modules installed. Language: dBase II plus compiled in Clipper. Drive should be a 286 or higher processor. An incredible buy at only $59.95!

SPECIAL SAVINGS ON TOTAL PACKAGE: Individuals can purchase the complete package (3 books and 2 software programs) for $139.95. Institutions requiring organizations version (unlimited users) of *Quick and Easy 171s* can purchase this complete package for $489.95. Please add $7.00 shipping for complete package. If ordering individual titles, add $4.00 for first item and $1.00 for each additional item. Send your order to: IMPACT PUBLICATIONS, 9104-N Manassas Drive, Manassas Park, VA 22111 or Fax 703/335-9486 (Visa/MasterCard).

THE COMPLETE CITY AND STATE RELOCATION KIT

Where would you really love to live and work during the next five or ten years, or perhaps the rest of your life? Florida? California? Colorado? Arizona? San Diego? Washington, DC? Seattle? Houston? Atlanta? What will it cost? What job opportunities are available? Who should you contact for employment opportunities? Several key directories and books answer these and many other key relocation questions. They provide expert guidance on identifying and selecting the best place to live and work.

- **PLACES RATED ALMANAC.** *Richard Boyer & David Savageau.* Newest edition of the definitive guide to selecting the best place to live in America from among 333 metropolitan areas. Analyzes communities by several *"quality of life"* criteria. 1993. $21.95

- **MOVING AND RELOCATION SOURCEBOOK.** *Omnigraphics, Inc.* This definitive reference guide to 100 metropolitan areas in the U.S. profiles everything from population, climate, taxes, transportation, education, and arts to sports, media, health care, and government. 623 pages. 1992. Cloth: $149.95

- **THE COMPLETE RELOCATION KIT.** *Howard K. Battles.* Outlines everything you need to know about changing jobs, homes, and communities. Includes charts and checklists for making intelligent relocation decisions. "Invaluable advice and helpful hints."—**Mobility Magazine.** $17.95

- **THE _NEW_ RELOCATING SPOUSE'S GUIDE TO EMPLOYMENT.** *Frances Bastress.* Addresses critical employment issues facing millions of mobile families in corporations, the military, the foreign service, academia, the ministry, and other work settings. Shows how to approach the job search under adverse circumstances. Includes everything from identifying skills to writing resumes, networking, and interviewing. 1993. $14.95

- **100 BEST SMALL TOWNS IN AMERICA.** *Norman Crampton.* A nationwide guide to the best in small-town living. Offers a coast-to-coast tour of wonderful, thriving small towns that are ideal places to live, work, and raise a family. Each town is profiled in detail: history, economy, job possibilities, recreational and cultural opportunities. 1993. $12.00

- **FINDING A JOB IN FLORIDA.** *Bond L. Parkin.* Addresses all levels of the Florida job market. Identifies training programs, apprenticeships, work/study, and financial aid. Includes addresses of newspapers, personnel consultants, chambers of commerce; jobs in government; and a directory of over 100 companies. 1993. $14.95

- **COUNTRY CAREERS.** *Jerry Germer.* Explores the entrepreneurial opportunities for professionals who want to work and live in small towns and rural areas. Includes all the practical information you'll need to turn your dreams of moving to the country into economic reality. Packed with dozens of tips on starting a variety of country careers—from operating a bed and breakfast to performing complex market research. 1993. $14.95

- **GUIDE TO MILITARY INSTALLATIONS.** *Dan Cragg.* A comprehensive guide to U.S. Army, Navy, Air Force, and Marine Corps installations both stateside and overseas detailing their facilities, services, and attractions. 3rd edition. $17.95

- **50 FABULOUS PLACES TO RETIRE IN AMERICA.** *Lee and Saralee Rosenberg.* Evaluates locations on factors retirees consider most important when relocating: cost of living and taxes, crime and safety, housing costs and availability, climate, access to health care, proximity to airports, special services, culture, recreation, and more. Includes maps, climate charts, comments from retirees, and hundreds of useful tips. 1993. $17.95

- **JOB BANK GUIDES TO SELECTED CITIES AND STATES.** *Bob Adams, Inc.* This set of 18 job bank directories provides information on over 500 firms in each city or state, including key names, addresses, and telephone numbers; descriptions of business; job requirements; and fringe benefits. Ideal resources for contacting major employers in each location. 18 directories include: Atlanta, Boston, Chicago, Dallas/Fort Worth, Denver, Detroit, Florida, Houston, Los Angeles, Minneapolis, New York, Ohio, Philadelphia, Phoenix, San Francisco, Seattle, St. Louis, and Washington, D.C. Updated annually. 1994. $15.95 for each volume or $287.10 for all 18 volumes.

- **JOB SEEKERS SOURCEBOOKS TO REGIONAL EMPLOYERS.** This set of 10 directories includes employment agencies, executive search firms, career counselors, data/base/network/referral services, outplacement firms, and resume preparation firms in key regions, states, and cities. Includes Boston & New England; Chicago & Illinois; Los Angeles and Southern California; Mid-Atlantic; Mountain States; New York & New Jersey; Northern Great Lakes; Pacific Northwest; Southern States; and Southwest. $14.95 each or $149.50 for complete set of 10 volumes.

SPECIAL OFFER ON COMPLETE SET: Purchase the complete set of 37 books for $699.95. Please add $25.00 shipping for complete package. If ordering individual titles, add $4.00 for first item and $1.00 for each additional item. Send your order to: IMPACT PUBLICATIONS, 9104-N Manassas Drive, Manassas Park, VA 22111 or Fax 703/335-9486 (Visa/MasterCard).

START YOUR OWN BUSINESS START-UP KIT

If you want to become an entrepreneur and start your own success business, get started by consulting some of the best advice on the subject. Fourteen key books provide sound advice on getting started in the right direction—from assessing your entrepreneurial skills to deciding which business is best for you.

- **HOW YOU GOT WHAT IT TAKES? The Entrepreneur's Complete Self-Assessment Guide.** *Douglas Gray.* Outlines 7 practical guidelines for assessing one's suitability as an entrepreneur—assessing the critical factors that make the difference between success and failure. Includes numerous useful checklists, quizzes, and worksheets. 1993. $12.95

- **HOW TO START, RUN, AND STAY IN BUSINESS.** *Gregory & Patricia Kishel.* Over 100,000 copies sold, this bestselling guide has put businesses all over the country on the road to success. Its unique interactive format with scores of checklists, usable forms, and examples of every aspect of business operations, leads small business entrepreneurs step-by-step through crucial decisions on every aspect of business operations. 1993. $12.95

- **10 BEST OPPORTUNITIES FOR STARTING A HOME BUSINESS TODAY.** *New Careers Center with Reed Glenn.* Presents 10 realistic opportunities for successful home employment. Basic business advice supplements the specific strategies provided for each endeavor. 1993. $14.95

- **KIPLINGER'S WORKING FOR YOURSELF.** *Joseph Anthony.* Provides key information for anyone considering self-employment. Includes invaluable resource information and discusses how the change to self-employment will affect family, finances, and taxes. 1992. $13.95

- **101 BEST BUSINESSES TO START.** *Sharon Kahn & Philip Lief Group.* Provides a wealth of practical advice on 101 businesses. Includes start-up and operating costs, project projections, and staffing needs, plus real-life stories on both the pitfalls and rewards of starting a business. 1992. $15.00

- **THE BEST HOME-BASED BUSINESSES FOR THE 90s.** *Paul & Sarah Edwards.* Shows everything you need to know to start a profitable company from home: what they are, how much can be earned, knowledge, and budget required, products, customers, and franchises. 1991. $10.95.

- **THE ENTREPRENEUR'S GUIDE TO STARTING A SUCCESSFUL BUSINESS.** *James W. Halloran.* Presents everything you need to know to get started, from generating the initial idea to realizing a profit. Includes models, formulas, strategies, and systems for starting out right. 1992. $16.95

- **THE MID-CAREER ENTREPRENEUR.** *Joseph R. Mancuso.* Explores the experience of starting a business in mid-career from three different angles: starting a new business from scratch, buying a franchise, and acquiring a business that someone else has started. 1993. $17.95

- **STARTING ON A SHOESTRING.** *Arnold S. Goldstein.* New edition outlines the necessary skills and requirements for starting a business with limited resources. Useful advice for anyone starting a business. 1990. $14.95

- **ENTREPRENEUR'S ROAD MAP TO BUSINESS SUCCESS.** *Lyle Maul & Dianne Mayfield.* New edition includes tips on how to prepare a business plan, find financing, develop marketing and management strategies, and use advisers productively. 1992. $14.95

- **HOW TO REALLY START YOUR OWN BUSINESS.** *David E. Gumpert.* Based on the experience of eight growth companies, this book is a comprehensive step-by-step guide to launching a successful business. 1992. $14.95

- **184 BUSINESSES ANYONE CAN START** (2nd Edition). *C. Revel.* Leading entrepreneur identifies different types of businesses that can be started with limited investment. Provides practical advice along with informative start-up guides. 1990. $12.95

- **168 MORE BUSINESSES ANYONE CAN START.** *C. Revel.* New edition of this classic book outlines more businesses that can be started with limited investment. 1991. $12.95

- **WHEN FRIDAY ISN'T PAYDAY.** *Randy W. Kirk.* Assesses business skills and clarifies key business issues (partnerships, location, hiring, training, advertising, promotion, marketing, planning, problem solving). 1993. $12.99

SPECIAL OFFER ON COMPLETE SET: Purchase the complete set of 14 books for $189.95. Please add $9.00 shipping for complete package. If ordering individual titles, add $4.00 for first item and $1.00 for each additional item. Send your order to: IMPACT PUBLICATIONS, 9104-N Manassas Drive, Manassas Park, VA 22111 or Fax 703/335-9486 (Visa/MasterCard).